Robert Falck and Timothy Rice are members of the Faculty of Music at the University of Toronto.

Mieczyslaw Kolinski, to whom this volume is dedicated, was aware throughout his life that musicologists are trapped by terminology, notation, and conceptions that properly apply only to a limited segment of their own musical tradition; he sought to find new methods and terminology which would be free of the limitations of traditional musical analysis, and thus adequate to describe and systematize music found anywhere in the world. This collection of twelve essays represents not a working-out of Kolinski's methods and assumptions, but rather studies done in the same spirit, facing important questions and problems in new ways. The results are engaging and controversial.

The essays are presented in three sections. In 'Systematic Perspectives' Nettl, Dowling, Waterhouse, and Rahn try to set up new, all-embracing ways of looking at particular aspects of music. In 'Comparative Perspectives' Boilès, McGee, Song, Sawa, and Nattiez take the utility of comparison for granted and go to the heart of a particular problem or relationship, gathering support for what likely began as an intuitive feeling. In 'Problematic Perspectives' Hopkins, Marshall, and Merriam focus on the problems inherent in comparison, and in fact, often conclude that comparison is not always warranted.

Edited by Robert Falck and Timothy Rice

Cross-Cultural Perspectives on Music

University of Toronto Press
Toronto Buffalo London

© University of Toronto Press 1982
Toronto   Buffalo   London
Printed in Canada

ISBN 0-8020-5510-9

Canadian Cataloguing in Publication Data

Main entry under title:
Cross-cultural perspectives on music

"Essays in memory of Mieczyslaw Kolinski from his students,
colleagues, and friends."
Bibliography: p. xx
ISBN 0-8020-5510-9

1. Kolinski, Mieczyslaw, 1901-1981 - Addresses, essays, lectures.
2. Ethnomusicology - Addresses, essays, lectures. I. Rice, Timothy,
1945-   II. Falck, Robert, 1937-   III. Kolinski, Mieczyslaw, 1901-
1981.

ML3799.C76   781.7   C82-094074-7

Essays in memory of

Mieczyslaw Kolinski

from his students,

colleagues, and friends

Contents

Acknowledgments ix

Introduction Robert Falck and Timothy Rice xi

Kolinski: An Appreciation and List of Works John Beckwith xvii

I SYSTEMATIC PERSPECTIVES

Types of Tradition and Transmission Bruno Nettl 3

Musical Scales and Psychophysical Scales: Their Psychological Reality W. Jay Dowling 20

Towards a New Analysis of Rhythm in Music David Waterhouse 29

Simple Forms in Universal Perspective Jay Rahn 38

II COMPARATIVE PERSPECTIVES

A Paradigmatic Test of Acculturation Charles Lafayette Boilès 53

Eastern Influences in Medieval European Dances Timothy J. McGee 79

Sanjo versus Rāga: A Preliminary Study Song Bang-song 101

Bridging One Millennium: Melodic Movement in al-Fārābī and Kolinski George D. Sawa 117

Comparisons within a Culture: The Example of the Katajjaq of the Inuit Jean-Jacques Nattiez 134

III PROBLEMS AND PROSPECTS

Aural Thinking Pandora Hopkins 143

Towards a Comparative Aesthetics of Music Christopher Marshall 162

On Objections to Comparison in Ethnomusicology Alan P. Merriam 174

Contributors 191

Acknowledgments

When we first sent out the call for papers to be published in a volume honouring Mieczyslaw Kolinski, we were more than gratified by the large number of scholars who replied, some with papers and others with words of encouragement and support. To all those who responded so enthusiastically, particularly those whose papers did not find a place in the volume, we extend our thanks. Dr Kolinski was grateful to both the contributors and the well-wishers and until his death on 7 May 1981 - unfortunately while the book was still in press - followed the progress of the project with keen interest.

This volume has been published with the help of a grant from the Canadian Federation for the Humanities, using funds provided by the Social Sciences and Humanities Research Council of Canada, and a grant from the Publications Fund of the University of Toronto Press. We should especially like to thank these organizations for this assistance, and the University of Toronto's Office of Research Administration, which contributed two short-term grants for the preparation of the manuscript. We acknowledge with gratitude the contributions of the anonymous readers who assessed the volume for the federation and the University of Toronto Press, many of whose thoughtful suggestions were incorporated in the final version. Finally, we should like to thank Deborah Kinzer, who typed the manuscript (some of it twice), and John Fodi, who autographed the musical examples.

While this volume was in preparation, we received the news of Alan Merriam's tragic and untimely death. We feel privileged to count among our contributors this man to whom the discipline of ethnomusicology owes so much.

Introduction

Throughout his career Mieczyslaw Kolinski was a leader in the effort to develop better ways of discussing music. Long aware that musicologists were trapped by conceptions, terminology, and notation that properly applied to only a limited segment of their own musical tradition, Kolinski sought methods and terminology that were free of the limitations of traditional musical analysis and thus were more useful for describing and systematizing music of any part of the world. Although his is almost the only attempt in our time to solve some of the fundamental terminological problems of ethnomusicology, Kolinski fought an uphill and, usually, lonely battle. Most ethnomusicologists seem to be eager to formulate and analyse, but generally unable to solve, the problems and limitations of their discipline and almost always reluctant to accept those solutions that have been suggested. The result is a tacit agreement to continue to distort other musical systems, if only because it makes communication among themselves easier.

A scholar who uses the traditional methods and terminology is always ethnocentric, in effect filtering all music through categories and conceptions proper only to one music. For the last twenty years or so, the most popular way out of this undesirable practice has been the intensive study of a single culture, supposedly in its own terms and for its own sake. This method has had the valuable effects of increasing the amount of information available about various musical cultures and of making scholars aware of the special qualities of each. Another, less fortunate, effect has been the neglect of cross-cultural comparison on the grounds that more, better, and more directly comparable data were needed. Such a tactic implies that, though postponed, comparison and synthesis never really disappeared as the distant goal of the efforts of all ethnomusicologists. The situation in historical musicology is comparable. Large-scale historical synthesis has not entirely disappeared but, for at least a generation, more specialized work on the individual musical cultures - which are labelled, for example, Renaissance or Baroque - has prevailed. In both ethnomusicology and historical musicology, the time seems ripe for a return to comparison, if only to see whether the detailed descriptive work done in the last twenty years or so will yield a more persuasive synthesis than similar attempts in the early part of the twentieth century. If present-day scholars do not from time to time attempt such a synthesis, or at least compare notes with one another, they run the risk that their careful descriptions will appear to future scholars as narrow and biased as nineteenth-century missionary accounts of 'African guitars' or the naively evolutionary models of earlier music historians seem now.

These essays dedicated to Dr Kolinski are an attempt to contribute to such a renewal and re-evaluation. It must be pointed out, however, that comparison has not completely died out in ethnomusicology. The works of Alan Lomax, Kolinski, John Blacking, and Walter Wiora, though stemming from completely different theoretical perspectives, represent the continuing effort to keep comparison alive. Attempts to borrow analytical techniques from such disciplines as linguistics and semiotics can also be seen as an analogous process, because they show ways of breaking the bounds of traditional musical analysis and point towards new ways of comparison.

In his search for new methods, Kolinski seems often to have been guided by just such considerations. Many scholars have questioned the particular assumptions he used, yet articulating a position on the issues is surely the first step towards solving the problems that they raise. The essays that follow represent work done in the spirit, rather than a working out, of the methods and assumptions of Kolinski. The authors of these essays deserve to be applauded for facing problems and questions in new ways: the results in many cases are both engaging and controversial.

The first section (Systematic Perspectives) presents papers that try to set up new, all-embracing ways of looking at a particular aspect of music. These papers do not engage directly in comparative study, but the systematic models that they suggest can provide the basis for comparison of individual pieces, genres, and, eventually, whole musical cultures. Obviously the number of possible points of comparison between repertories and pieces of music is almost limitless, and there is no claim that these essays have exhausted the subject. They do, however, cover aspects of four basic elements of music: melody, tonal structure, rhythm, and form.

In 'Types of Tradition and Transmission,' Bruno Nettl uses melody as the main criterion to analyse the ways in which a specific tradition has come to life and lived. Once these ways are known, they provide a basis for a comparison of the nature of whole traditions, rather than simply a comparison of single elements within those traditions. Nettl chooses melody because it has been one of the most thoroughly studied dimensions of music but, as he says, other elements might profitably be approached in the same manner. His essay ends with the salutary warning that it is easier to construct models than to test their validity in a convincing way.

Jay Dowling's 'Musical Scales and Psychophysical Scales' is an approach to the problem of tonal structure from a psychological point of view. His claims are based largely, though not exclusively, on evidence obtained in the laboratory. Using the Western diatonic scale as his model, Dowling distinguishes four levels of abstraction that seem to be operative in the psychological organization of tonal structures. Like Nettl, he suggests various applications, including the study of where systems of mode and pitch adopted by various cultures are precise or imprecise. The result is an elegant analytical tool that should yield comparable data and stimulate similar attempts to develop empirically valid levels of abstraction for other dimensions of music.

David Waterhouse, in 'Towards a New Analysis of Rhythm in Music,' establishes a framework for analysing what he calls 'rhythm-in-performance.' His premises do not emerge from the laboratory but from a logical, structural model. In his attempt to list and exhaust the possibilities for manipulation of rhythm in performance, Waterhouse works in the spirit of Kolinski's classification of tonal structures and appropriately and generously acknowledges his indebtedness.

Rounding out the first section, Jay Rahn's 'Simple Forms in Universal Perspective' is a rigorously logical epistemic approach to the problem of musical forms large and small. After showing that current terminology is a hopeless confusion of unrelated criteria, Rahn develops a model that requires only four neatly nested factors to account for all simple forms in any kind of music.

The second section (Comparative Perspectives) consists of essays by the active comparers, each of whom goes right to the heart of a particular problem and tries to marshal evidence in support of what probably began as an intuitive feeling. While the first group of writers felt the need to elaborate a system before comparing (and actually compared in a casual way only to indicate possible future applications), the second group takes the utility of comparative study more or less for granted. Writers in the latter group rarely feel the need to expound a model or framework for comparison and seek no larger context than the one set up for the purposes of their study. This approach results in what appears at first to be a series of unrelated, two-sided comparisons. At the deeper level of method, however, the essays in this section in fact represent a rather thorough cross-section of possible theoretical approaches to comparison.

Charles Boilès, in 'A Paradigmatic Test of Acculturation,' uses the comparative method to evaluate a previous claim concerning influence among musical traditions. Rejecting the facile conclusion that some acculturation must have taken place simply because cultures have been in contact, he seeks to test for specific relationships between the music of different cultures. To this end, Boilès devises a new technique for comparing the character of different melodies. This allows him to conclude that, although acculturation has surely occurred in many dimensions of culture, melody seems to have remained stable and uninfluenced.

Timothy McGee's case for 'Eastern Influence in Medieval European Dances' is similar to that of Boilès in that McGee, too, is seeking the 'cultural origin of a musical artefact.' The remoteness of the subject and the lack of directly comparable data make his task somewhat more difficult, however. Whereas Boilès treats only the melodic dimension and finds no relationship, McGee gathers evidence from as many areas as possible to build a case for the origin in another culture of a nominally European repertory. The linchpin of the comparative argument is a provocative attempt to characterize the differing ideals of melodic composition in European and Middle-Eastern culture.

The next two essays also constitute a comparison in a two-sided way, but the goals of their authors are fundamentally different from those of the two foregoing writers. Neither suggests that similarities between cultures or aspects of musical practice or theory imply any kind of cultural connection. In 'Sanjo versus Rāga,' Song Bang-song looks at music in two cultures in order to illustrate that comparison can illuminate without directly suggesting acculturation or influence. The similarities he uncovers, however, are so striking that it would seem worth while to seek further explanations for them. George Sawa, in 'Bridging One Millennium,' compares two analytical treatments of melody. Sawa finds similarities where few or none would be expected, which suggests both the fundamental soundness of the analytical procedures of al-Fārābī and Kolinski and the potentially universal importance of the melodic features analysed.

'Comparisons within a Culture,' by Jean-Jacques Nattiez, is based on the notion that comparison is at the root of all scientific thought. Nattiez here looks within what normally is thought of as a single culture for evidence of striking dissimilarities. He finds the way out of the resulting difficulty by comparing data on one genre separated widely in both time and space. The analysis shows how evolution and diffusion work within a single culture and as such provides an interesting example of a normally comparative, cross-cultural perspective at work at the intracultural level.

The final section (Problems and Prospects) focuses on the problems inherent in comparison. As several of the authors in sections I and II recognized, comparison is not without its dangers and limitations. The contributors to this final section take these problems and doubts as their points of departure and seek to clarify the nature of the obstacles. Such awareness is obviously a prerequisite to overcoming these limitations and eventually to doing useful comparative work.

Pandora Hopkins' 'Aural Thinking' treats the familiar problem of cross-cultural musical perception. Her original and systematic approach - like Dowling's, a laboratory project - provides engaging verbal evidence of the mind's working to bridge the gap from one musical culture to another. These cross-cultural comparisons tend to reveal differences that, unless fully acknowledged and understood, can make comparative description difficult.

Christopher Marshall's 'Towards a Comparative Aesthetics of Music' is concerned with the problem of how to isolate really comparable data. Marshall responds to the dilemma posed by Merriam in 1964 - of how to consider musical value in a culture that lacks a formal musical aesthetic - and suggests a basis on which a comparison can be made within such a culture. These 'aesthetics of music' will have to be constructed one by one on the foundation of each culture's epistemology, and cannot be patterned after a preconceived or explicitly Western-inspired model. He presents at the same time a case study of the sort of work that must be done if this kind of cross-cultural comparison is to be made on a rational basis.

The final word is left to Alan Merriam, who reviews past and present 'objections to comparison in ethnomusicology' and finds them all wanting in one way or another. Merriam argues that comparison is at the heart of the kind of generalizing that most scientific and scholarly disciplines espouse and comes down firmly in favour of the kind of study embodied in this volume. He concludes that, although comparison is not the only legitimate goal of ethnomusicology, scholars in this field must seek to make it a usable tool rather than abandon it altogether.

These problems have been granted the last word not because we, the editors, believe that, in the end, we must conclude that comparison is not justified, but precisely because we believe that comparison is an open-ended process and an open-minded philosophical position. Any attempt to give an artificially rounded and systematic view of the subject would deny the best impulses upon which the discipline is founded: the willingness to get beyond our own culture and our own time, without, at the same time, losing sight of our obligation to make some larger statement about man the music maker.

Robert Falck
Timothy Rice
Toronto, September 1980

JOHN BECKWITH
Kolinski: An Appreciation and List of Works

Mieczyslaw Kolinski, of Jewish ancestry, was born in 1901 in Warsaw. He received his early education, both general and musical, in Hamburg, and it was there that he composed his first pieces, some of which were given public performances while he was still in his teens. It was in Hamburg that he first attained recognition as a pianist when, at the age of eighteen, he appeared as soloist with the Oldenburg Symphony Orchestra in a performance of Tchaikovsky's First Piano Concerto. He completed his studies in Berlin, first at the Hochschule für Musik (composition, piano) and later at Berlin University (musicology, anthropology, psychology). He attracted attention in Berlin with performances of his own works and those of others and became active in non-Western music studies as assistant to Erich M. von Hornbostel at the Staatliches Phonogramm-Archiv.

In the first of two major moves forced on him by the rise of Nazism, Kolinski went in 1933 to Prague, where a brother was living. During his years in the Czech city, he developed further as pianist and composer: his major piano works were composed and premiered, and a ballet was successfully produced in Prague and taken on tour by a noted modern-dance troupe. Kolinski found Prague a suitable milieu for transcribing a large body of non-Western songs that had been offered him, through Hornbostel, by the American anthropologists Melville Herskovits and Franz Boas. He concentrated more and more fully on transcription work (in which he was immersed from then on, with numbers now in the thousands and embracing many cultures), and published some of his first articles on theory, including an important study on consonance and dissonance.

In 1938, at the threat of the Nazi take-over of Czechoslovakia, Kolinski was uprooted once again. On the advice of friends, he went to Belgium, without proof of citizenship but hoping for confirmation of an appointment in the United States, which Herskovits and others were trying to arrange for him. During the uncertain waiting period, his musical curiosity was far from idle: finding himself in the homeland of the carillon, he learned to play this instrument and wrote some compositions for it and an article (unpublished) in which he suggested ways in which it might be improved.

The outbreak of war prevented his emigration to the United States. Soon the Nazis advanced into Belgium and Kolinski was compelled to register, to wear the Star of David, and to submit to such restrictions as an 8:00 P.M. curfew, confiscation of his radio set, and prohibition against the use of public benches. In 1942 he received an order from the Nazi authorities to present himself for deportation to a labour camp in northern France. The day before he was to leave, he accidentally met a woman friend who, though Jewish like himself, was among the few who, by failing to register, escaped persecution. She warned him that the French camp was an interim gathering point for Jews who were to be conveyed to the notorious concentration camps, such as Auschwitz and Buchenwald.

During the succeeding two-and-a-half years Kolinski lived in hiding, thanks to the family of the well-known Belgian painter Fritz van den Berghe, who made a closed-off room in the house for him. Later he and Edith van den Berghe, the painter's daughter, were married. Though living amid constant danger and unable to go outdoors except for rare trips to the country, Kolinski found during this odd and tense existence that he was able to concentrate and work regularly and well. After the war he became active in many areas of Belgian musical life, composing another ballet (to his wife's scenario), performing as soloist and accompanist in new compositions, and publishing articles and reviews on theoretical and ethnomusicological topics. In 1946 he played his own Piano Sonata in Amsterdam's Concertgebouw, and in 1947 a concert devoted to his music was given at the Palais des Beaux Arts in Brussels. In an introduction to the program, musicologist Charles van den Borren wrote of Kolinski's musical output as 'already extensive, and rich in qualities which are far from being solely of a cerebral order,' and went on to note the 'spontaneity and freshness' of Kolinski's style, and its 'strangely expressive vital breath.'

Kolinski emigrated to the United States finally in 1951 (he became an American citizen in 1961) and moved in a number of new career directions. He became an editor of Hargail Music Press and for the next decade not only edited but composed and arranged numerous practical and educational publications for this firm - especially for their considerable recorder catalogue - often drawing on his folk-music transcriptions as source material. He became attached to a large veterans' hospital near New York as music therapist, developed techniques in this field, taught, and directed such group activities as the patients' own production of South Pacific. He performed and recorded his works with New York musicians and at the same time continued to transcribe and to work on scholarly articles. In the early 1950s, he became one of the dozen or so founding members of the Society for Ethnomusicology. (Kolinski in fact was responsible for suggesting its name, changed at the last moment from the originally proposed American Society for Comparative Musicology.) He served as vice-president of the society for two years (1956-7) and as president from 1958 to 1959, and remained an executive board member and adviser for over a decade afterwards. The experience put him in the centre of a vital scholarly development, and the period coincided with the publication of his most important and seminal studies: the writings on analysis of melodic movement and classification of tonal structures, and the allied writings on tempo and on tuning, which form the core of his systematic view of music.

In 1966 the Kolinskis again changed their country of residence. Invited by the University of Toronto to establish a program in ethnomusicology at its Faculty of Music, Mieczyslaw Kolinski began a full and challenging round of undergraduate and graduate teaching. He became a Canadian citizen, a busy transcriber and analyst of Canadian folk-music repertories (sometimes on commission from the National Museum of Man), and a sought-after adviser to Canadian musical organizations. Although he retired in 1976, with the title of 'scholar emeritus,' he continued to give guest lectures and seminars and to write and compose, with no visible slackening of pace until his death on 7 May 1981.

Kolinski's life possessed many qualities shared by other European liberals, Jewish and non-Jewish, of his generation: serenity and sweetness combined with toughness and shrewdness, extraordinary tolerance and kindness with a fierce intellectual pride. One waited long for those rare moments when he was inclined to speak of the years in Berlin, Prague, and Brussels; when he did, it was with a low-key, almost deprecating air which belied the very real dangers that in those times threatened him, his family, and his work.

Those who have worked closely with Kolinski are familiar with his keen enjoyment of, and sharp skill in, intellectual discussion and debate. One had only to ask a question implying one's fundamental uncertainty or an area of dispute to prompt him to review all the positions and polish off the untenable ones with 'but I refuted that' - said not boastfully but with a rather childlike satisfaction in the neatness of his logical conclusion.

Kolinski's curiosity and his sense of exploring questions to their fullest led him to traverse many broad musical areas and to consider many issues. Whenever a supposedly new subject was touched on, his acquaintances became used to the sudden appearance of extensive but hitherto unknown (perhaps still unpublished) work of an original, problem-solving sort from phases of his past life. Once, in speaking of the teaching of musical rudiments, he produced the Harmonone, which he patented in Prague in the 1930s (and which was put into production just shortly before he had to leave Czechoslovakia). This contraption consists of a series of concentric cardboard wheels, the upper ones revealing through cut-out windows what is printed at certain points on the lower ones - a tool for teaching such fundamentals as the circle of fifths, key signatures and relations, leading notes, and major/minor relations. Again, during a discussion of the problems of the beginning piano student, he produced his three-volume new approach, which included an original device for mastering the reading of the lines and spaces and also many attractive original pieces (as yet still unpublished). Highly characteristic is his suggested reform for notation, integrated with an ingenious new vocabulary of sight-singing syllables (CAUSM Journal, Spring 1976) - a sweeping solution that, however hard it might be to put to practical use, makes one look deeply at the imperfections and incongruities of the conventional Western musical-staff and sol-fa notations.

Among the writings of his Canadian years, besides the published items noted in the list that follows, are an analytical study of a large French-Canadian collection; an application of Kolinski's analytical method to a body of medieval church music; and a two-volume chord study, which proposes, characteristically, a scheme for classifying all the simultaneities possible in a twelve-note temperament system, from those of two notes to those of twelve.

His music also has a special flavour. Van den Borren was quick to note its spontaneity, but its gracefulness is controlled and its harmonies and rhythms fascinate and entrance rather than electrify. The piano works are closest to Hindemith and Bartók in their unusual harmonic formations clearing into a tonal centre at section ends and in their love of continuous patterns in asymmetrical metre. In the first two movements - Lydian Variations and Chaconne - of the Sonata (1966), and in the ingenious Dances in Etude Form, melodic lines have their intervals expanded and changed, or take on new and complicated details of chromatic decoration, without losing their strong basic shape. Both melody and rhythm in these pieces in fact often suggest a model from some folk repertory, though specific and acknowledged borrowings of this sort are few. The larger works - for example, Encounterpoint and Dance Fantasy - are denser and more elaborate in linear activity. Encounterpoint (called by Kolinski 'a contrapuntal encounter between tonal and atonal forces') is especially interesting for its successful fusion of musical types, the 'tonal' being represented by a distinct quotation, a Crimean Tatar theme. The more fully folk-derived pieces, whether arrangements or suites inspired by folk models (such as the much-played Dahomey Suite or the recent suites of Canadian, German, Dutch, Slovak, Hebrew, Yiddish, Sephardic, French, and American tunes set for voice with flute and piano), are elegant examples of their genre and suggest by their sensitive and tasteful harmonic emphases a sheer enjoyment of line which Kolinski the scholar would be too scrupulously objective to permit himself - even though their form has certainly not been achieved without a careful analysis of the given originals.

WORKS BY MIECZYSLAW KOLINSKI

Note: The following list revises and brings up to date Raymond Kennedy's 'A Bibliography of the Writings of Mieczyslaw Kolinski' Current Musicology 1966: 100-3.

Articles
1929a 'Zum Problem der musikalischen Temperatur' Die Musik 21: 345-9
1929b 'Musikalische Völkerkunde' Jüdische Rundschau 25: 345
1930 'Die Musik der Primitivstämme auf Malaka und ihre Beziehungen zur samoanischen Musik' Anthropos 25: 585-648
1936a 'Konsonanz als Grundlage einer neuen Akkordlehre' Veröffentlichungen des musikwissenschaftlichen Instituts der Deutschen Universität in Prag 7

1936b 'Suriname Music' in Melville and Frances Herskovits Suriname Folk-lore (New York, Columbia University Press) 489-740
1945 'Nouvelles Perspectives du jazz' Coulisses (Bulletin mensuel de l'Agence artistique internationale A. Licart, Brussels)
1949 'La Musica del oeste africano: musica europea y extraeuropea' translated by Francesco Curt Lange Revista de estudios musicales 1 (2): 191-215
1956 'The Structure of Melodic Movement: A New Method of Analysis' Miscelánea de estudios dedicados al Dr. Fernando Ortiz por sus discipulos, colegas y amigos (Havana) 2: 881-918
1957a 'The Determinants of Tonal Construction in Tribal Music' Musical Quarterly 43 (1): 50-6
1957b 'Ethnomusicology, Its Problems and Methods' Ethnomusicology 1 (10): 1-7
1959a 'The Evaluation of Tempo' Ethnomusicology 3 (2): 45-57
1959b 'A New Equidistant 12-Tone Temperament' Journal of the American Musicological Society 12 (2-3): 210-14
1960 'Notes on Christensen's article, "Inner Tempo and Melodic Movement"' Ethnomusicology 4 (1): 14-15
1961a 'The Origin of the Indian 22-Tone System' Studies in Ethnomusicology 1: 3-18
1961b 'Classification of Tonal Structures, Illustrated by a Comparative Chart of American Indian, African Negro, Afro-American and English-American Structures' Studies in Ethnomusicology 1: 38-76
1962 'Consonance and Dissonance' Ethnomusicology 6 (2): 66-74
1965a 'The Structure of Melodic Movement: A New Method of Analysis, Revised Version' Studies in Ethnomusicology 2: 95-120
1965b 'Gestalt Hearing of Intervals' in Gustave Reese and Rose Brandel, eds. The Commonwealth of Music (New York, The Free Press of Glencoe) 368-74
1965c 'The General Direction of Melodic Movement' Ethnomusicology 9 (3): 240-64
1967 'Recent Trends in Ethnomusicology' Ethnomusicology 11 (1): 1-24
1968 '"Barbara Allen": Tonal versus Melodic Structure' part 1, Ethnomusicology 12 (2): 208-18
1969 '"Barbara Allen": Tonal versus Melodic Structure' part 2, Ethnomusicology 13 (1): 1-73
1972a 'An Iroquois War Dance Song Cycle' Journal of the Canadian Association of University Schools of Music 2 (2): 51-64
1972b 'An Apache Rabbit Dance Song Cycle, as Sung by the Iroquois' Ethnomusicology 16 (3): 415-64
1973a 'How about "Multisonance"?' Ethnomusicology 17 (2): 279
1973b 'A Cross-cultural Approach to Metro-rhythmic Patterns' Ethnomusicology 17 (3): 494-506
1974a 'Obituary: Arnold M. Walter' Bulletin of the International Folk Music Council 44: 13-15
1974b 'Modes, Musical' Encyclopaedia Britannica 12: 295-8
1976a 'Herndon's Verdict on Analysis: tabula rasa' Ethnomusicology 20 (1): 1-22
1976b 'A Co-ordinated Denomination and Notation of Pitch' Journal of the Canadian Association of University Schools of Music 6 (1): 11-28

1977 'Final Reply to Herndon' Ethnomusicology 21 (1): 75-83
1978a 'The Structure of Music: Diversification versus Constraint' Ethnomusicology 22 (2): 229-44
1978b '"Malbrough s'en va-t-en guerre": Seven Canadian Versions of a French Folk Song' Yearbook of the International Folk Music Council 10: 1-32
1980a 'Indians: Eastern Woodlands' Encyclopedia of Music in Canada (Toronto, University of Toronto Press) 452-3
1980b 'Haiti' The New Grove Dictionary of Music and Musicians 8: 33-7
1981 'Afro-Surinam Music' (revised and enlarged reprint of Kolinski's contribution to Melville and Frances Herskovits Suriname Folklore, New York, 1936) in Frank Harrison, ed. Source Materials and Studies in Ethnomusicology 11 (Buren, Netherlands. Frits Knuf Publishers)
1982 'Reiteration Quotients: A Cross-cultural Comparison' Ethnomusicology 26 (1): 85-90

Reviews

1929 'Robert Lachmann: Musik des Orients' Die Musik 22: 131-2
1950a 'Otto Johannes Gombosi: Tonarten und Stimmungen der antiken Musik' Revue belge de musicologie 4 (4): 217-18
1950b 'Walter Howard: Die Tonmittel der Musik in ihren natürlichen Beziehungen' Revue belge de musicologie 4 (4): 219-20
1957a 'Bruno Nettl: Music in Primitive Culture' Musical Quarterly 43 (2): 246-8
1957b 'Studia memoriae Belae Bartók sacra' Ethnomusicology 11 (1): 30-3
1960a 'A.M. Jones: Studies in African Music' Musical Quarterly 46 (1): 105-10
1960b 'Fritz Bose: Die Musik der Chibcha und ihrer heutigen Nachkommen: Ein Beitrag zur Musikgeschichte Südamerikas' Ethnomusicology 4 (2): 90
1960c 'William P. Malm: Japanese Music and Musical Instruments' Ethnomusicology 4 (3): 154
1962 'Alan P. Merriam and R.F.G. Spier: Chukchansi Yokuts Songs' Journal of the International Folk Music Council 14: 137-8
1963 Review-essay: 'Curt Sachs: The Wellsprings of Music' Ethnomusicology 7 (3): 272-86
1965 'Heinrich Husmann: Grundlagen der antiken und orientalischen Musikkultur' Ethnomusicology 9 (1): 59-60
1968 'UCLA, Institute of Ethnomusicology: Selected Reports' Ethnomusicology 12 (2): 277-83
1970 Review-essay: 'Alan P. Merriam: Ethnomusicology of the Flathead Indians' Ethnomusicology 14 (1): 77-99
1971a 'Kurt Reinhard: Einführung in die Musikethnologie' Yearbook of the International Folk Music Council 3: 161-2
1971b Review-essay: 'Mantle Hood: The Ethnomusicologist' Yearbook of the International Folk Music Council 3: 146-60
1973 'Wolfgang Wittrock: Die ältesten Melodietypen im ostdeutschen Volksgesang' Ethnomusicology 17 (3): 551-4

xxiii Kolinski: An Appreciation

1974 'Bruno Nettl: <u>Folk and Traditional Music of the Western Continents</u>' <u>The Canadian Music Educator</u> 15 (4): 33-4

Musical Transcriptions
1934 New Guinea examples 38-59, Samoa examples 109-13 and 115-20 in Marius Schneider <u>Geschichte der Mehrstimmigkeit</u> 1 (Tutzing, Germany, H. Schneider)
1949 Transcriptions and analysis: in phonorecording <u>Folk Music of Palestine</u> Folkways P408
1959 Transcriptions and commentary: in phonorecording <u>Dahomey Suite</u> Folkways FS3855
1960 186 Haitian songs and drum rhythms in Harold Courlander <u>The Drum and the Hoe</u> (Berkeley, University of California Press) 205-313
1963 19 folk songs in Harold Courlander <u>Negro Folk Music, U.S.A.</u> (New York, Columbia University Press)
1964 Transcription II in 'Symposium on Transcription and Analysis: A Hukwe Song with Music Bow' <u>Ethnomusicology</u> 8 (3): 241-51

Unpublished Writings
'Die Musik Westafrikas' 464 music examples (transcribed and analysed from field recordings by M. Herskovits)
'Transcription of 309 Haitian Songs Recorded by M. Herskovits' deposited at the American Folklife Center, Library of Congress, Washington, DC
'Transcription of 152 Kwakiutl Songs Recorded by Franz Boas'
'Transcription and Analysis of 117 French-Canadian Folk Songs and Versions' commissioned by the Canadian Centre for Folk Culture Studies, National Museum of Man, Ottawa
'A Study in Melodic Analysis, as Applied to a Collection of Medieval Tunes' (based on a selection of sequences of Adam of St Victor)
'The Shape of Melody: an Intercultural Study' comprising 4000 music examples
'The Universe of Chords' classification of chords based on the cycle of fifths, encompassing all simultaneous tone configurations conceivable within the twelve-tone system (897 music examples from Bach to Bartók)
'Music Therapy: Selected Case Histories from a Naval Hospital'
'Should the Carillon Be Perfected, and Can It Be?'

Musical Compositions
1917 <u>Stimmungsbilder Suite</u> pf.
1918 <u>14 Songs</u> voice, pf.
1919 <u>Sonata</u> pf.
1922 <u>5 Songs</u> sopr., pf.
1924 <u>Sonata Based on a Russian Folk Song, First Version</u> vln., pf.
1926 <u>Sonata</u> vlc., pf.
1927 <u>String Quartet</u>
1929 <u>First Suite</u> pf.
     <u>Lyric Sextet</u> sopr., fl., str. qt.
1931 <u>Bu Ru Bu</u> (ballet) full orch.

1933	Little Suite	vln., pf.
1934	Second Suite	pf.
1935	Railway Fantasy [Expresszug-Phantasie] (ballet)	2 pfs.
1936	Third Suite	pf.
1937	Chamber Sonatina	vln., vla., vlc., pf.
1938	A Day and Its Seven Faces (Variations)	pf.
	4 Dances in Etude Form	pf.
1939	8 Preludes	carillon
1944	3 Songs	sopr., pf.
1946	Fourth Suite	pf.
	Sonata Based on a Russian Folk Song, Second Version	vln., pf.
	Sonata, First Version	pf.
1947	Four-Hand Conversations [Divertimento]	pf. duet
1948	Man and His Shadows (ballet)	full orch.
1949	American Suite, Based on 12 Spirituals	med. voice, str. qt. (or pf.)
1950	3 Three-Part Inventions	sopr. vocalise, vla., vlc.
1951	Dahomey Suite	fl. (rec.), pf. (arr. for fl., str. orch. [1953] and for ob., pf. [1959])
1956	Concertino	sopr. vocalise (or ob.), str. qt., pf.
1958	Prelude	full orch.
	Fun with Recorder Duets (20 pieces)	2 sopr. recs.
	Fun with Recorder Duets (20 pieces)	sopr. and alto recs.
1959	Fun with Recorder Trios (12 pieces)	sopr., alto, ten. recs.
1960	Hatikvah Variations	str. qt.
1963	Snapshots (7 pieces)	pf.
1966	Sonata, Second Version	pf.
1968	Dance Fantasy (based on Man and His Shadows)	str. orch.
1973	Encounterpoint.	org., str. qt. (arr. for fl., cl., vln., vla., vlc., pf. [1974], and for 2 pfs. [1979])
1976	Concertino	sopr. vocalise, cl., pf.
1977	2 Songs to Texts by Canadian Poets	sopr., fl., pf.
1978	Settings of 14 Canadian Folk Songs	high (med.) voice., pf.

Plus:
Eight items of original teaching compositions for piano, violin, recorder(s), accordion, including The New Piano Method Based upon the Four-Line Approach 3 vols., and Let's Discover Music: A Method for Recorder 2 vols.

Over twenty collections of folk-music settings for various media (six to twenty settings in each collection)

Recordings
1959a Dahomey Suite ob., pf. Folkways FS3855
1959b Music for the Ballet Studio (41 pieces) pf. Folkways FC7673
1979 29 Folk Songs in Concert Form sopr., fl., pf. Folkways FTS31314

I / SYSTEMATIC PERSPECTIVES

BRUNO NETTL
Types of Tradition and Transmission

One of the characteristics of scholars in ethnomusicology has always been their interest in processes.[1] Defined by some as a field in which music is viewed synchronically, as opposed to history, in which a diachronic view is taken (Chase 1958: 7), ethnomusicology nevertheless exhibits, through its literature, a very lively concern with the way in which changes are made, encouraged, or inhibited in the history of music - or of a music, a genre, type, piece, or song. The ethnomusicologist's interest has been more general than specific, in the sense that it has been theoretical, and of course, in most instances, it has been hampered by the absence of records that could enhance an understanding of historical processes viewed over long periods. Ethnomusicologists have therefore revealed something about the kinds of processes that may be expected to operate but not much about the specific changes that take place in a given situation. Among the many obvious reasons for this state of affairs that one can cite is the particular kind of role that the musical artefact plays in the thinking of ethnomusicologists; for them, a piece of music is more likely to be conceived as comprising all versions, variants, and performances of something once created (but probably no longer available) than as only the original version created by the composer. Thus, the typical ethnomusicologist's view of processes is different from that taken by the music historian; but the interest in processes is surely there.

The term most used to lump together all of the various processes that may be found in the history of a musical repertory is <u>tradition</u>, a concept that combines the stable nature of a culture's way of life with the implication that by its very existence over long periods of time this way of life is subject to change. The way in which a tradition is passed on is called <u>transmission</u>, and the two terms are sometimes used, informally and perhaps colloquially, to emphasize two sides of the character of a culture or indeed of a music - its stability on the one hand, its tendency to change on the other.

My purposes here are to present some thoughts on the nature of musical tradition, and to speak speculatively on some rather basic questions: how is a musical repertory transmitted; what can we learn about the process of transmission; and how can that process itself affect the nature of a music? I shall try to approach the

questions in the broadest sense, dealing in a theoretical and
generalizing way with some elemental concepts of musical thought,
such as compositions, genetic and other kinds of relationships among
musical artefacts, and ideas about innovation. I should like to suggest a model for the comparative classification and study of musical
repertories based on their structure and integral interrelationships
and on the types of transmission that are used, and to guess at what
a study of the structure of a contemporary repertory might tell us
about its genesis and life.

A SAMPLING OF PUBLICATIONS

The ethnomusicological literature on this subject provides a picture
of ambiguity on the part of scholars. In some respects there is a
vast body of written material that touches upon the nature of musical
tradition and transmission and reveals many approaches: it is an
issue in the back of everyone's mind. In other respects, not overly
much of the literature addresses itself specifically to the question.
The purpose here is not to survey this literature thoroughly. A
sampling, however, shows us that the problem of the nature of traditional transmission has been treated by groups of scholars representing
a number of contrastive specialties, and provides several avenues of
approach. It also shows us that the nature of tradition and transmission, with the associated questions of authenticity, stability, and
change, has come increasingly to the awareness of ethnomusicologists,
who may thus be ready for a more concerted effort in this direction.
  Let us look briefly and very selectively at some examples in the
literature of historical musicology. Generalizations about change in
individual repertories and traditions appear in some of the classics
of this field. For example, Curt Sachs (1943; 1940: 25-66; 1946;
1948; 1962), in many of his works, provides a basically evolutionistic
view of world music, derived from cultural evolutionism which postulates separate and easily discerned stages, each of which might indeed be regarded as an independent tradition. A similar view, that
history consists of a group of separate, more or less disjointed
traditions, appears in the work of many historians of European
music, as, for example, the venerable Guido Adler (1930: 68-71; 1934:
174), whose belief in 'musical periods' is surely responsible for
much of the later emphasis on periodization. Paul Bekker, another
historian whose work had considerable impact, accepted the periodic
view but suggested that 'musical culture moves in a wave-like motion,
now universal, now national, now back to a common unity' (1927: 107),
evidently implying or emphasizing gradual and constant change. Subsequently, other views have come to the forefront. In a fairly recent
opus, which takes an essentially Marxist view, Georg Knepler (1961;
1972: 234, 238) ties musical change closely to social change and
seems to take a more conjunct view of history and musical development.
In a more recent work, Charles Rosen (1972: 20), speaking of 'style'
in a historical context as something akin to a language, again implies
the establishment of one style and its later abandonment for another,
illustrating the interest in separable periods or traditions in
modern Western scholarship.

5 Types of Tradition and Transmission

The classics of ethnomusicology also touch on the subject but their thrust is more in the direction of cultural continuity and gradual change than is the case in small samplings of the works of historians. Thus Alan Merriam (1964: 277-319) devotes a chapter of The Anthropology of Music to 'Music and Culture History' and another to 'Music and Cultural Dynamics' and, citing a broad range of ethnomusicological literature, shows that for this branch of the field a 'tradition' or 'a' music might be parallel to a population. Change always occurs, but it is never 'wholesale or overnight' (ibid.: 303). This statement by its implication provides an interesting contrast to the prevailing view of the historian of European music who most typically gives greater emphasis to the alternation of periods of stability with those of rather sudden change.

The nature of tradition and transmission is a subject with which Charles Seeger, perhaps more than anyone, has dealt in numerous general treatises and specific studies. His discussion of degrees and types of variance in a musical repertory (1950) at one extreme, and his detailed analysis of 'Barbara Allen' tunes at the other (1966), illustrate his range of interest. Seeger's article on oral tradition is basic (1950), distinguishing specifically between the oral and the written, an issue also treated by Hood (1971: 90-3), whose 'Hipkins solution' to problems of transcription bridges the gap between written and oral traditions. Hood (1959) also introduces the notion of reliability of one tradition, again distinguishing between written and oral, presumably more and less reliable, more and less stable.

The studies that deal more specifically with transmission and with the way a tradition moves or remains stable come mainly from two overlapping areas of the literature: classification of melodies, and attempts to show genetic relationship. The first of these areas is a long-established tradition in European folk-music research, going back to works of Krohn (1903), Hustvedt (1936; see also Bayard 1942), then moving on to Bartók (1931: 6-11) and eventually to the highly sophisticated studies of recent Eastern European scholars (see, for example, Elschek 1966, 1969; Várdányi 1962). The purposes of classification are described by Herzog (1949) as involving the rational arrangement of a large body of material, the creation of finding lists, and the assembling of genetically related material. It is this kind of classification that allows us to have adequate overviews of entire repertories in order to be able to treat them as systems, or organisms.

In further sections of this paper I shall work towards the establishment of a framework for comparing repertories thus internally classified; the various classification systems would seem therefore to be of enormous use in following and testing the framework to be established. It is interesting to note that most of the classification work involves melodic components, and little (Bartók [1931: 7] and Brailou [1973: 151-342] notwithstanding) involves rhythm. What can one make of this? No doubt the prominence of melody over rhythm in the development of Western musical theory has provided the context for the development of ethnomusicological procedures. In this Western-oriented context it is interesting to find that Marius Schneider

(1957) – who distinguishes sharply between simple and high cultures
– believes that basic differentiation of units of musical thought
is rhythmic, at least in the simplest cultures. But, as I have already pointed out, the ethnomusicological literature that tries to
classify repertories largely ignores rhythm, except for cultures
that are surely not very simple and that rhythmically are very
sophisticated, such as those of India and West Africa.

This incomplete discussion of relevant literature would be far
less adequate if I failed to mention the studies of Kolinski (1959;
1961; 1965a; 1965b), who tries to provide frameworks for the comparative classification of repertories by melodic, scalar, rhythmic,
and temporal parameters. His approaches have frequently not been
followed but, although I have not attempted here to follow his plans
specifically, they have certainly provided much of the stimulus for
this paper.

The literature on problems of genetic relationship of similar contemporary materials inevitably treats segments of repertories. Olsvai
(1963) has provided terminology that shows the continuum of relationships between total repertory and individual performance in European
folk music – and in a way that could be transferred to other kinds
of musical cultures. Various degrees of relationship are described.
A repertory consists of a number of 'tune strains,' each of which
is a group of 'tune families' that resemble each other; a tune family
consists of a number of specimens, each of which in turn consists of
variants. This is analogous to Kemppinen's (1954: 7) analysis of texts,
as illustrated in his study of one ballad, 'Lady Isabel and the False
Knight.' In this study he gives a hierarchy of relationships – type,
form, variant, version – likewise moving from general to special.
Bayard (1954), in a brilliant study of two tune families, also
develops the similar concept syndrome of family, form, and tune. And
the notion of a tune type, the specific interrelationships of whose
members are not specified, is also used by Wiora (1953: 48-53), who
for this purpose draws upon the entire body of European folk (and
some art) music as a single repertory or tradition.

Studies of specific tune families and analogous kinds of related
groups are prominent in the literature dealing with Anglo-American
folk music. The work of Bayard is most important, and his 'Prolegomena
to a Study of the Principal Melodic Families of British-American Folk
Song' is the classic beginning of this movement (1950). Bronson's
vast collection and study of tunes associated with Child ballads (1959-
71) provides data that are interesting, since tunes are shown to be
related within the framework of a text type, but incomplete since
the relationship of the tunes across textual boundaries is – understandably, given Bronson's basic purpose – not demonstrated. Porter
(1976), in contrast, gives a detailed study of the relationship problem in microcosm, showing the way in which a single singer develops
one song over a period of about a decade. A similar study was made by
Christensen (1975: 4), who used a small group of Kurdish songs to show
that various performances of a piece differ from each other to some
extent in correlation with differences in the social context of the
performance. Similar materials from Iran are discussed by Blum (1974:

7 Types of Tradition and Transmission

90), who concerns himself with the issue of melody type as a focus of closely related tunes recognized as such by the culture.

What Porter observes directly in an Anglo-Scottish folk song over a short period, is reconstructed for the Spanish song 'Don Gato' over a long, undetermined period by Boilès (1973), one of the few authors besides Bayard bold enough to try to reconstruct the history of a song from a comparison of its contemporary versions. There should be more attempts of this sort in order to test the usefulness and validity (though final proof will forever elude us) of Boilès's approaches. But the recent literature has definitely moved onto two tracks: the microcosmic, dealing with individual songs, and the classificatory - eventually entrusted to computers - involving the musical universe of a culture. Incidentally, the issues of classification of repertories and of genetic relationship play a much smaller role in the literature of European music history than in the ethnomusicological literature. But they are certainly not absent, as indicated by, for example, Jan LaRue's (1959) proposal of a union thematic catalogue of eighteenth-century symphonies or Nicholas Temperley's (1961) espousal of the use of statistics in the assessment of the significance of thematic relationships (assuming the term significance to be somewhat analogous to the folk-music scholar's use of the term genetic).

One might expect entire musical repertories to have been classified comparatively in terms of their internal interrelationship, but this seems not to have been attempted. It is curious not to find classes analogous to, say, the old classification of languages (agglutinative, isolating, inflective); such attempts were presumably deemed unproductive. Among those few that are extant, I shall mention Becking's (1928: 23-81) classification of composers by rhythmic type, Fischer's (1915) melodic typology (Lied and Fortspinnungs types), and Nettl's (1974) attempt to set repertories at various points of a continuum from composition to improvisation. It is this kind of classification to which I would like to address myself here, now that I have presented this brief and to some extent random survey of the literature dealing with types of musical traditions and types of transmission, in macrocosm and microcosm.

I should like to consider now entire repertories and the processes that cause them to have a certain shape and a certain mode of life and change. We must recognize, however, that the tendency of ethnomusicologists, perhaps understandably enough, has been to concentrate on the musical artefact, the song, the piece. Taking our cue from historians of European music and of art, we have considered the pieces of music as the nodes and as the most convenient stopping places at which to assess the progress of tradition. But despite the theoretical interest in processes, we have not given much practical attention to the way in which they may lead to 'a piece,' or away from it to another piece, or perhaps to another version of the same piece. We know little about composition, variation in performance or improvisation, or learning and forgetting. And furthermore, while a good deal of literature approaches the question (sometimes as a by-product), we have not really had much to say about the organic and genetic interrelationship of pieces in a repertory as clues to the nature of these processes. We have not developed an internally comparative method for telling us about the genesis of a repertory and of individual pieces in that repertory. Certainly the descriptive component of ethnomusicology has prevailed, and the interest in process, while there, has stayed in a corner.

Perhaps we have not had much choice. Literature and recordings present us with individual artefacts and establish little in the way of relationship among them, a relationship that would shed light on their history. Ethnomusicologists have thus come up with very little theory regarding the types of histories that individual pieces, genres, repertories, and even entire musical cultures experience. Among the few exceptions, we have mentioned the development of the tune-family concept, the notion that there is in essence something different between oral and written transmission, and the thought that consensus, compatibility, and syncretism have something to do with the concept of communal re-creation, which is itself a specialty of oral rather than written tradition. Indeed, there has been an attempt in much literature from Phillips Barry[2] to Mantle Hood (1959) to Leo Treitler (1974) to lump oral traditions in a single syndrome of behaviour patterns. I refer to, for example, Treitler's speculation that composition in an oral tradition results in similar but not identical types or, in our terms, pieces. Inevitably ethnomusicologists have had their own system of values, and the reliability or stability of oral tradition has been accepted at least unconsciously as a positive value, especially as it seems the best hope for the extrapolation of history from the present.

There is one more general consideration that must be mentioned. The ethnomusicologist always works with two sides of a coin, the one side being his own perception of the cultural and musical realities with which he is concerned, and the other, the perception shared by a consensus of the members of the culture whose music and behaviour are being studies. Hood (1971) has presented these two sides of the field lucidly, and the recent proposal of a special 'cognitive ethnomusicology' gives emphasis to the recognition of the issue by many scholars. Thus, in all of the following considerations, the existence of this 'coin' is a continuing problem (see, for example, Blacking 1973: 98-9 et passim; Herndon 1974: 248 et passim).

TYPES OF TRANSMISSION

In attempting to present a model for the comparative study of repertories, let me begin with the microcosm, the individual composition, and its history. Let me propose that there are at least four different types of history that an individual musical composition may experience. In Type I, the composition, once created, may be carried on without change, more or less intact. Or, in Type II, it may be transmitted and changed but only in a single version or a single direction, so that it continues, different from its original but without the proliferation of variants. In Type III, it may experience the kind of transmission that produces many variants, some of which

9 Types of Tradition and Transmission

eventually are abandoned and forgotten, others remain stable once they become differentiated, and yet others change constantly. In all three of these types, the history of the composition is essentially self-contained, all forms being derived specifically, perhaps exclusively, from the original creation. A fourth type is similar to Type III, developing within the family principle but borrowing specific materials from other, unrelated compositions.

It is important to bear in mind that this typology is hypothetical and speculative, a model that sets forth extreme cases. We have some idea, from our perusal of the literature, that the tune family-type history, Type III, really does exist. So perhaps does the fourth, the borrowing type, but we can construct it only on the basis of conjecture. In both types we hypothesize, as did Charles Boilès, the existence of a parent composition for tunes that appear to be related. We cannot be as sure that the first two types of history really exist in their pure forms. Surely, just because we find a tune without known relatives does not necessarily indicate that we have an example. But translated into tendencies, the four types may have credibility.

The other side of the coin is always a culture's own perception of musical identities. For example, suppose we find what appears to us to be a true tune family of Type III, with all variants directly derived from the parent. It is conceivable that the performers do not recognize this process of derivation at all but ascribe to each variant a separateness of creation. I found a bit of evidence of this kind of situation among the Blackfoot Indians.

The old pattern of dreaming songs - composing them, as it were, in visions - provides some insights. Each person who had a vision was likely to have recieved songs from his guardian spirit. In fact, many of the songs thus learned by different individuals - albeit perhaps from the same guardian spirit - may, to the objective outside observer, be alike. It is true that this outsider may not be cognizant of the phenomena by which the Blackfoot differentiate songs. Students of Plains-Indian music have sometimes reported upon the difficulty of understanding why a singer regards two similar songs as unrelated and two quite different ones as variants of a single entity. But aside from that, it seems possible that the very act of separate creation which is experienced by these two songs may be enough to give the songs status as two different units of musical thought, quite in opposition to the fact that by our standards they are almost identical.

A contrastive experience happened to me in Iran. A performer claimed to play a piece - or, one might say, improvise upon a mode - identically each time, despite the fact that to any outside observer the performances sounded completely different, having in common only certain motifs and scalar patterns. In other words, the thing I called the other side of the coin can really be very distinctly another side. The obvious solution for a classification of transmissions could therefore be the assumption that the four types mentioned above are present in both systems but perceived differently in each system. One culture might regard a song as existing in numerous variants of the family-tree sort; another might consider the same group of variants as individual, separately created songs; and a third culture again might regard them as being in essence alike and belonging to a single-version, unchanging tradition.

Now that I have established the four hypothetical kinds of history that a composition can experience, the next step is to see whether entire traditions or repertories can be thus classified. There is no doubt in my mind that each repertory exhibits a mixture of at least some of the four types of compositional history, and it might be possible to find a dominant type for each repertory. But we are first faced with still another major problem on which I can only touch: the differentiation of genetically related units in a repertory with a limited musical vocabulary. One might state the problem simply by asking what relationship is significant and what is due to chance. A number of the publications already mentioned deal at least implicitly with this question.

Let us take an example. If we examine all peyote songs in most of the various American-Indian repertories that contain them, we find that many or most of the songs are very much alike. In composing new songs, any composer would have to produce something very similar to what already exists. A certain tonal range, a small number of note values (normally just two), and a typical melodic contour would have to be used. And the singer would have to use a very characteristic delivery and accompanying drum-and-rattle beat. Should one not therefore say that there are certain style elements, a simple musical vocabulary, on which the composer must draw? And is not such a vocabulary the basis of each musical tradition? Indeed some repertories evidently have large vocabularies of this sort, others much smaller, somewhat in the manner of languages. Materials that do not come from the vocabulary either are musically not understood or are accepted in the way languages accept neologisms or loan words. As a suggested nomenclature we could say that this vocabulary constitutes the thing we call <u>style</u> in music, while we might use the term <u>content</u> for those things that distinguish one compositon - a song perhaps - with all of its variants, or relatives, as it were, from other compositions in the same repertory. Incidentally, this distinction is perhaps parallel to the social model of a homogeneous cultural unit composed of a group of biologically related families, and to the problems of identifying the biological relationships from personal appearance or behaviour.

There are objections to this analogy, of course. In each culture the scope of the musical organism and its social role may differ. It may be a song, a group of songs, a phrase, a line. In some cultures, the musical unit is identical with what is socially regarded as a 'performance.' In others - as in the case of musical lines that have, as it were, an existence of their own - a unit is performed only in conjunction with other units. In a group of Czech jesting songs, I found the possibility of 'line families,' analogous to tune families, that have a distribution throughout otherwise unrelated groups of songs; yet a line is evidently never performed by itself.

11 Types of Tradition and Transmission

DENSITY AND DYNAMICS

The idea of a model for a type of tradition based in part on analogy with historical linguistics, and for types of relationships among mucical creations based on aspects of social structure, is attractive despite the problems already discussed. It leads, however, to two other considerations: <u>density</u> of a repertory and the <u>dynamics</u> of change.

By density, I mean the degree to which separate units of a repertory are similar, whether or not genetically related. Or, putting it another way, how close or how far apart, musically, are the units, pieces, songs, from each other? To illustrate the concept, imagine two tune families whose internal relationship has been proved by observation of the process, beginning with the composition of the parent tune. One family will develop variants, versions, and forms that are in the aggregate very different from each other; there may be considerable difference between one variant and its closest neighbour. This family would be lacking in density or could be called, for want of a better term, sparse. The ultimate classification of a family as sparse would depend on the classifier's having a complete knowledge of all its members; but this is only theoretically or experimentally possible. The other tune family has variants that are very similar to each other, and its closest neighbour-variants are almost identical. Such a family would be classified as dense.

Of course, this definition leads to other considerations. It is possible for a family to be dense, that is, to have a vast number of variants covering a great many points that are musically far apart in terms of any of a large number of components. But it would also be possible to find a family that is sparse but that, because of the small number of variants in it, still covers, musically speaking, very little ground. Samuel Bayard (1954) has illustrated these two types admirably; his 'Brave Donnelly' is dense, and his 'Job of Journeywork' is relatively sparse and much more extensive or broad than 'Donnelly.'

The same kind of thinking may be extended to an entire repertory. There are perhaps dense and sparse repertories, and there are, musically speaking, broad and narrow ones, and the two co-ordinates do not necessarily correlate. Thus, speaking impressionistically and giving exmples for which I have not more evidence than some first-hand acquaintance, I would say that twentieth-century Western art music is a broad repertory, and eighteenth-century Italian music less broad but very dense. Blackfoot-Indian music of the nineteenth century, from what we know about it, was probably broad and dense, at least as compared to Blackfoot music of the recent past, which is much less broad but equally dense. The English and Czech folk-song repertories are possibly more or less equally broad, but the English repertory seems to me to be denser and perhaps also larger. This mode of thinking should lead some day to a way of comparing repertories in accordance with the criteria mentioned. I do not know whether or not this will ever be possible, but it seems to me useful to consider different kinds of music from this point of view, realizing that the internal relationships among the units of musical thought in a repertory tell us something about its nature and genesis. But, again using the two sides of the coin, our understanding of these concepts must involve a culture's attitude towards individual compositions, innovation and its value, and the idea of delimiting a repertory.

A concept analogous to spatial density is historical density, that is, the speed with which a piece or a repertory changes. We might call this component the dynamics of the tradition. Admittedly we are able to learn even less about historical density than about some of the other dimensions of our subject because of the lack of precise historical documentation of world music. Still, one should be aware of it, and the reconstructions of evolutionists, classifiers, and tune-family proponents may help to increase our knowledge. Obviously, for example, one song may change very quickly but another - or the identical one in other circimstances - might undergo approximately the same changes but with the process requiring three times the amount of time. The dynamic distinction is relevant to all the model types discussed at the beginning of my remarks, except perhaps for the first, that of the piece that simply does not change at all.

At this point, the relative dynamics of oral and written traditions should be mentioned. Looking at the whole literature of ethnomusicology, we find two contrasting implications, one of which is that written traditions change slowly because they are able to preserve their artefacts in a way not possible for oral traditions, which are thought to change involuntarily, as it were, as a result of, for example, faulty memory. The other implication is that oral traditions change slowly because the simplicity of their cultural context makes them inert, and written traditions, because of the very sophistication of their apparatus (the notation system itself), move quickly (see, for example, Herzog, 1949: 1033; Hood 1959: 201). Within the history of a written tradition, speed varies, as is well known from a quick perusal of Western art music, whose tempo seems gradually to have accelerated but with much variation and many tempi rubati. Can we find out anything about speed of change in a culture for which only a contemporary repertory is known? It is to be hoped that analysis of the interrrelationships of related units some day will tell us something; so far there is little we can say concretely that is not the result of intuition, a brief historical record going back to the nineteenth century, or statements made by elderly informants. It will be more than usually necessary to exercise extreme caution.

EXAMPLES

I have set up a complex model for the comparison of musical traditions. Let me recapitulate: the history of the individual units of musical thought can be classified; I have proposed the existence of at least four major types: the unchanging, the changing but unvaried, the genetically related family, and the borrowing family. This same model can be magnified to characterize an entire repertory. Each unit and

13 Types of Tradition and Transmission

each repertory can be further classified in accordance with the dynamics of change and with density. But each classification has two aspects, again like the two sides of a coin: that of the outside observer whose findings are based on his special perception and on comparison; and that of the insider who uses the values of his own culture and its attitudes towards such things as creation, stability, change, and the special nature of music to create his own folk taxonomy.

Are these classifications practical? Given the small amount of information available for each musical culture and for each unit of musical creation in its history, probably not yet. But I imagine that each scholar with knowledge of more than one tradition could make a stab at trying them out. Like Alan Lomax,[3] I have tried to divide the concept of transmission into parameters, and would like to see a very rough, gross classification of musical repertories to establish them somehow within the framework of world music. Let me try it with some traditions with which I have some small amount of acquaintance and for whose types of transmission there seems to be at least a bit of direct evidence.

First, the modern music of the Blackfoot Indians and perhaps other Plains Indians of North America, primarily the social dance songs now intertribally current. These songs are very similar to each other; they are learned quickly because their forms are standardized; they are composed, so informants say, in considerable numbers (and their existence on many LP records testifies to their large quantity). Most of them do not remain in the repertory very long and do not undergo much change. Many of the songs seem to belong to Type II, the type that does not diversify but that experiences some change; some songs would seem to fit readily into Type III, the tune-family concept - but this is not very common - and some into Type IV, the family type that borrows components from extant songs, somewhat more common. Thus, the repertory cannot be regarded easily as being dominated by one type of transmission. The density is considerable, as implied above, and the dynamic component indicates considerable speed and a great deal of turnover. Now, since many 'new' songs may, on our side of the coin, be simply variants of existing songs, perhaps the statement of dynamics should be changed to reflect this observation. Obviously, the assessment of density and dynamics depends on the side of the coin from which we classify the transmission type of an individual song in the first place.[4]

The Blackfoot Indians themselves seem to have a view somewhat similar to the outsider's view presented here; but there are differences. The Blackfoot do not appear to feel that songs change very much but seem rather to regard each song as specially created and remaining essentially unchanged; similar tunes are separate. Thus, their view might differ from my analysis in that they would consider many songs as belonging to the unchanging Type I. Some informants agree that their songs are quite similar to each other and that two separate songs may indeed sound almost alike. And they agree that turnover is quick, although they believe that this was not so in the past. Presumably they would view their music history as moving increasingly rapidly.

There is another repertory of Blackfoot music, a repertory consisting of older religious music and associated material that, in contrast to the newer songs, is not shared with other Plains-Indian tribes (Nettl 1967: 304). This repertory exists on older recordings of Blackfoot music and in the memories of older informants, but it is not performed widely. From scanty sources of information one might guess that this music lived to a large extent in a tradition of Type I, that it was quite dense and also broad, and that it changed rather slowly, having far less turnover than the modern repertory.

As a contrast, consider the peyote songs sung by Plains Indians. These songs are quite different in sound from the general repertory of the Blackfoot, for in each Plains culture they constitute only a part of the repertory of the entire population; only some individuals participate, and for each of these individuals peyote music constitutes only a part of the musical experience. On the other hand peyote music is intertribal, and such groupings as tune families cross cultural, tribal, and linguistic boundaries. Nevertheless, this tradition can - with this boldly impressionistic approach that I am following here - perhaps be described as well.

The idea that peyote songs are made up from existing materials by combining and recombining phrases from a limited vocabulary is encountered in the literature and among singers. I once tried my hand at making a lexicon of musical lines found in a limited number of Kiowa and Arapaho peyote songs, attempting to identify lines that appeared in several songs. I must confess that, except for the normal closing formula and several penultimate formulae to which the last four notes are attached, I did not find a staggering number of such widely distributed lines, even if variants were liberally accepted. The results are somewhat different and more encouraging if one takes into account only the rhythmic material - the rhythms of the various vocal phrases.

On the other hand, one does not find large numbers of differentiated variants of individual songs or even of lines. The conclusion would be that this is a repertory that belongs in large measure to Type I, the unchanging, single form - with modifications, of course, and particularly with evidence of the process of Type IV borrowing. It is interesting that the statements of Indians themselves imply that they regard this as an essentially borrowing repertory, belonging primarily to Type IV, in contrast to their other music, such as the contemporary Blackfoot repertory described above. The peyote repertory is not as dense as that of the modern Plains songs but more so than the older Plains repertory. Again, it should be remembered that my hypotheses are made on the basis of small amounts of evidence. Speed of change and development can perhaps be assessed on the basis of comparing older with more recent recordings and of comparing variants of the same song from different tribes. Again on the basis of a small amount of information, I regard this as a slowly changing repertory whose songs do not change very much, whose materials

15 Types of Tradition and Transmission

remain extant for long periods, and in which there is little turnover. All of this, of course, is not easy to square with the ideas that this tradition creates new songs by combining material from existing ones and that its practitioners say so.

As indicated in the first part of this paper, the most-studied repertory of music for our purposes is that of Anglo-American folk song, for which B.H. Bronson and Samuel Bayard have developed sophisticated ways of studying tune relationships. These folk songs - they occupy a role in their cultures similar to that of peyote songs in Plains-Indian cultures in the sense that they constitute only a portion of the musical experience but are shared by a number of related cultural units - live mainly in the tune-family tradition, Type III, and in some cases they borrow material with the process of Type IV. The scope of the repertory is wider, perhaps, than is true of the two Indian repertories mentioned, but nevertheless it is not very broad. And considering the number of available variants of some tune families, it is quite dense, for the variants are similar and partake of a very limited number of modal, rhythmic, and form types. The style is limited even when the content is not. It appears to be a rather rapidly moving repertory in which individual songs change quite quickly, but the turnover of songs is slow and old material is retained while a small amount of new material is, or was, periodically introduced.

Moving to another culture, I had an opportunity to analyse a small number of Czech jesting folk songs. Like the peyote songs and the Anglo-American ballads, this group of Czech songs is an imcomplete repertory in the sense that Czech folk singers do not seem to regard it as a self-contained repertory but at best, perhaps, a genre with no specific boundaries. Nevertheless, the results, preliminary though they are, may be interesting as a contrast to the other materials discussed here. A significant portion of the material - particularly the third line of four-line songs - is in the Type IV, or borrowing category. There is, as already mentioned, the possibility of line families that move independently through the repertory. The basic units, or families of entire tunes, are small and dense, and the entire repertory is also dense, for tunes that are evidently unrelated genetically are nevertheless similar in content and style. The speed of change in recent tunes is something that also may attest to the importance of the written tradition in this culture. Unfortunately I have found no data for folk taxonomy.

My last examples are from Iran. Here the concepts held in the culture may well be quite different from those held by the outside investigator; moreover, in Persian culture there are substantial differences among the various strata of musical experience. Let me contrast the classical tradition of Tehran with one genre of folk music, the <u>chaharbeiti</u>, a four-line song form studied in Khorasan by Stephen Blum, to whom I am grateful for this information (1972; 1974).

The Persian classical system has as its central repertory the <u>radif</u>,[5] a collection of pieces that are used as the basis of improvisation and composition. In a sense, the <u>radif</u> is the 'content' of the music. Each of its parts, or <u>gushehs</u>, has variants and is in fact a small tune family. Each part, at the same time, has organic and genetic relationships to others in its mode, or dastgah, and to certain ones in other dastgahs. Thus the entire radif, or at least large parts of it, could be regarded as a single creation, or family, analogous to the Anglo-American tune family, with many internal interrelationships. The performances of each gusheh, improvised though they are, are in themselves also like a very, very sparse tune family. On the other hand, a performer produces in the course of his career a tightly knit, dense subgroup comprised of all of his performances of one gusheh. And each such sparse tune family maintains only a few content elements, such as thematic and closing formulae, to hold it together. The total group of performances or improvisations is a broad, sparse repertory, one that changes rapidly, while the radif itself changes only slightly. Here, then, are two structures superimposed on one another, to be analysed separately, and they exhibit more or less contrastive behaviour. The folk taxonomy, let me say very briefly and without discussion, seems here to be quite different from my analysis.

In certain portions of the Persian folk-music repertory in Khorasan, one may find a kind of microcosmic replication of what occurs in the classical music. The use of a small number of tunes to serve as musical vehicles for a vast number of texts is the basis of the repertories. The outsider perceives instantly, for example, that about half of the tunes used for chaharbeiti genre are very similar; indeed, the Iranian refers to such tunes collectively as one tune, the chaharbeiti tune (Blum 1974: 90). Of course, this tune exists in variants but these have not become developed to exhibit broad differences; the outside listener has no problem in keeping them under one hat, so to speak. Here we have, perhaps, a tradition that in a certain sense may be classed as Type I, the relatively unchanging type. And this is true, generally speaking, of a number of other melodies and genres in the Khorasan repertory. Each family, thus, is dense and seems to move slowly through time, changing but little. The entire repertory varies in density, and the families remain different from each other in varying degrees and exhibit the influences of the many cultures that play a part in Khorasan.

These various examples are taken at random, and their classification is hypothetical, awaiting better samplings and analytical methods. But ethnomusicologists, concerned as they are with the music of entire cultures, populations, and total repertories, should work towards finding ways of comparing the music of all cultures to each other as a whole, and also, of course, towards finding the reasons, inherent no doubt in the culture and its system of values, for differences and similarities. It is not too difficult to come up with models. The difficulty lies more in seeing whether they correspond in any way to reality, whether reality can be squeezed into them without too much distortion, and whether one knows enough about reality - the reality of the analyst and that of the culture's own perception.

17 Types of Tradition and Transmission

NOTES

1 An early draft of this paper was read at the annual meeting of the Society for Ethnomusicology, 17 October 1975, in Middletown, Connecticut. I should like to express thanks to Stephen Blum, who was my associate as a research assistant several years ago; to Sandra Moore, my research assistant in 1975-6, for helping to compile and abstract bibliographical materials for this study; and to the University of Illinois Research Board for making the help of these assistants available. This paper is in part the result of work done while I was an associate of the University of Illinois Center for Advanced Study in 1973-4, at which time I made preparations for a series of papers dealing with historical components in ethnomusicological study.
2 The rather voluminous work of Phillips Barry is often overlooked now by students of oral tradition, but his studies, published early in the twentieth century, do much to develop the concept. See, for example, Barry 1914.
3 In a number of ways I feel indebted to the spirit - though not the method and style - of recent work by Alan Lomax and his associates in the so-called cantometrics project. See, for example, Lomax 1968: 34-74, 117-69.
4 For more information on Blackfoot culture see Nettl 1967-8. The question of the size of repertories has hardly been touched in the literature. I am indebted to Alan Merriam for illuminating conversations regarding the comparative sizes of Blackfoot and Flathead repertories; the latter appears to be much smaller, despite the large number of uses of music and the similarity of style. Although he does not draw these conclusions in print, he does discuss the problem in Merriam 1967: 161-9.
5 For an explanation of the radif concept, see, for example, Zonis 1973.

REFERENCES

Adler, Guido 1930 Handbuch der Musikgeschichte 2d ed., vol. 1 (Berlin, H. Keller)
- 1934 'Style Criticism' Musical Quarterly 20: 172-6
Barry, Phillips 1914 'The Transmission of Folk Song' Journal of American Folklore 27: 67-76
Bartók, Béla 1931 Hungarian Folk Music (London: Oxford University Press)
Bayard, Samuel P. 1942 'Ballad Tunes and the Hustvedt Indexing Method' Journal of American Folklore 55: 248-54
- 1950 'Prolegomena to a Study of the Principal Melodic Families of British-American Folk Song' Journal of American Folklore 58: 1-44
- 1954 'Two Represenative Tune Families of British Tradition' Midwest Folklore 4 (1): 13-33

Becking, Gustav 1928 *Der musikalische Rhythmus als Erkenntnisquelle* (Augsburg, Ichthys Verlag)
Bekker, Paul 1927 *The Story of Music: An Historical Sketch of the Changes in Musical Form* (New York, W.W. Norton)
Blacking, John 1973 *How Musical Is Man?* (Seattle, University of Washington Press)
Blum, Stephen 1972 'Musics in Contact: The Cultivation of Oral Repertories in Meshed, Iran' PhD dissertation, University of Illinois, Urbana
- 1974 'Persian Folksong in Meshed (Iran), 1969' *Yearbook of the International Folk Music Council* 6: 86-114
Boilès, Charles L. 1973 'Reconstruction of Proto-Melody' *Yearbook for Inter-American Musical Research* 9: 45-63
Brailou, Constantin 1973 *Problèmes d'ethnomusicologie* (Geneva, Minkoff Reprints)
Bronson, Bertrand H. 1959-71 *The Traditional Tunes of the Child Ballads* (Princeton, Princeton University Press)
Chase, Gilbert 1958 'A Dialectical Approach to Music History' *Ethnomusicology* 2 (1): 1-8
Christensen, Dieter 1975 'On Variability in Kurdish Dance Songs' *Asian Music* 6 (1-2): 1-6
Elschek, Oskar 1966 'Methodological Problems in Slovak Ethnomusicology' *Ethnomusicology* 10 (2): 191-8
- 1969 *Methoden der Klassifikation von Volksliedweisen* (Bratislava, Slovakischen Akademie der Wissenschaften)
Fischer, Wilhelm 1915 'Zur Entwicklungsgeschichte des Wiener klassischen Stils' *Studien zur Musikwissenschaft* 3: 24-84
Herndon, Marcia 1974 'Analysis: The Herding of Sacred Cows' *Ethnomusicology* 18 (2): 219-62
Herzog, George 1949 'Song' *Standard Dictionary of Folklore, Mythology, and Legend* (New York, Funk and Wagnall) 1032-50
Hood, Mantle 1959 'The Reliability of Oral Tradition' *Journal of the American Musicological Society* 12 (2-3): 201-9
- 1971 *The Ethnomusicologist* (New York, McGraw-Hill)
Hustvedt, Sigurd 1936 *A Melodic Index of Child's Ballad Tunes*, Publications of the University of California at Los Angeles in Languages and Literature 1 (2) (Berkeley, University of California Press)
Járdányi, P. 1962 'Die Ordnung der ungarischen Volkslieder' *Studia Musicologica* 2: 3-32
Kemppinen, Iivar 1954 *The Ballad of Lady Isabel and the False Knight* (Helsinki, Akateeminen Kirjakauppa)
Knepler, Georg 1961 *Musikgeschichte des 19. Jahrhunderts* (Berlin, Henschel)
- 1972 'Music Historiography in Eastern Europe' in Barry Brook et al., eds., *Perspectives in Musicology* (New York, W.W. Norton)
Kolinski, Mieczyslaw 1959 'The Evaluation of Tempo' *Ethnomusicology* 3 (2): 45-56
- 1961 'Classification of Tonal Structures' *Studies in Ethnomusicology* 1: 38-76

19 Types of Tradition and Transmission

- 1965a 'The Structure of Melodic Movement' Studies in Ethnomusicology 2: 95-120
- 1965b 'The General Direction of Melodic Movement' Ethnomusicology 9 (3): 240-64

Krohn, Ilmari 1903 'Welche ist die beste Methode, um Volks- und volksmässige Lieder nach ihrer melodischen (nicht textlichen) Beschaffenheit lexikalisch zu ordnen?' Sammelbände der internationalen Musikgesellschaft 4: 643-60

LaRue, Jan 1959 'Union Thematic Catalogue of 18th-Century Symphonies' Fontes Artes Musicae 4: 18-20

Lomax, Alan 1968 Folk Song Style and Culture (Washington, American Association for the Advancement of Science)

Merriam, Alan P. 1964 The Anthropology of Music (Evanston, Ill., Northwestern University Press)
- Ethnomusicology of the Flathead Indians (Chicago, Aldine)

Nettl, Bruno 1967-8 'Studies in Blackfoot Indian Musical Culture' Ethnomusicology 11 (1): 141-60, 12 (2): 192-207
- 1974 'Thoughts on Improvisation: A Comparative Approach' The Musical Quarterly 60 (1): 1-19

Olsvai, I. 1963 'Typical Variations, Typical Correlations, Central Motifs in Hungarian Folk Music' Studia Musicologica 4: 37-70

Porter, James 1976 'Jeannie Robertson's "My Son David": A Conceptual Performance Model' Journal of American Folklore 89: 7-26

Rosen, Charles 1972 The Classical Style (New York, W.W. Norton)

Sachs, Curt 1940 The History of Musical Instruments (New York, W.W. Norton)
- 1943 The Rise of Music in the Ancient World, East and West (New York, W.W. Norton)
- 1946 The Commonwealth of Art (New York, W.W. Norton)
- 1948 Our Musical Heritage (New York, Prentice-Hall)
- 1962 The Wellsprings of Music (The Hague, Martinus Nijhoff)

Schneider, Marius 1957 'Primitive Music' in E. Wellesz, ed. Ancient and Oriental Music, New Oxford History of Music, vol. 1 (London, Oxford University Press) 1-82

Seeger, Charles 1950 'Oral Tradition in Music' Standard Dictionary of Folklore, Mythology and Legend (New York, Funk and Wagnall) 825-9
- 1960 'On the Moods of a Music-Logic' Journal of the American Musicological Society 13 (1-3): 224-61
- 1966 'Versions and Variants of the Tunes of "Barbara Allen,"' Selected Reports (Institute of Ethnomusicology of UCLA) 1 (1): 120-63

Temperley, Nicholas 1961 'Testing the Significance of Thematic Relationships' Music Review 22: 177-80

Treitler, Leo 1974 'Homer and Gregory: The Transmission of Epic Poetry and Plainchant' The Musical Quarterly 60: 333-72

Wiora, Walter 1953 Europäischer Volksgesang (Cologne, A. Volk)

Zonis, Ella 1973 Classical Persian Music: An Introduction (Cambridge, Mass., Harvard University Press)

W. JAY DOWLING
Musical Scales and Psychophysical Scales: Their Psychological Reality

This article presents a psychologist's view of musical scales to an audience of ethnomusicologists. It represents an expansion of the argument I have made elsewhere (Dowling 1978) that an actual melody - perceived or produced - is the result of hanging a particular melodic contour (pattern of ups and downs) on a modal-scale structure. It is fitting that this article should appear in a volume in honour of Mieczyslaw Kolinski, since his conceptualization of the analysis of melodic structure strongly influenced my thinking.[1]

To discuss the psychology of musical scales I shall introduce several levels of abstraction from the actual tones of empirically observed melodies. These levels of abstraction roughly parallel those of such schemes as Hood's (1971: 322 ff.), though I shall use more levels than Hood and also define certain terms differently. The scheme I shall use is illustrated in figure 1. The levels of abstraction are (1) psychophysical scale, the general system by which pitches are related to the frequencies of tones; (2) tonal material, the entire set of pitch intervals available in a given musical culture; (3) tuning system, a selection of a subset of the available pitch intervals made by choice of instrument or genre, for example; and (4) mode, the organization of the intervals of a tuning system into the sort of 'musical scale' that can provide the pitch material of an actual melody, with all the ramifications that might occur in a given culture.

PSYCHOPHYSICAL SCALE

The most abstract level of analysis is that of the psychophysical scale. This is the only level where I shall use the term scale, because it has been used so often at all of the other levels that to attempt to use it there in a more precise way would only be misleading. I hope that this abstract level is sufficiently remote from those other uses to avoid any confusion. By psychophysical scale I mean a system by which psychological pitches are assigned to physical frequencies of tones. We need to distinguish between frequency and pitch because various ways have been suggested for assigning pitches to frequencies, not all of which would strike the

Musical Scales and Psychophysical Scales

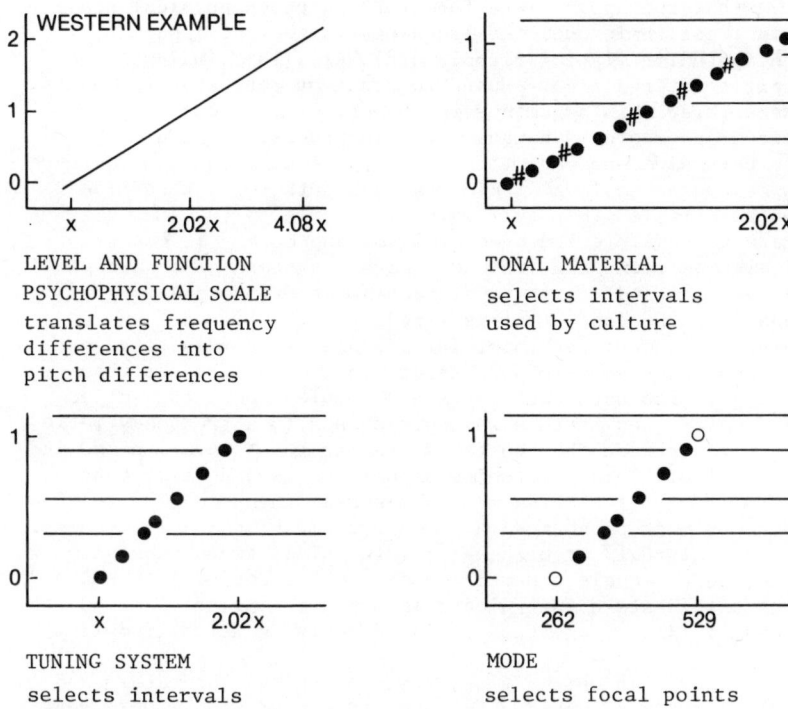

Figure 1. An outline of the levels of analysis of the pitch material of music presented in the text. In each of the graphs pitch in octaves is plotted against frequency in hertz. The horizontal lines are the lower four lines of the treble stave.

musician or psychologist as sensible. In this context, I mean a measurement system in which pitch intervals are assigned to differences between frequencies. We must think in terms of pitch intervals because, with the exception of a person with absolute pitch, there is no absolute anchor for the scale on the psychological side. In fact, at all levels except that of mode it will be preferable to think of sets of intervals rather than sets of fixed pitches. Ideally, a psychophysical scale should be like a foot rule, able to slide around among frequency differences and convert those differences into intervals of pitch. (Shepard 1964: 2351 and Attneave and Olson 1971: 148 make essentially the same point.) In its measurement operations the scale mirrors the operation of the human auditory system. The scale should be a movable rule and not a fixed co-ordinate system like longitude and latitude. (Of course, if the rule should prove empirically impossible to achieve, the alternative will be not metric co-ordinates but rather a system of arbitrary place names at odd distances from one another.)

I believe that the appropriate form for the psychophysical scale of pitch is logarithmic over the frequency range most important in music, and approximately logarithmic elsewhere. That is, constant sizes of pitch intervals correspond to constant ratios of frequency. I shall make three main arguments in support of this position: first, octave judgments by humans are both precise and cross-culturally pervasive; second, the intervals of well-known melodies are transposed along a logarithmic scale; and third, alternative approaches have failed to provide a useful scale.

Humans are generally quite precise in making octave judgments. In a typical experiment the listener hears a pattern alternating between a low tone and a high tone, each about one second long. The frequency of the lower tone is fixed, and the listener can adjust the frequency of the higher tone. The listener's task is to adjust the higher tone so that it sounds exactly one octave higher than the lower tone. With both pure tones and complex tones the subjective octave determined in this way corresponds to a frequency ratio of about 2.02/1 between the two tones, rather than the 2/1 harmonic ratio (Ward 1970). This stretching of octaves is generally constant across the midrange of hearing most often used in music (200 to 2000 Hz) and becomes more pronounced at more extreme high and low ranges. This approximately 0.1% stretching of intervals between successive tones (relative to equal-tempered tuning and 2/1 octaves) is characteristic of both Western instrumentalists playing melodies (Sundberg and Lindquist 1973) and the tuning of Indonesian gamelans (Dowling 1978).

The consistency with which it appears in both the laboratory and the musical practice of various cultures recommends the 2.02/1 subjective octave as a basis for a psychophysical scale of pitch. And the fact that this rule assigns equal differences in pitch (subjective octaves) to equal ratios of frequency (2.02/1) determines the form of the function as logarithmic. In Western music this octave would be used to derive an equal-tempered scale in which the semitone represents a frequency ratio of $2.02^{1/12} = 1.060$ (vs the usual semitone ratio of 1.059).[2]

Humans transpose familiar melodies along a logarithmic scale. This happens every time people sing 'Happy Birthday,' beginning on some arbitrarily selected frequency. Attneave and Olson (1971) studied this phenomenon more precisely by having listeners reproduce the NBC-chimes pattern by adjusting sine-wave oscillators. The advantage of using the NBC chimes was that they had never been played over the radio at any pitch level other than g-e-c, ending on middle c (262 Hz). Therefore the transpositions produced by the listeners would have to be extrapolations along their own internal pitch scales, and not the result of having heard the chime pattern at different pitch levels. Attneave and Olson provided the listeners with one tone out of the pattern and had them adjust the other oscillators to the frequencies of the other two tones. The pitch intervals of the pattern, up nine semitones and down four, were transposed accurately along a logarithmic scale from about 100 to 8000 Hz, and very precisely up to about 3000 Hz. In line with the studies of the subjective octave, these logarithmic intervals were stretched slightly relative to equal-tempered intervals based on the 2/1 octave.

Finally, the logarithmic pitch scale has no serious rivals in terms of consistent replicability and precision of human judgment. Stevens's 'mel' scale (Stevens and Volkman 1940), popular among psychologists, is based on listeners' ratio judgments of pairs of tones - whether one tone is twice as high as another, or one third as high, for example. But people do not make these judgments with nearly the precision with which they make octave judgments. As Ward (1970: 412) says in comparing the mel scale to the octave scale, 'Measuring pitch in mels ... is analogous to pacing off a room for wall-to-wall carpeting when a steel measuring tape is handy.' And Stevens's type of scale does not always replicate. Null (1974), for example, using a variety of methods very similar to those of Stevens, found scales that are best approximated by logarithmic curves. Both within the laboratory and across cultures the logarithmic musical scale appears to be the best candidate for a psychophysical scale of pitch.

I am claiming that the level of psychophysical scale with its logarithmic scale based on subjective octaves represents something that is almost cross-culturally universal. An overwhelmingly large number of musical cultures in the world uses the octave as a basic feature of their pitch systems. The fact that there are few cultures in which the octave is not a prominent feature does not preclude the very likely possibility that the octave is built into the structure of the human auditory system. Just because the ear is good at making octave judgments does not mean that all cultures must use the octave in their music. But although the interval of the octave is found almost universally, the ways in which the octave is filled in with smaller intervals vary widely from culture to culture. These smaller intervals are still transposed in a generally logarithmic manner, but it would be mistaken to suppose that anything like the equal-temperament systems developed by Chinese and Western theorists (Needham 1962) is found more than rarely outside those two cultures. The remaining three levels are concerned with how the octave is divided in various cultures.

TONAL MATERIAL

The next-less abstract level of describing the pitch components of music is that of tonal material. At this level are found all of the pitch intervals that are used in a musical culture. In Western music this would constitute the set of semitone intervals of the equal-tempered scale as represented, for example, on the piano keyboard. At this level also appear intervals that are not necessarily represented in the tuning of instruments, such as the neutral third, which appears in certain blues vocal performances in Western music but which lies between two notes on the piano. Indonesian music uses 'vocal tones' that lie outside the tunings of the gamelan instruments (Hood 1971); Indian music uses 'ornament tones' that lie between tones in the system of seven-note modes (Jairazbhoy 1971). These intervals will be omitted from the next level, that of tuning systems, but will reappear at the level of mode. This is because their use is heavily conditioned by the other dimensions of a mode besides its pitch-interval set. Tonal material is less abstract than psychophysical scale in that it specifies certain intervals within the octave that are characteristic of the culture. It is more abstract than tuning system in that it specifies all the intervals available in a culture, not just the ones used in a particular genre or on a particular instrument.

TUNING SYSTEM

The tuning system consists of intervals selected from the tonal material that are used in the various modes in the culture. Tuning systems are more general than modes in that they do not involve the imposition of a hierarchy of tonal functions on the intervals chosen. This selection is analogous to a set consisting of the white notes on the piano, which forms the basis of the major, minor, or church modes in Western music; or to a set of the black notes, which can be the basis of several pentatonic modes. In Indonesian music the tuning system corresponds to either the sléndro or the pélog system, which selects either five or seven pitches for each octave.

In cultures that do not use equal-tempered tuning and that do use instruments whose tuning fixes the pitches of the interval series, the tuning system is the appropriate level at which to make the transition from interval sets to fixed pitches. This is not true in Western music. In Indonesian music, however, the tuning of a particular gamelan fixes pitches and remains stable over very long periods of time. There is another aspect of the tuning of the gamelan that makes it an especially good example for the discussion of the tuning-system level. Hood (1966) has described the details of gamelan tuning, showing that within each octave the pattern of intervals between tones deviates from the pattern in the other octaves. At the level of the psychophysical scale these tuning deviations average out to the 2.02/1 subjective octave (Dowling 1978); at the tuning-system level the deviations constitute a musically important pattern which helps give individual character to each gamelan. This difference in tuning systems points to an important difference between Indonesian and Western music. In Western music the constancy of relationships of intervals across octaves is absolutely essential; in Indonesian music this constancy is not preserved and the variability is used for musical purposes. Hood (1971) points out that this variance is intentional and not just the result of non-Westerners' disregard of a musical dimension (precision of intonation) that Westerners consider all-important; all the various sets of instruments are tuned very precisely to the same skewed scale. In fact, in one sense the Indonesian musician is attending more precisely to pitch than the Westerner: he uses precise intonation that both matches the psychophysical scale overall and follows systematic deviations from it within octaves.

25 Musical Scales and Psychophysical Scales

MODE

Mode is determined by the convergence of values along several dimensions. One of these dimensions is pitch material, the central dimension of mode for this article. The pitch aspect of mode involves the imposition of a tonal hierarchy on the tuning system, as well as omissions and additions of pitches. Two other dimensions of mode less familiar to the Western musician must ultimately be considered as well - namely, characteristic melodic patterns and extramusical contexts - even though they are not dealt with here.

There are several ways in which a tonal hierarchy is imposed on a tuning system. The first is the selection of a tonality. The process of selection of a tonality does two things. First, it determines the absolute-pitch level at which performance will occur. Second, it determines where the tonal centre or centres will occur in relation to the intervals of the tuning system. If the tuning system has not already specified pitches, tonality selection will do so. In Western music, mode can be specified by tonality selection in the tuning system in two ways. If the tuning system is thought of as specifying the pitches of the white notes on the piano, then tonality selection will determine mode by choosing one of the notes as the tonic: for example, c for major, a for minor, d for dorian. Note that in this process the pitch level of the tonic changes with the mode. This sort of tonality selection is most characteristic of those cultures that use large sets of instruments with fixed tuning systems, such as the Indonesian gamelan. The second way of selecting tonality is to choose a pitch level as the tonic and then to adjust the tuning system's interval pattern with respect to the pitch level to determine the mode. If c is selected, the tuning-system pattern of intervals, ascending in semitones, of 2-2-1-2-2-2-1 determines the major mode. If this interval pattern is shifted down one notch, still starting on c, it becomes 2-1-2-2-2-1-2 and determines the dorian mode. This is equivalent to flatting the third and seventh degrees. This sort of tonality selection is more characteristic of cultures that use small sets of flexibly tuned instruments, such as the Indian sitar. Both methods of selecting tonality determine two things: fixation of the tuning system at some absolute-pitch level, and selection of a tonal focus in the tuning system.

The move from tuning system to mode entails more than just the fixing of tonality. The pitches of a mode are organized into a hierarchy of tonal functions. The various pitches have dynamic tendencies that make them gravitate towards others in the hierarchy. These tendencies have a psychological reality that goes beyond the increase and decrease of tension as a melody departs from and then returns to the tonal centres. Francès (1958) carried out an experiment in which he flatted two notes on a piano, e-flat (d-sharp) and a-flat (g-sharp). Then he played a piece in C minor, in which these notes have generally downward dynamic tendencies, and another piece in E major, in which the tendencies are upward. Listeners tended not to notice the flatting of the notes in the C-minor piece, but the flatting was quite apparent

26 W. Jay Dowling

in the E-major piece. Later I shall discuss the relationship of
humans' pitch-discrimination ability to the pitch material of music.
Here it is important to note that how small an alteration of pitch
can be reliably noticed (the just noticeable difference, or JND)
depends in Francès's experiment on melodic context. The JND seems
much larger when going in the direction of the dynamic melodic tendencies of the tone than when going against them.

The tonal hierarchy can determine omissions of pitches found in
the tuning system. Both the Indian and Indonesian modal systems are
characterized by tones that are omitted in certain modes (Hood 1971;
Jairazbhoy 1971). The omission is not absolute, however, and the
customarily omitted notes may be introduced for special musical
effects. Tones are also added to the set of pitches in the tuning
system in generating a mode. In Western music this is most evident
in the altered sixth and seventh degrees added to the harmonic and
melodic minor. Bronson (1976) notes that altered sevenths occur in
about four per cent, and altered thirds and fourths each occur in
about one per cent, of the Child ballad tunes. The vocal tones of
Indonesian music and the ornament tones of Indian music are added
at this level from the level of tonal material. These additions are
governed by the structural rules of the mode.

The dimension of pitch material in the definition of mode is
familiar to Western musicians; the remaining two dimensions are
less so. In numerous cultures mode is defined in terms of characteristic melodic patterns, such as the rāgs in Indian music
(Jairazbhoy 1971). In fact, in some cultures the dimension of
melodic pattern is completely dominant. Becker (1969) notes that
although a Burmese harpist may change open-string tunings in going
from mode to mode, the notes are altered by fingering. The result
is that the interval patterns of the various modes can be more or
less the same. (In my scheme, these customary fingerings would have
to be included in the tuning system.) Modes differ in their characteristic melodic patterns, and the retunings facilitate playing of
the different patterns. Some ethnomusicologists argue that there is
a similar predominance of melodic pattern in Indonesian music.

MULTIDIMENSIONALITY AND TRADE-OFFS

From this discussion of mode it should be clear that I do not think
that any one dimension is a sufficient basis for a definition. It
should also be clear that different cultures put different emphases
on the different possible dimensions. In terms of the pitch material
of music, those differences in emphasis can be seen where the culture
chooses to achieve precision in the multilevelled and multidimensioned
pitch system, and where it allows fuzziness. The human auditory
system is capable of discriminating a change of less than one per
cent in frequency of tones in the midrange where most of the pitches
of music occur (Shower and Biddulph 1931). The JND is thus much
smaller than any of the intervals used by the music of any culture.
For example, a 'quarter-step' interval in Western equal-tempered
tuning represents a 2.9 per cent frequency change. But this more or

less universal frequency-resolving power of the ear is used in different cultures for different purposes. Pitch categories may be left fuzzy at some levels and made precise at other levels. In my example of Indonesian gamelan tuning, pitch categories were necessarily fuzzy at the level of tonal material, since the details of the interval sizes varied from octave to octave and different gamelans are tuned to slightly different patterns. At the level of tuning system the pitches were made precise in the tuning of the actual pitches of a particular gamelan. Here pitch discrimination in terms of JNDs comes into play - the pitches of all the various instruments falling in the same octave are brought very closely into tune with each other.

Not all examples of fuzziness and precision fall in the same direction on the sequence of levels going from abstract to concrete. In the above example, the abstract level was fuzzy and the concrete level precise. The opposite relationship holds in the following example. In Western opera performance, singers typically use a wide, strong vibrato. This has the effect of making their pitches fuzzy, since it physically produces a spread of sound energy around the centre frequency. Thus pitches that are precisely defined at the more abstract levels of tonal material and tuning system, become much less sharply defined in the sung melody. A similar situation holds for the pitches of timpani in Western orchestral music and the large, low-pitched gongs in Indonesian music.

I think it is useful to distinguish between the several dimensions of musical pitch, such as those illustrated in figure 1, and the various dimensions of musical-performance practice characteristic of cultures. Cultures vary in such aspects as customary precision of intonation, degree of synchrony, and amount of dynamic contrast. Musical performance in a culture is determined by how that culture values many of these dimensions. With respect to pitch, different cultures choose to achieve precision of tuning at different levels and in different dimensions. I like to think that there are trade-offs involved in these cultural choices: achieving precision along one dimension means allowing fuzziness along another. But we do not know enough yet to know if that is really true. I believe it is true that no culture achieves perfect precision along all possible dimensions. I suspect that if that did happen the result would be most unmusical.

NOTES

1 The conceptual scheme presented in this paper was worked out with Dane Harwood. I also wish to thank James Bartlett, Kelyn Roberts, Darlene Smith, Leanne Hinton, Ron Lah, and Klaus Wachsmann for comments and encouragement.
2 Shepard (1964) and Krumhansl (1979) present persuasive arguments that octave equivalence should lead us to structure the psychophysical scale as a helix rather than as a two-dimensional line. The present formulations are compatible with that view but easier to draw, as shown in figure 1.

REFERENCES

Attneave, F. and Olson, R.K. 1971 'Pitch as Medium: A New Approach to Psychophysical Scaling' *American Journal of Psychology* 84: 147-66

Becker, J. 1969 'The Anatomy of a Mode' *Ethnomusicology* 13 (2): 267-79

Bronson, B.H. 1976 *The Singing Tradition of Child's Popular Ballads* (Princeton, Princeton University Press)

Dowling, W.J. 1978 'Scale and Contour: Two Components of a Theory of Memory for Melodies' *Psychological Review* 85: 341-54

Francès, R. 1958 *La Perception de la musique* (Paris, Vrin)

Hood, M. 1966 'Sléndro and Pélog Redefined' *UCLA Selected Reports in Ethnomusicology* 1 (1): 28-48

— 1971 *The Ethnomusicologist* (New York, McGraw-Hill)

Jairazbhoy, N.A. 1971 *The Rāgs of North Indian Music* (Middletown, Conn., Wesleyan University Press)

Krumhansl, C. 1979 'The Psychological Representation of Musical Pitch in a Tonal Context' *Cognitive Psychology* 11: 346-74

Needham, J. 1962 *Science and Civilization in China*, vol. 4, part 1 (Cambridge, Cambridge University Press)

Null, C.H. 1974 'Symmetry in Judgments of Musical Pitch' PhD dissertation, Michigan State University

Shepard, R.N. 1964 'Circularity in Judgments of Relative Pitch' *Journal of the Acoustical Society of America* 36: 2346-53

Shower, E.G. and Biddulph, R. 1931 'Differential Pitch Sensitivity of the Ear' *Journal of the Acoustical Society of America* 3: 275-87

Stevens, S.S. and Volkmann, J. 1940 'The Relation of Pitch to Frequency: A Revised Scale' *American Journal of Psychology* 53: 329-53

Sundberg, J.E.F. and Lindquist, J. 1973 'Musical Octaves and Pitch' *Journal of the Acoustical Society of America* 54: 922-9

Ward, W.D. 1970 'Musical Perception' in J.V. Tobias, ed., *Foundations of Modern Auditory Theory* (New York, Academic Press) 1: 405-47

DAVID WATERHOUSE
Towards a New Analysis of Rhythm in Music

In proposing a new approach to the analysis of rhythm,[1] I am conscious of my temerity. The literature of the subject is strewn with carcasses, and what I have to say could easily become food for carrion crows. But in reading what a number of authors have said about the theory of rhythm - though I have not picked through all the bones - I find grave shortcomings. In the first place, nobody can agree what rhythm is; and such associated terms as <u>metre</u>, <u>accent</u>, <u>stress</u>, <u>beat</u>, <u>time</u>, and so on are generally used without precision. In the second place, most essays on the <u>general</u> theory of rhythm (as opposed to descriptions of the rhythm systems of particular cultures) treat the subject from the standpoint of West European classical music; and today all musicologists (not only those who call themselves ethnomusicologists) have a duty to fight that bias continually. Thirdly, nobody - not even ethnomusicologists - pays more than lip service to the element of rhythm <u>in performance</u>: that is to say, to the way in which a rhythm is actually expressed, whether in the unwritten rules of a musical culture or in the art of an individual great performer. This third point, which is crucial to my approach, will be made clearer presently.

Rhythm is, however defined, one of the most important components of music; and in developing a vocabulary for musical analysis that could be applied to the music of any culture we should treat it as seriously as we have come to treat melodic analysis, the structure of tone systems, and the classification and description of musical instruments. There are today enough specialists in non-Western music to make possible a fresh and concerted attack on the problem; but it needs a theoretical backing that will be both less ethnocentric and less inhibited by the old analogy of rhythm in poetry.

I shall not take space here to review earlier definitions and theories. My own theory, in the light of what has just been said, is put forward as a contribution to epistemology and to musicology. It is <u>not</u> genetic: that is, I am not concerned with psychology, psycho-analysis, physiology, sex, evolutionary theory, or any other non-musical historicist consideration. Mine is a theory of rhythm in <u>music</u>, not a theory of 'Rhythmik' that would embrace the whole of human existence. Further, my theory is not a linguistic or mathematical model, because I do not believe that music can be reduced to language or mathematics. It is, rather, a structural, even structuralist, theory, in the broadest sense of those terms; but is not, I think, overtly metaphysical. I have chosen to cast it in basically Aristotelian terms, but it could also be phrased in Lévi-Straussian language. That might appeal to many readers nowadays - and having realized the possibility I was attracted by it myself - but I decided to retain my original framework, as a demonstration that structures are not absolute, but are to some extent like alternative systems of logic.

If it is charged that by citing Aristotle I am myself made guilty of ethnocentrism, one should also deplore the fact that I am using English for my analysis, rather than a non-Indo-European language - or, ideally, a universal one. Philosophy too has its socio-linguistic context, and, even if his terminology now sounds a little quaint, Aristotle's thought is presupposed in the structures of most later European philosophy, including what is said by some admired theorists of modern anthropology. The fact that it would be difficult to translate my own theory into Japanese does not invalidate it: it simply indicates the point of view and perhaps the limitations of the analytic method of Western philosophy.

Rhythm is a word, and like any word it is not defined by its etymology or by some objectively existing fact or concept, but by the way we decide to use it. My usage is relative to my theory, in which <u>rhythm-in-performance</u> (or simply <u>rhythm</u>) is paired and contrasted with <u>metre</u>. I treat these two terms as interdependent in the same way as Aristotle's terms Matter and Form; but I hasten to add that Aristotle, his disciple Aristoxenus, and other Greek writers do not make this connection. Aristotle himself mentions rhythm and metre quite often, but he nowhere gives us a fully developed theory of rhythm; and I do not speculate about what he would have said, even if my theory is Aristotelian.

To Aristotle, Matter and Form are <u>correlative</u>: they can be conceived of separately, but do not exist independently of each other. Aristotle does, however, distinguish between Prime Matter and Secondary Matter, the former of which <u>is</u> capable of separate existence. Treated as an epistemological distinction rather than as a piece of primitive physics, and as applied to my theory of musical rhythm, this would mean that rhythm-in-performance may exist independently of metre, as in music with free rhythm: an acceptable conclusion, I think.

More usually, however, rhythm-in-performance is associated with some kind of metre. Again consulting Aristotle, we find that he distinguishes between <u>sensible</u> Forms and <u>intelligible</u> Forms, and that they are arranged in a hierarchy. From a musical point of view, this suggests that metres too should be arranged in a hierarchy, from simple to complex: again, I think, an acceptable conclusion.

Actually, Aristotle's theory is much more complicated than I have made it appear to be. Form and Matter are related to each other in an inverse ratio, so that the greater the predominance of Form in an entity, the more refined and ethereal the Matter will be. In musical terms, this implies that the more a metrical system constricts

Towards a New Analysis of Rhythm in Music

the performer, the less room he has to manipulate rhythm-in-performance. On the other hand, in Aristotle's system Matter is the principle of individuation. The particular depends for its particularity on the Matter of which it is constituted. There are some striking parallels between Aristotle's theory of individuation and that proposed in recent years by P.F. Strawson, for whom the ultimate individual particulars of our conceptual system are 'things' and 'persons.' In music, which exists in time rather than space, the corresponding individual particulars are <u>performances</u>; and in rhythm, what makes a performance individual is what I am provisionally calling 'rhythm-in-performance.' Without this element, rhythm is merely metre: lifeless, mechanical, and not very interesting.

To Aristotle, the individual is not definable, but is recognized through intuitive thought or by perception. Intelligible individual particulars are recognized by the former, sensible particulars by the latter. If we think of rhythm-in-performance from this point of view, it appears to have both sensible and intelligible aspects, depending on the size or ranking of the rhythmic unit. Aristotle's basic point is that individuals are not to be known by universal propositions, however many: and I would say similarly that the total rhythm of a great performance cannot be understood by analysing only the metre; further, that any developed musical tradition has unwritten rules of rhythmic interpretation, which give individuality to the treatment of metres it may share with other cultures.

If these unwritten rules are analysed - and I do insist that they are in principle capable of analysis - that is not to say that we can give a <u>total</u> explanation of rhythm. Aristotle discusses different kinds of Matter, but he maintains that Matter is not fully knowable; and so for us too the rhythm of a great performance within any musical tradition cannot be reduced to formulae. To use another piece of Aristotelian language, <u>potential</u> knowledge is of the universal, but <u>actual</u> knowledge is of the individual and presupposes insight. It is not just the grasping of a set of laws, but presupposes a nonverbal awareness or recognition of particulars. As Wittgenstein's aphorism has it, 'Whereof one cannot speak, thereof must one be silent': and this is a philosophical truth, not a piece of mysticism.

This lesson in elementary philosophy need not be prolonged. We are now ready to consider in more detail the two basic components I have distinguished of rhythm in music - namely <u>metre</u> and <u>rhythm-in-performance</u>. I shall pass over metre somewhat briefly, since that is what most works on rhythm are about, and it would take us too far afield. I shall content myself with three general observations.

First of all, as Kolinski (1973) has shown quite well, the analogy between musical and poetic metres is misleading and ultimately false. The metrical schemata of prosody, whether quantitative, accentual, or syllabic, cannot easily be adapted to describing the subtle and varied rhythmic segments of a musical performance. In my theory, an additional reason for the inadequacy of the analogy is its total neglect of rhythm-in-performance. Poetry, I believe, has its own rhythm-in-performance; but in music the range of possibilities is so much greater, and in this respect prosody can hardly distinguish between music and poetry.

Secondly, how shall we arrange our scheme of metres? Deryck Cooke has suggested that all musical metres can be derived from two basic ones: duple and triple. Unfortunately he is thinking purely of Western music, but his theory bears examination. His reductionism is surely on the right lines: he does not go far enough, however, and like so many writers is misled by the analogy with prosody. Students of non-Western music would probably wish to add the <u>single</u>-beat metrical unit; and we may also find a use for the established terms <u>isometric</u> and <u>heterometric</u>. It should also be pointed out that the distinction between two- and three-beat units is not absolute. There are trochaic rhythms with a long first beat and short second beat, for example the Scottish jig, which fall between the two; and in still other cases we might wish to construe a three-beat metre as 2 + 1. Beyond that, however, the reduction of all metres to combinations of 1-, 2-, and 3-time would appear to be a truth of logic or mathematics, rather than an empirical theory; and as such it is ultimately trivial.

A third observation concerns unusual or more specialized types of metre. I am thinking especially of <u>polymetric</u> schemes such as one commonly finds in African music and, in less obvious form, in many other cultures; and irregular or asymmetric metres, for which I prefer the Turkish term <u>aksak</u> (literally 'limping' or 'lop-sided'). In polymetric music, it turns out, on analysis, that more than one metrical scheme is proceeding simultaneously, whether or not performed by a single player. Kolinski, under the influence of Gestalt psychology, would say that the ear cannot perceive more than one metre at any time: and before dismissing what he says, adherents of Freud or of J.B. Watson should go back and read Wertheimer, Köhler, and Koffka. Kolinski does allow, however, that we can perceive polyrhythm; and, redefining this as polyrhythm-in-performance, I agree emphatically.

Another type of simultaneous metre is logically distinct from the African type of polymetre, but in practice may sometimes be hard to distinguish from it, and may indeed frequently coexist with it. This is when two or more metrical schemes whose periods are of ever greater duration appear to be arranged in a hierarchy. The pattern formed by these periods, which may or may not correspond to the melodic phrase-pattern of the music, constitutes a higher-order metrical system, whose units are related vertically rather than horizontally. An appropriate general term might be <u>stratified</u> metre.

<u>Aksak</u> metres should present no special theoretical problems, but there may be practical difficulties in understanding their effect as rhythm-in-performance. Using combinations of simple, polymetric, stratified, and <u>aksak</u> schemes, it should be possible to develop a model - quite possibly topological or at least transformational - that will take account of all existing and most hypothetical metres. Some specialized metres have been created by twentieth-century composers, notably Stravinsky, Bartók, and Messiaen: it would be necessary to allow for such things as Messiaen's principle of <u>rétrogradation</u>, and for the new possibilities generated by electronic and

33 Towards a New Analysis of Rhythm in Music

computer music. For ordinary purposes, however, fairly simple models should suffice.

Syncopation is an auxiliary term which we may find useful as a way of characterizing particular metres - whether regular, irregular, or polymetric. In ordinary language, however, it also suggests features which more strictly belong to rhythm-in-performance, and for the present theory it would have to be redefined slightly. Tempo is another word with ordinary-language associations: but Kolinski (1959) has given a precise definition of it, which should be adopted generally.

I turn now to rhythm-in-performance. The problem as I see it has two aspects. What makes distinctive the handling of a particular metre within some musical culture, so that all representatives of that culture interpret it similarly? And what can we say from a rhythmic standpoint about the way in which a great artist, from any developed musical tradition, achieves his expressive effects? As I have hinted earlier, the second of these questions is on philosophical grounds less amenable to analysis; and we may be thankful for that, since otherwise our pleasure and interest in music could evaporate. The first, however, is a practical difficulty confronting any ethnomusicologist who aspires to 'bi-musicality'; and it is my contention that we can and should try to analyse this aspect of a musical culture. I have tried to list the possibilities as exhaustively as I can:

1.1 Accentuation (sfz.) of note on a primary beat
1.2 Accentuation (sfz.) of note on a secondary beat

2.1 Ornamentation of note on a primary beat
2.2 Ornamentation of note on a secondary beat

3.1 Lengthening of note on a primary beat
3.2 Lengthening of note on a secondary beat

4.1 Shortening of note on a primary beat
4.2 Shortening of note on a secondary beat

5.1 Anticipation of note on a primary beat
5.2 Anticipation of note on a secondary beat

6.1 Delay of note on a primary beat
6.2 Delay of note on a secondary beat

7.1 Silence before a primary beat
7.2 Silence after a primary beat
7.3 Silence before a secondary beat
7.4 Silence after a secondary beat

Under seven main headings, this gives sixteen methods of expressing a metre; and there may be others I have not though of. It would, I think, be rather dull to use only one method, and in actual practice we can expect to find some combination. This is, however, subject to the limitations of the musical instrument being used. One non-rhythmic component which has rhythmic affect, and so must be mentioned, is <u>pitch</u>. Where changes of pitch are correlated with the metric pattern in some way, one's perception of the rhythm is often enhanced. This applies to both monophonic and polyphonic music; and a typical case would be the coincidence of primary beat and tonic - as in many musical traditions. The European harmonic system, too, has rhythmic implications which should not be overlooked.

My terms 'primary beat' and 'secondary beat' refer to metre, and for particular metres it may be convenient to subdivide the types of beat further. I choose the terms 'primary' and 'secondary' as being the most neutral available, and reject such descriptions as 'stressed' and 'unstressed.' In case there is some objection to my use of the term 'note,' I should say that I am thinking of music in which pitch is an element. This would include most percussion music, but I realize there may in certain cases be difficulty in defining just what a note is. I do not think this affects my theory, however, because in music with this degree of indeterminacy rhythm-in-performance is likely to be fairly undeveloped.

I shall now consider briefly each of the seven factors. <u>Accentuation</u> is a momentary loudening. The degree of loudness, and the way in which it is produced, will depend on the culture, the performer, and the type of instrument. This type of rhythmic expression is perhaps the most common, and it is certainly the one that is best understood in the West European classical tradition, which has notational symbols for it. Even in European music, however, there are instruments, such as the organ, harpischord, and bagpipe, which are incapable of it.

<u>Ornamentation</u> serves to enhance melody as well as rhythm, and in many music cultures it is a principle of formal organization, the basis of sets of variations. It may also be an integral aesthetic feature of the music. From a rhythmic point of view, however, it is one way in which the harpsichord or bagpipe, for example, compensate for their inability to accentuate notes. From a rhythmic point of view, one also has to consider that ornaments take time to execute, and thereby may displace a main note forwards or backwards. It has become customary to ask whether ornaments begin on or before a beat, but this is too simplistic an approach to the problem, since the beat may fall anywhere between the beginning of an ornament and its resolution onto a main note.

<u>Lengthening</u> and <u>shortening</u> of a note only make sense in relation to a rigid metrical scheme. They are most easy to detect if the metrical values are indicated by a notation that prescribes the duration of notes, as does Western staff notation. The lengthening and shortening of note values will then appear as <u>systematic deviations</u> or departures from the expected proportional norms. For non-Western music, however, it will not always be clear what durational grid can be imposed, and we should be cautious in using Western notational symbols, with their binary divisions of duration. It is

35 Towards a New Analysis of Rhythm in Music

important to realize, too, that Western notation is not wholly adequate even for Western music, since there are unwritten conventions that govern the lengthening and shortening of notes in dance rhythms especially. One may contrast the Viennese waltz and the minuet, the polka and the march, and so on.

Similar considerations apply to the <u>anticipation</u> or the <u>delay</u> of a note. Both devices serve to draw attention to the note; and, within a particular musical tradition, one may be used rather than the other, both may be used, or neither. Anticipation is the converse of lengthening; delay is the converse of shortening. It may be possible to make generalizations about the aesthetic and psychological effects of these four expressive devices of rhythm-in-performance: but I am not yet confident that I can do so myself.

The last category, <u>silence</u>, is self-explanatory. Next to accentuation, silence is the most common device performers resort to when they try to express a rhythm. Any rest or any staccato implies a silence; and silence also helps a performer to phrase his melody. It was remarked earlier that phrase <u>structure</u> may have metrical implications; in <u>practice</u>, however, phrasing may be considered as an aspect of rhythmic expression, since in addition to using silence one can also phrase by use of lengthening, shortening, anticipation, or delay.

I was tempted to include in my list the converse of accentuation, which would be a sudden but temporary diminuendo; and its more extreme form, which would be silence <u>on</u> a primary or secondary beat. The former, however, does not seem capable of enhancing a rhythm; and the latter would be even less effective, though as an aspect of <u>metre</u> it is important in syncopation. Logic, however, does demand that these further possibilities be included in the list; and perhaps somebody can think of an application for them. This would raise the total number of factors to twenty.

Just as metres can be arranged in a hierarchy, so there is a hierarchy for rhythm-in-performance. The seven types of rhythmic expression we have been considering belong to the lowest level; and above them we can distinguish other ways of departing from strict metre. The two main types seem to be the familiar <u>accelerando</u> and <u>rallentando</u>; also occasional, as opposed to systematic, application of some one of the seven types - as in a cadential pause. Over these one can superimpose such culturally conditioned forms as <u>rubato</u> (which Matthay has shown to be capable of analysis and indeed of notation), and the 'staggered' or 'stretched' rhythms which one encounters in Japanese court music (<u>gagaku</u>) and in classical music for Highland pipes (<u>piobaireachd</u>). Both <u>rubato</u> and stretched rhythm seem to be associated with, and perhaps depend on highly organized and symmetrical musical forms. On a higher level still, we may place the performer's choice of tempo and his overall rhythmic conception of what he is playing. The relationship between these levels of rhythmic interpretation can probably be stated quite formally, as can the relationship between scientific laws of lower and higher order.

The reader may be wondering how the abstract system presented above will work out in practice. The answer is twofold. First, in any developed musical tradition, the application of all sixteen factors of rhythm-in-performance to whatever metrical schemes there may be is a difficult and subtle business. When one adds to this the higher factors of rhythmic interpretation, the analysis becomes still more complex. Where the metrical scheme too is complex, as in different ways it is in Indian, or Balkan, or Korean, or Balinese, or African music, we can only marvel at the artistry of a great performer, in whose music there is an interplay between a hierarchy of metrical factors and a hierarchy of factors of rhythmic import.

Secondly, I contend that the best way to become aware of what I have been calling rhythm-in-performance is <u>from the inside</u>: that is, to immerse oneself in the tradition, not only as listener but as performer too. In theory, it should be possible to measure both metre and rhythm with a machine - one which might be somewhat simpler than the Melograph; but though this would be very helpful, one would still have to analyse the results, and to assess the relative importance of the different factors (Ed. note: see Hopkins' article in this volume). This could not be done without an intimate knowledge of the tradition. Thus comparative study of rhythm, using my method, depends on collaboration between specialists.

I was myself first made aware of the importance of rhythm-in-performance when many years ago I began to study the Highland bagpipe, which uses the straightforward metres of European music, but which interprets them in quite a surprising way, by emphasizing a different set of rhythmic factors. Highland pipes are incapable of accentuation or of silence (at least while they are being played!). They can sound only <u>fortissimo</u> and <u>legatissimo</u>. This being so, the piper has to use ornamentation, lengthening, shortening, anticipation and delay, if he is to play expressively. A glance at any page of pipe music will show one that it is even more ornamented than that of Couperin; but of course the notation does not indicate the other factors, which the novice piper learns subconsciously, if he learns them at all. Most pipers play no other instrument, and a master piper cannot easily explain what he is doing. I was made painfully aware of the difficulty when, with a conventional music training - and not a little exposure also to ethnomusicology and non-Western music - I tried to play 6/8 and 2/4 as written, and found that it did not sound right. I was fortunate in having good teachers, and did eventually learn what one was supposed to do; but then found myself unable to analyse it - and not always able to execute it! This was the genesis of the general theory of rhythm which I have outlined in the present paper.

I am precluded from giving here a detailed analysis of the structure and interpretation of rhythm in Highland pipe music, since it could fill a large book. At this stage I am not even sure of the best way in which to present such an analysis: it would be necessary to devise special notational symbols and technical terms, and it would be unintelligible without reference to recorded examples. Even then, the untrained ear - that is, the ear of a non-piper -

might find it hard to respond to certain fine discriminations.

I believe that similar considerations apply to the study of any highly developed performance tradition, and not only to rhythm but also to melodic and tonal analysis. In these cases too we need an analytical method which will take heed of contemporary performance practice - the melodic progressions and temperaments actually preferred by skilled instrumentalists and singers - as well as of theoretical structures. Indeed, the latter may turn out often to be ex post facto and even anachronistic. Further discussion of these topics, however, would take us beyond the boundaries of the present essay, whose main purpose has been to advocate the serious analysis of rhythm-in-performance, and to propose informally a structural model for it.

NOTE

1 The text of this essay is a slightly revised version of a paper read at the conference of the Society for Ethnomusicology in San Francisco in 1974. Since then, the pressure of other work, and a natural disinclination from rewriting, have prevented me from making extensive alterations, though I have tried to take account of the comments of friends who heard it or read it, notably Dr Mieczyslaw Kolinski and Dr Laurence Picken. I also like to think that in its original, aphoristic form, the leading ideas of the paper stand revealed more clearly. At a later date I hope to treat the subject more fully.

REFERENCES

Cooke, Deryck 1959 The Language of Music (London, Oxford University Press)
Kolinski, Mieczyslaw 1959: 'The Evaluation of Tempo' Ethnomusicology 3 (2): 45-57
- 1972 'A Cross-cultural Approach to Metro-rhythmic Patterns' Ethnomusicology 17 (3): 494-506
Matthay, Tobias 1912 Musical Interpretation (London, Joseph Williams)
Strawson, P.F. 1959 Individuals. An Essay in Descriptive Metaphysics (London, Methuen)
Wittgenstein, Ludwig 1955 Tractatus Logico-Philosophicus, 6th impression (London, Routledge & Kegan Paul)

JAY RAHN
Simple Forms in Universal Perspective

A great deal has been accomplished in music theory of late. In contrast to previous efforts at theorizing, recent endeavours have attempted to lay foundations for discussing not just twelve-tone music or major-minor music or any other kind of music but all music. Indeed, Benjamin Boretz in 'Meta-Variations' has referred to his work as an 'all-music theory,' that is, a theory for all music rather than just some music. In quite different spheres are Maury Yeston's The Stratification of Musical Rhythm and Robert Erickson's Sound Structure in Music, in which temporal, textural, and timbral aspects of music are discussed not only with respect to the standard repertory of the Common Practice period or the emerging standard repertory of contemporary art music, but also music outside the Western elite tradition. Such a tendency to include all, or any, music is most encouraging to ethnomusicologists who are called upon to consider literally all music from a unified perspective. Indeed, such a tendency should be exciting to both types of specialist: the theorist mostly preoccupied with Western art music just might discover that his findings are put to a severe test when they are held up against other music; and the ethnomusicologist, who has for too long made do with rather makeshift formulations, can certainly learn something from the rigour[1] of current theory.

One potential area for co-operation involves the forms that music can take. Although there is a considerable amount of information on forms throughout history and across cultures, the special topic of forms has been largely neglected by theorists. One reason for this neglect would appear to lie in the type of discourse that has been employed with regard to forms. For example, several otherwise promising accounts founder when they arrive at such locutions as 'The form of the piece is ...' Usually, in such cases it is not a question of 'the' form but of several coterminous forms. Consider, for instance, the following micropiece:

Simple Forms in Universal Perspective

The form with regard to pitch succession is ABCDEF, but with respect to timbral succession it is ABA, and with regard to interval content it can be interpreted as AA. From this example two things are to be learned: different forms can coexist temporally, and only the form of some specific variable - such as the succession of pitches, timbres, or intervals - can be spoken of convincingly. It also seems useful to consider the forms in a part of a piece as well as those of the whole. A given span might be characterized as containing given forms. It also seems profitable to consider the forms of the contents of non-contiguous spans. This, in fact, is what is done when the rhyme scheme of a poem is described as, for example, abba: here the timbres of special spans corresponding to the last syllables of lines are compared.

To summarize, several forms can coexist; it is always a question of the form of a specific variable; and the spans considered in a form need not be contiguous. Though the questions surrounding multiple coterminous forms are highly interesting, their significance cannot be understood until the individual constituent forms have been accounted for. Accordingly, the present paper will focus on individual, simple forms, the sort that can be represented by such letter formulas as AAB, ABCA, and ABABA.

Several types of simple form are found, and various terms have been used to classify these different types. Forms consisting exclusively of one value that is repeated for different spans (for example, AA, AAA, AAAA) have been termed iterative (Herzog 1935; Nettl 1956; Sachs 1961; Chenoweth 1974). Forms in which no values are repeated have been described variously as progressive (Herzog 1935; Nettl 1956, 1974; Sachs 1961; Chenoweth 1974), through-composed (Merriam 1967; Besmer 1970), or strophic (Wade 1973). The terms recursive (Herzog 1935; Sachs 1961), reverting (Nettl 1956, 1974; Chenoweth 1974), rondo (Wade 1973), and strophic (Merriam 1967; Besmer 1970) have been used to describe forms in which there is repetition among such non-adjacent spans as ABA, ABAC, and ABCCB.

Beyond this elementary typology, various authors have described special types for special repertories. Thus, Herzog (1935), Sachs (1961), and Merriam (1967) refer to forms marked by paired repetition (for example, AABB, AABBCC), and Nettl (1954) and Merriam (1967) distinguish incomplete repetition (for example, ABC/BC, ABCD/BCD). Chenoweth (1974) describes forms that mix iterative and recursive relationships, such as ABCADEB, as progressive, and forms that can be analysed into iterative segments (for example, AABB/AABB/AABB, AABA/AABA/AABA) as strophic. Finally, forms in which the first and last values are identical (for example, ABA, ABCA, ABABA) have been termed symmetrical by Nettl (1974).

Even this cursory review of the designations of eight writers is sufficient to demonstrate that there is little agreement among them on the terms used to describe even the most basic types of forms. Furthermore, some formal types seem to be found all over the globe and others are more restricted in distribution.

Ethnomusicologists, however, are not the only students of music who are engaged in describing simple forms. For example, Bar form

(AAB), binary or bipartite forms (for example, AA, AB), and ternary or tripartite forms (for example, ABC, ABA) are widely recognized by historians of Western music. With regard to the latter two kinds of forms, one can observe little agreement about their meaning or significance.

There is great diversity not only in the terminology used to describe simple forms, but also in criteria considered significant to describe types of forms. The notion of symmetry depends on the concept of extremity since the extreme spans must be identical; the number of spans is considered significant if such terms as ternary or tripartite are used; a distinction between adjacency and non-adjacency is involved if iterative repetition is to be distinguished from recursive repetition; and the terms progressive and reverting have the connotation of 'forward motion in time,' which is lacking in such terms as symmetry, paired repetition, incomplete repetition, and binary or bipartite. Moreover, some theorists avoid letter notation altogether in their discussions of form, because they feel that letter notation produces too static an impression of the allegedly dynamic processes of music (Meyer 1956; Cone 1968).

This terminological and critical confusion and the opposing formal, or static, and processive, or dynamic, approaches create a fundamental problem for any consideration of form. I propose a solution that gets back to basics, namely, an epistemological solution. A more comprehensive view is possible, I believe, if one steps back and tries to describe only those relationships that are necessary to identify a given form. For example, although one cannot identify the form ABA if one compares only adjacent spans, one can identify the form AA in this way. It follows that a form such as ABA requires more types of relationships, or more concepts, in order to be identified.

Not only does an epistemic approach help to identify forms; it also aids in describing the relationships among forms. For example, ABBA and ABCA intuitively appear to be similar, as do ABA, ABABA, and ABACA. But what types of relationships and concepts must be invoked to describe determinately their similarities and differences? An epistemic approach provides a clear answer.

The epistemic solution offered here also transcends the formal-processive dualism inherent in many discussions of form. Formal and processive approaches are merely two sides of a single coin. The formal approach corresponds to the notion of cardinality, which implies the notions of adjacency and sequence, which in turn correspond to the processive approach. Furthermore, the distinction between processive and formal approaches involves a distinction between local and more remote relationships. If it is easier to perceive local relationships than it is to perceive more remote relationships, the approach offered here will also clarify problems in the psychology of form.

In theoretical discussions, it is customary to cite examples. Often these examples are works divorced from the context of the repertory in which they are found. In this study, however, the examples consist of formal types that are found throughout entire repertories, and analytical techniques that have been applied to

41 Simple Forms in Universal Perspective

entire corpora of music, both Western and non-Western. Moreover, this discussion is not restricted to melodic forms but also considers relationships between any non-simultaneous spans to which single values have been assigned. For example, the succession of pitches in g a b g might be considered an instance of ABCA form, as might the succession of durations in ♩ ♩. ♪ ♩ and the succession of timbres in on y u on (a rhyme scheme).

Throughout the discussion, values will be compared with one another in terms of only two relationships: identity (A = A) and non-identity (A ≠ B). The positions of the spans in which various values are found will be compared to one another according to four types of relationship: diversity, adjacency, immediate and referential sequence, and cardinality. If two spans are positionally diverse, they simply occur at different times; if they are adjacent, they are next to each other. If two spans are in immediate sequence, one just precedes the other. Finally, if two spans are related cardinally, their positions are numbered.

Positional relationships of diversity identify only the most basic forms: those that are purely iterative or progressive and made up of only two spans. Adjacency identifies more complex forms than does diversity. Sequence is more powerful than adjacency, and cardinality is the most powerful type of relationship.

DIVERSITY

The most basic interpretation of formal relationships is one that is restricted to diversity, that is, one where the positions within a span are considered to be merely different. For example, AA can be described as a form in which spans at different positions have identical contents, and AB as a form in which spans at different positions have different contents. The same could be said of such forms as AAA and AAAA and ABC and ABCD, respectively: in each case, there is a uniform relationship of identity or non-identity among contents at different positions. In these forms, only two types of relationship are possible: repetitive and non-repetitive.

Such an interpretation seems fine for the schemes AA, AB, AAA, and ABC, but it fails to distinguish among AAB, ABB, and ABA. All that it can tell us about these is that there is one repetitive relationship and two non-repetitive relationships:

```
 ┌ = ┐         ┌ = ┐       ┌ = ┐
 A  A  B,    A  B  B,    A  B  A
    └ ≠ ┘       └ ≠ ┘       └ ≠ ┘└ ≠ ┘
 └── ≠ ──┘   └── ≠ ──┘
```

As far as this kind of interpretation is concerned, all three types of form are the same.

In summary, diversity suffices for all two-position forms (AA and AB). It fails, however, to distinguish among non-uniform, 'mixed' three-position forms (AAB, ABB, and ABA).

42 Jay Rahn

Examples of diversity   In scale formulas for monophonic pieces, such as those in example 1, the pitch classes or pitches that appear at various positions of a piece are merely listed. From such formulas, nothing can be inferred concerning which pitches or pitch classes appear adjacent to one another; which appear immediately before or after others; which is the first or last of a piece; which is referential for the piece; or which appears at any given position, such as the third or twelfth position. All that can be inferred is that the given pitches or pitch classes occur at different positions.

Example 1. Scale formulae: (a) pitch classes of the diatonic collection of C-major; (b) pitches in the Japanese scale of zoku-gaku (after Peri 1934)

Similarly, in the theory of atonal music, one discusses so-called unordered sets of pitch classes (for example, 014): these also imply mere diversity of position (compare Forte 1973). Analyses of music in which the durations of tones are listed with no consideration for their further ordering, reduce rhythmic relationships to a mere sum of duration and positional diversity (see, for example, Nettl 1954). And finally, in a number of contemporary aleatoric pieces, sections may be arranged by the performer in any order; that is, the composer specifies positional diversity as the only basis for formal relationships on the sectional level.

ADJACENCY AND EXTREMITY

The relationship 'adjacent to,' which includes the category 'different from,' is symmetric, since if X is adjacent to Y, Y is adjacent to X. It is also intransitive, for if X is adjacent to Y and Y is adjacent to Z, it does not follow that X and Z are adjacent to each other. In the form AA, the two As are adjacent to each other; in AB, A and B are adjacent to each other. Since A = A and A ≠ B, the iterative relationship of immediate repetition can be inferred from AA, and the progressive relationship of immediate contrast from AB. In AAA, there are two iterative relationships; in ABC, there are two progressive relationships. ABC can be considered to represent a chain or process of progression, and AAA a process of iteration.

According to an interpretation based strictly on adjacency, ABA cannot be distinguished from ABC, and AAB cannot be distinguished from ABB. ABA, however, can be distinguished from AAB and ABB, a fact that marks adjacency as an improvement on the discriminatory powers of mere positional diversity. ABC and ABA both represent processes of progression, since the contents of adjacent spans are always in contrast. All that can be stated about AAB and ABB is that in both forms one pair of positions is repetitive and one pair is non-repetitive:

```
┌ = ┐           ┌ = ┐
A  A  B,      A  B  B
  └ ≠ ┘         └ ≠ ┘
```

<u>Examples of adjacency and extremity</u> The notion of juxtaposition (as in the statement that works in the Classical style feature juxtaposition of different textures more often than do those in the late Baroque style) depends on the concept of adjacency. All of the examples of 'long songs' collected by Bartók in northern Romania can best be interpreted by adjacency. If this is done, it is found that within the strophes of all the songs, relations among adjacent phrases are marked by a process of musical progression (compare Rahn 1976).

Finally, it can be noted that recursive or recapitulating forms, which require for their distinction a recognition of extremes, dominate entire repertoires. For example, most of the standard forms in the Classical style, such as the rondo, minuet-and-trio, and sonata, feature recurrence, as do the ABBA 'utility tunes' of the 'Come-all-ye' type in Anglo-American song (compare Rosen 1971).

If the notion of adjacency is extended to its corollary concept, extremity, one can infer a distinction between ABC and ABA. The extremes of a group of spans can be defined in terms of adjacency as the only spans of the set that are adjacent to only one other member of the set. For example, in ABC, the spans represented by A and C are extremes in contrast with the span represented by B. Accordingly, one can infer a distinction between ABC and ABA on the basis that the extreme spans in ABC differ whereas in ABA they are the same. The special status of extremes also makes them fair game to be considered referential for the rest of the positions. As referential positions they can be compared with all others. When the notion of sequence is added to one's conceptual vocabulary, what were merely extremes take on new meaning as the first and last positions of a form.

SEQUENCE

The next most basic relationships possible between the various positions of a form are sequential: positions can be described as before and after, in the senses of immediately preceding and immediately following, respectively. If A immediately precedes B, it follows that A and B are in different positions and adjacent to each other. If the positions of the two As in AA are described in terms of immediate sequence, it can be asserted that the first A anticipates the second and the second A confirms the first. If A immediately precedes B, or B immediately follows A, it can be said that A prepares B or B resolves A.

44 Jay Rahn

In a sequential interpretation AAB and ABB can be distinguished, since anticipation precedes preparation in AAB, whereas the reverse is true in ABB. This is an example of processive logic.

Examples of sequence   Scale formulas of the type developed by von Hornbostel and Kolinski depend on immediate before-after relationships (Kolinski 1976). Example 2 shows not just the pitch events of the piece according to order identity (as was done in example 1) but also the relative positions of pitches in the leaps. Thus, the arrow joining g and d indicates that g appears immediately before d.

Example 2. Scale formula for an East African song (after Kolinski 1976). Lines join pitches that immediately precede or follow each other; an arrow joins two pitches of which the first precedes the second but the second does not precede the first. The fermata indicates the last tone of the piece; the inverted fermata, the first.

In atonal music theory, the notion of interval succession depends on sequence, and such concepts as tension, resolution, anticipation, and suspension in Common Practice theory similarly depend on notions of immediate precedence or sequence (compare Forte 1973). Recently, these relationships have been explained as 'defined relations of succession,' and as such they form the basis for the interpretation of voice-leading and melodic dissonance (Boretz 1969-71).

In French monophonic song around 1500, the rhyme schemes of half strophes are all distinguishable by processive logic: aa, ab, aaa, aab, abb, and abc are all found; aba is not (see Rahn 1978; 1981). Further recognition of the importance of first and last positions, which depend for their definition on the notion of sequence, is found in modal theory of medieval Europe and the prescriptions for Arabian maqamat and Indian rāgas (compare Tinctoris 1967; d'Erlanger 1930-59, vol. 5).

CARDINALITY

The ultimate interpretation of formal relationships involves the cardinality of the positions in a form. Cardinal numbers can be assigned to all the positions of a form.

In forms composed of two, three, or four positions, cardinality need not be invoked for one form to be distinguished from another. This can be seen in the case of the four-position forms. The repetitive and iterative scheme AAAA is distinguished by a chain or process of iteration. The schemes AAAB, ABBB, and AABB can all be distinguished by the processive logic of adjacent and sequential relationships. If either the first or last position is considered referential and before-after relationships are invoked, the following schemes can also be

45 Simple Forms in Universal Perspective

distinguished: ABBA, ABBC, AABC, AABA, ABAA, ABCC, and ABCA. If both the first and last positions are considered referential, ABAB, ABCB, ABAC, and ABCD can be distinguished from one another and from other forms.

Five-position forms present greater difficulties in distinguishing one form from another. Even if two positions, such as the first and last, are considered referential and sequential relationships are allowed, one relationship between a pair of positions will still remain undefined. For example, if the first and last positions are referential and sequential relationships are introduced, the forms ABABA and ABACA are indistinguishable because there is no place in the interpretation for relationships between the second and fourth positions. In order to distinguish such forms, two approaches are possible: a resort to cardinality, whereby each position can be related to every other position, or a breaking down of the forms into more manageable form. Accordingly, AAABB, AABAB, and ABBBA might be broken down into pairs of three- and two-position forms: AAA/BB, AAB/AB, and ABB/BA.

In order to distinguish such forms fully, one must be able to describe, in each pair, the relationships between the two forms, that is, between AAA and BB, between AAB and AB, and between ABB and BA. In all three pairs, the component forms are distinguishable by processive logic. In AAA/BB, both component forms are repetitive and iterative, and the form as a whole is distinguishable by processive logic. In AAB/AB, the contents of the first and last positions of the component forms are identical. In ABB/BA, the contents of the first position of the first component and the last position of the last component are identical; also, the contents of the last position of the first and the first of the last are identical. This is a case of inverse parallelism, or <u>mirroring</u>.[3] Beyond such simple forms, however, recourse must be made to cardinality, by which relationships among all forms can be fully described.

We have already seen how large forms can be broken down into smaller forms and described in terms of pre-cardinal relationships. It remains to be shown how larger forms can be parsed according to purely cardinal relationships. The familiar forms for the rondo, ABABA and ABACA, have been mentioned earlier. These forms can be described and distinguished efficiently by recognizing that the five positions can be partitioned into odd- and even-numbered positions, that is, by a modulo-2 cycle: positions one, two, three, four, and five become two sets: (1 3 5) and (2 4). Thereupon, the members of each set can be compared: $A = A = A$ and $B = B$ or $B \neq C$. That fascinating recursive form, ABA, can also be described in terms of modulo-2 partitioning: positions one, two, and three become the two sets (1 and 3) and (2), and the relationship of ABA with the rondo or alternating forms is clear.

Beyond this point lie partitionings modulo 3, 4, and so on. Also possible under a cardinal interpretation are relationships in order-determinate music, such as order inversion and retrograde in its narrowest sense (see Boretz 1971).

46 Jay Rahn

<u>Examples of cardinality</u> Since cardinal interpretations can describe the relationships within and among all forms in any music, there is no need to recite many instances where cardinality has been or can be invoked: it is implicit in almost all interpretations. Nevertheless, some of the special cases deserve exemplification. The ubiquitous <u>ouvert-clos</u> period structure noted by Curt Sachs (AA', BB', CC', etc.) is in fact an example of parallelism, as in ABAC, DBDC, EBEC (see Sachs 1961). The complementary four-position forms AABB, ABAB, and ABBA dominate the rhyme schemes of quatrains in French monophonic songs around 1500, and close variants of these - for example, AABC, ABAC, and ABCA - dominate the musical settings of these songs. The polyphonic repertory of the same period preferred the five-position form AAB/BA to its cognate AB/BA, which is found to predominate as a rhyme scheme in the monophonic repertory. In the same corpus, forms of more than four positions are also found. These, however, can all be broken down into shorter forms and described in pre-cardinal terms (see Rahn 1978a, 1981). Finally, the ABBA - ABCA - ABBC group of forms recurs frequently in the Hungarian 'New Style' songs and has been considered a group on these and other grounds (see Bartók 1931).

  Finally, the special forms of paired repetition and incomplete repetition mentioned above can be dealt with by breaking down forms into component parts. The paired repetition in AABB can be analysed into a pair of iterations joined by non-repetition: AA/BB. Only positional diversity need be invoked to analyse such a form. The intuitively more complex form AABBCC demands the notion of extremity in order to be defined, a fact that confirms its intuitively greater complexity. The incomplete repetition in ABCBC can be captured by recognizing the need to invoke extremity in order to define the initial component ABC and invoking a modulo-2 partitioning to capture the identity of the Bs and Cs. This form, as well as the more complex ABCDBCD, can also be dealt with by collapsing the distinctions among B, C, and D and considering the forms as instances of AB/B, which is definable more simply in terms of sequence. This brings up the question of what analytical motivation might lead one to consider a form to be ABCBC or ABCDBCD rather than ABB. If B, C, and D each corresponded to a temporal unit, however broadly defined (as for example in Rahn 1978b and in press), one might wish to characterize the form by means of the extended formula. If one wished to capture the unity underlying ABCBC and ABCDBCD, one might want to rewrite both as ABB. These, however, are analytical questions that lie outside the immediate scope of this study.

CONCLUSIONS

Two questions remain. Do the simple formal types illustrated above recur over and over in repertories around the world and through history because they embody special relationships, or are they noticed by analysts simply because they are special? In other words, do they represent universal ways of making music or universal ways of interpreting music? In either case, the answer would appear to be that

47 Simple Forms in Universal Perspective

the special qualities of the formal relationships on which these types are based seem to point to some deep-seated cognitive or perceptual processes.

The second question can be answered more directly. If cardinality can handle all cases, why bother to specify relationships based on diversity, extremity, adjacency, or immediate or referential sequence? At least three responses can be given. First, the desire for economy discourages the search for a more powerful relationship when a weaker one will suffice. Second, in an interpretation, a weaker formal relationship (such as one based on sequence) might correlate with other relationships that are also based on the weaker relationship. This correlation would result in the capture of an isomorphism that might have been overlooked, adding elegance to the interpretation. Example 3 illustrates an instance where a formal anticipation defined in terms of sequence is coterminous with a tonal resolution that also is defined sequentially. Finally forms that are special in terms of a weaker notion are not necessarily special in terms of a stronger concept. For instance, in terms of cardinality, the three-position forms AAB, ABB, and ABA form a homogeneous set. In terms of adjacency, however, AAB and ABB would be grouped together in contrast to ABA, which would be placed with ABC.

Example 3. Formal anticipation mixed with tonal resolution. Circled notes consist of an anticipation and its confirmation; the tonal resolution is from V^7 to I.

As we have seen, there is a progression within the ordering of formal relationshsips. Cardinality implies referential sequence, which is invoked when extremity fails to distinguish among forms. Extremity in turn implies adjacency, which in turn implies mere positional diversity. Each lower form of interpretation is embedded, or 'nested,' in each higher form. From these relationships (cardinality, sequence, extremity, adjacency, and diversity) as well as identity, the following phenomena can be accounted for, or 'generated': repetition, non-repetition, uniformity, iteration, progression, processive logic, recursion, anticipation, preparation, confirmation, resolution, 'first-ness,' 'last-ness,' symmetry, parallelism, mirroring, cycling, complementation, centrality, similarity of forms, alteration, inversion, and retrograde. Strikingly, the types of formal relationships to which scholars have in the past given special names are usually also special according to the development presented here. This is all the more surprising since none of the authors cited develops a thorough system for dealing with forms, but seems rather to have proceeded on the basis of intuition. Once again, then, theory can be seen to clarify and deepen the informal notions that have been used to describe music.

NOTES

1 As always the term <u>rigour</u> requires some clarification. In its most benign form the search for rigour can best be summarized by Nelson Goodman's dictum that to economize is to systematize. In practical terms, this means that as one reduces the number of 'primitive,' undefined concepts in a theory, it is almost inevitable that the theory will become more powerful - and probably more understandable as well. From the empirical point of view, one expects that as the number of concepts is reduced, the range of observables for which they can account will be increased. This, indeed, is one of the lessons of 'Meta-Variations.' Boretz's work, for example, establishes the unity of twelve-tone with major-minor music by reducing much of the relational complexity of both systems to the notion of partitioning and concepts directly derivable therefrom.
2 The seminal notion of <u>process</u> is used in slightly different ways by Noske (1969), Carpenter (1967), and Meyer (1973). A determinate meaning can be attached to the term if it is used to cover all values derived directly from the concept of adjacency and its successor, immediate sequence.
3 The term <u>mirroring</u> is used here in its broadest sense to include much more than the special cases of retrograde or order inversion.

REFERENCES

Bartók, Béla 1931 <u>Hungarian Folk Music</u>, translated by M.D. Calvocoressi (London, Oxford University Press)
Besmer, Fremont 1970 'An Hausa Song from Katsina' <u>Ethnomusicology</u> 14 (3): 443-59
Boretz, Benjamin 1969 'Meta-Variations: Studies in the Foundations of Musical Thought (I),' <u>Perspectives of New Music</u>, 8 (1): 1-74
- 1970 'Sketch of a Musical System (Meta-Variations, II),' <u>Perspectives of New Music</u> 8 (2): 49-111
- 1971 'Musical Syntax (II),' <u>Perspectives of New Music</u> 9 (2)/10 (1): 232-70
Carpenter, Patricia 1967 'The Musical Object' <u>Current Musicology</u> 5: 56-87
Chenoweth, Vida 1974 <u>Melodic Perception and Analysis: A Manual on Ethnic Melody</u> 2d ed. (Papua New Guinea, Summer Institute of Linguistics)
Cone, Edward T. 1968 <u>Musical Form and Performance</u> (New York, W.W. Norton)
Erickson, Robert 1975 <u>Sound Structure in Music</u> (Berkeley, University of California Press)
d'Erlanger, Baron Rodolphe 1930-59 <u>La Musique arabe</u> 6 vols. (Paris, Librairie orientaliste Paul Geuthner)
Forte, Allen 1973 <u>The Structure of Atonal Music</u> (New Haven, Yale University Press)
Herzog, George 1935 'Plains Ghost Dance and Great Basin Music' <u>American Anthropologist</u> 37: 403-19
Kolinski, Mieczyslaw 1976 'Herndon's Verdict on Analysis: <u>tabula rasa</u>,' <u>Ethnomusicology</u> 20 (1): 1-22

Merriam, Alan P. 1967 Ethnomusicology of the Flathead Indians (Chicago, Aldine)
Meyer, Leonard B. 1956 Emotion and Meaning in Music (Chicago, University of Chicago Press)
- 1973 Explaining Music (Berkeley, University of California Press)
Nettl, Bruno 1954 North American Indian Musical Styles (Philadelphia, American Folklore Society)
- 1956 Music in Primitive Culture (Cambridge, Harvard University Press)
- 1974 'Aspects of Form in the Instrumental Performance of the Persian Āvāz,' Ethnomusicology 18 (3): 405-14
Noske, Frits 1969 Forma Formans (Amsterdam, Frits Knuf)
Peri, Noël 1934 Essai sur les gammes japonaises, Serge Eliseev and Philippe Stern, eds., (Paris, Librairie orientaliste Paul Geuthner)
Rahn, Jay 1976 'Text-Tune Relationships in the hora lunga versions collected by Bartók' Yearbook of the International Folk Music Council 8: 89-96
- 1978a 'Melodic and Textual Types in French Monophonic Song, ca. 1500,' PhD dissertation, Columbia University
- 1978b 'Evaluating Metrical Interpretations' Perspectives of New Music 16 (2): 35-49
- 1981 '"Fixed" and "Free" Forms in French Monophonic Song, ca. 1480-1520' in Mary Beth Winn, ed. Musique naturelle et musique artificielle: In Memoriam Gustav Reese, Le Moyen français 5 (Montreal, Editions Ceres)
- in press A Theory for All Music: Problems and Solutions in the Analysis of Non-Western Forms (Toronto, University of Toronto Press)
Rosen, Charles 1971 The Classical Style: Haydn, Mozart, Beethoven (New York, W.W. Norton)
Sachs, Curt 1961 The Wellsprings of Music Jaap Kunst, ed. (The Hague, Martinus Nijhoff)
Tinctoris, Jean 1967 Concerning the Nature and Propriety of Tones, translated by Albert Seay (Colorado Springs, Colorado College Music Press)
Wade, Bonnie 1973 'Chīz in Khyāl: The Traditional Composition in the Improvised Performance' Ethnomusicology 17 (3): 443-59
Yeston, Maury A. 1976 The Stratification of Musical Rhythm (New Haven, Yale University Press

II / COMPARATIVE PERSPECTIVES

CHARLES LAFAYETTE BOILÈS
A Paradigmatic Test of Acculturation

Because of the work of Mieczyslaw Kolinski - and others who are as dedicated to musical scholarship - our knowledge of world musical phenomena is increasing vastly. Kolinski's imaginative efforts to create new analytical procedures have been a source of personal inspiration, and on this occasion it is my desire to honour him by using not only his techniques but also some of my own that exist because of indirect influence that he has had on me.

The problem at hand is one that has long fascinated ethnomusicologists: identification of the cultural origin of a musical artefact. It is my belief that ethnomusicology, properly applied, can solve this enigma, for it uses not one but several approaches to achieve its ends. Ethnomusicologists employ musicological data to answer ethnographical questions and ethnological data to answer musical questions; any other procedure might be historical, ethnological, or musicological, but it is not ethnomusicological. In this study, ethnohistory and musicology are used to discuss an ethnological question concerning origin and acculturation.

Cultural origin of a musical artefact is not often proved except on the basis of historical evidence, such as ancient scores and chronicles. Musicologists have not yet developed many analytical techniques of sufficient sophistication to discover in the music itself the elements that signify its cultural provenance. In the absence of historical data, musicologists, instead of developing types of analyses, sometimes turn to deductive logic to answer the question. However, deductive logic is a form of speculation and is not nearly as satisfactory a proof as is empirical data. Conjecture, at best, is merely that, and in cross-cultural studies is often disproved. Where concrete historical proofs do not exist except circumstantially, it therefore devolves upon the musicologist to retrieve from extant musical artefacts the empirical data needed for arriving at conclusions.

A PROBLEM OF ACCULTURATION

For this study, let us consider a question raised by Robert Murrell Stevenson (1968: 145-50) concerning the state of acculturation of a Cora-Indian melody transcribed by E.M. von Hornbostel and used by

Carlos Chávez as thematic material for his <u>Sinfonia India</u>.[1] The Cora melody was recorded by Konrad T. Preuss in 1905: when von Hornbostel transcribed it (see example 1), he was surprised to find in the melody what he thought was a large amount of European influence. In the usual indefatigable and meticulous standards of his scholarship, Stevenson proposes some trenchant historical facts that might support von Hornbostel's notions. As evidence of acculturation, Stevenson mentions the Spanish name of the informant, Ascención Díaz, and cites historical data proving that the Nayarit hamlet of Jesús María, Mexico - where the recording was made - was under 'overwhelming European influences' (1968: 149) by 1754 because it was the centre of Jesuit missions in Mexico. To these proofs Stevenson adds his assumption that the song betrays 'very strong European influences - in its interval and in its metrical and formal organization (1968: 149). Other ethnohistorical facts, plus the musical analysis presented in this paper, complement Stevenson's position but they also place his opinion in a different perspective.

With respect to the Spanish name of the Indian informant, the following information should be added to that of Stevenson. In order to record vital statistics in civil registries, both colonial-Spanish and present Mexican authorities have demanded that Indians take Spanish surnames in any area where no system of Indian surnames existed. One finds patrilineal surname systems among some Maya and Nahuatl groups but none among many others. Indians have informed me that as late as the 1950s they were faced with the necessity of selecting a surname. Thus it is obvious that the Cora, regardless of their state of acculturation, under heavy Jesuit domination would have adopted Spanish surnames. It is difficult, however, to estimate the degree to which Jesuit influence has remained entrenched in the Cora community during the past two centuries because, in 1767, Charles III of Spain issued a decree expelling the Jesuits from all Spanish lands, including the colonies. It has been my impression that even though they describe themselves as Christians and the priests have remained, many Indian groups in Mexico continue to be pagan and have maintained their culture at the margin of the nationally dominant culture.

Other ethnohistorical data may be adduced regarding the Indian's given name. It is well known that people of many of Mexico's pre-Columbian cultures gave their children names based on the name of the day on which the child was born, a custom reflected in their mythology: <u>makwili shochitl</u> ('five flower') is the calendar name of Shochipili, the deity of music, and <u>se akatl</u> ('one cane') is the birth-date name of Quetzalcoatl, the deified cultural hero. Colonial and present-day Mexican Indians have syncretized this custom by choosing their given names from the almanac known as the <u>Calendario del más antiguo Galván</u>, which exists in abundance in almost every Indian village in Mexico. In view of this fact, it would not be in the least surprising to learn that the Indian, Ascención Díaz, was born on 15 August and was therefore named after the Roman Catholic feast listed in the almanac for that date. Thus it is possible that the use of Spanish names might be attributed to reasons different

55 A Paradigmatic Test of Acculturation

from those of pure acculturation: the names might be an indexical sign of Spanish presence in the Cora community but they do not necessarily signify more than a marginal toleration of Spanish culture.

THE 'EUROPEAN' MUSICAL INTERVALS

Several factors might be mentioned with respect to the assumption that the musical intervals are European. Diatonicism was not at all unknown in ancient Mexico and, in the extant Mexican collections of pre-Columbian flutes, there are a few instruments that can even produce the exact gamut of tones found in the Cora song. This fact does not necessarily prove that the ancient Cora used this particular gamut, but it suggests that they could have known it and the intervals that can be generated from it.

Another factor concerns von Hornbostel's transcription. The original Preuss recording is not available to me but I have checked other transcriptions by von Hornbostel against the original cylinders. After I had taken several readings with a Stroboconn, it seemed to me that, other than in the most obvious exceptions, von Hornbostel normalized some of the tunings to conform more closely to the European diatonic system. This is to be expected because of ethnocentrism and the consequent fallibility of any human ear, and von Hornbostel did not have the sophisticated sound-measuring equipment now available in order to avoid this pitfall. It is, therefore, with a modicum of suspicion that I tentatively accept the statement that the intervals are indeed European.

CULTURAL SELECTIVITY AND MUSICAL ARTEFACTS

Diffusionism, supported by some historical data but no formal musical analysis, was the basis for the original assumptions about the nature of the Cora intervals. For this study, it is proposed to model the musicological paradigms on a different assumption: the principle of cultural selectivity.

When any musicological statement about origins or acculturation is made, it seems not only appropriate but logical to acknowledge cultural selectivity as one of the dynamics of any given musical system. Cultures are recognized as being different because of those things that are uncommon among them; if they are not different, no uncommonness can be shown to be present. However, it is axiomatic that, given the same set of artefacts or concepts, peoples of differing cultures choose different subsets of these things for their use; and they use them in differing ways. In our consideration of the Cora Indians, we want to know whether they use the same melodic intervals as the Europeans and Euro-Americans with whom they have been in contact, but we also wish to know which intervals are used and how they are used. Where there are little or no differences it may be assumed that common origin or acculturation exists, but should great contrasts appear, there can be no doubt that cultural selectivity is operative because of nomological differences among the respective cultures producing the musical artefacts.

The problem at hand requires investigative procedures of several types and stages. No single, simple operation will solve the problem, and thus the musical material has to be subjected to a process of several stages in order to arrive at a meaningful level of information. It is necessary to formulate procedural stages that are consonant with the assumption being investigated; in this study, it has been assumed that there is possible acculturation from Spanish and Mexican mestizo influences.

ANALYTIC RESTRAINTS

Analyses for proving similarities cannot be made if like things are not compared with each other. As stated by Kolinski (1961: 39), 'In order to assure adequate comparison, tonal structures belonging to a similar type should be represented within a similar section of the cycle of fifths.' His statement means that the specimens to be investigated should be homologous, not analogous. In order to maintain such rigour, the musical artefacts used for this study must be as similar as possible; that is, it is imperative to compare the Cora song with Spanish and Mexican songs having an identical tonal structure. In Kolinski's system (Kolinski 1961), the Cora song falls into the hepta-C mode, and all other songs used in this study must be in the same complex and not in any of the other 347 types he lists. While I do not subscribe fully to the philosophical basis on which Kolinski's tonal structure classification system is organized, I agree in principle with the analytic restraints he sets forth. Accordingly, all Spanish and Mexican specimens used in this study have the same tonal structure as the Cora melody: an ambit of one octave and an identical gamut of seven pitches in the same intervallic relationships to each other. If it were possible in studies such as this, all songs to be compared should also have the same metre, and, ideally, should be of the same functional type.

It was not quite possible to fulfil all these conditions. There are no Spanish or Mexican songs that are functionally identical with the Cora example, and it was therefore decided to settle upon some form of narrative song as the best alternative. For the Spanish corpus, 446 songs collected from all parts of Spain by J. Juan del Aguila (1959, 1960, 1966) were examined and examples 2 and 3 selected. The Mexican corpus of 154 <u>corridos</u> published by Vicente T. Mendoza (1964) yielded examples 4, 5, and 6 that could be used in this study. It was found that none of the metrical conditions existed in songs having the requisite tonal conditions and, because the investigation is concerned primarily with how the intervals are used, it was decided to ignore metrical organization as one of the qualifying criteria.

However, a commentary on the metre is in order. It is true that some Spanish songs use alternating metres in the manner found in the Cora song, and several varieties were found in 6.9 per cent of the 446 Spanish songs consulted for this study. In contrast, alternating metres seem to be rather common in North-American Indian music. In a sample of the several studies published by Frances

57 A Paradigmatic Test of Acculturation

Densmore (1910, 1913, 1918, 1929, 1932), seventy to ninety-five per cent of the songs have alternating metres. Alternating metres appear in many of the examples published in Kolinski's study (1972) of the Apache Rabbit Dance song cycle. Nettl (1968) has published a number of Blackfoot songs with alternating metres, and Kurath's study (1968) of Iroquois song and dance contains numerous examples of the same phenomenon. In addition, not only I myself but many other

Example 1. Cora melody as transcribed by E.M. von Hornbostel (Stevenson 1968: 146-7). Original gamut: $\underline{f}$'-$\underline{a}$'-$\underline{b}$-flat'-$\underline{c}$"-$\underline{d}$"-$\underline{e}$-flat"-$\underline{f}$".

Example 2. Melody Spain A, 'El sagrado nacimiento,' collected and transcribed by J. Juan del Aguila (1959: 29). Original gamut: f'-a'-b-flat'-c"-d"-e-flat"-f".

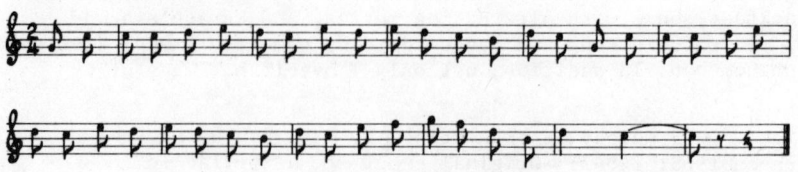

Example 3. Melody Spain B, 'Los reyes de la baraja,' collected and transcribed by Fernando García Lorca (Aguila 1966: 89). Original gamut: d'-f-sharp'-g'-a'-b'-c"-d".

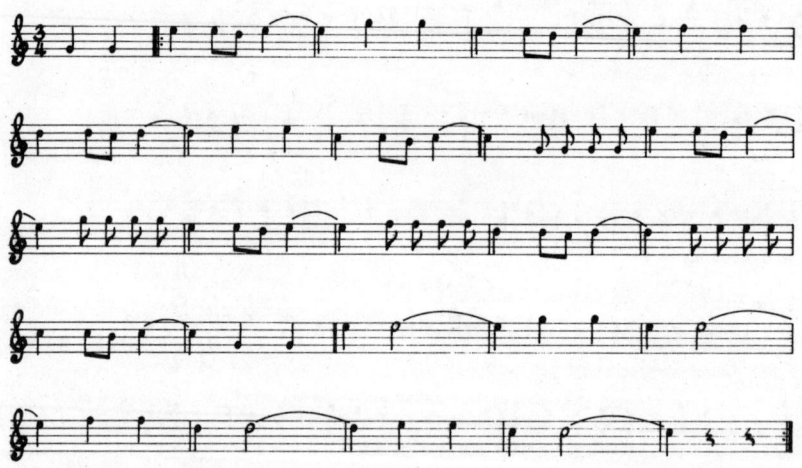

Example 4. Melody Mexico A, 'Orlachia,' collected and transcribed by Vicente T. Mendoza (1964: 110). Original gamut: f'-a'-b-flat'-c"-d"-e-flat"-f".

59 A Paradigmatic Test of Acculturation

Example 5. Melody Mexico B, 'Los tulisanes,' collected and transcribed by V.T. Mendoza (1964: 209). Original gamut: c'-e'-f'-g'-a'-b-flat'-c".

Example 6. Melody Mexico C, 'Lucrecia,' collected and transcribed by V.T. Mendoza (1964: 227). Original gamut: c'-e'-f'-g'-a'-b-flat'-c".

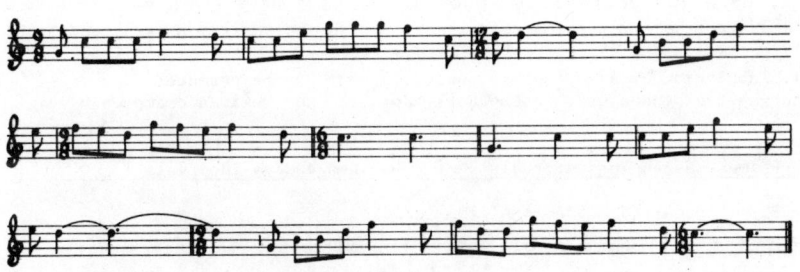

specialists on Mexico know the use of alternating metres to be widespread in Meso-America. It is not necessary to adduce more evidence from numerous other collections. From the few that have been mentioned, it is clear that alternating metre is not only a Spanish or European trait; although this metre might possibly exist as a result of acculturation, its presence in the Cora song might also indicate an affinity with a rather dominant tradition existing in aboriginal music throughout the North American continent.

Concerning the tonal structure that serves as the basis for these songs, the original gamut of the Cora example (transposed to concert C in example 1) consists of the pitches f'-a'-b-flat'-c"-d"-e-flat"-f" which can be expressed in the semitone system of cipher notation as 0-4-5-7-9-10-12, 0 being the lowest pitch and 12 the highest. In point of fact, this particular distribution of tones is rather rare in Spanish and Mexican traditions. Only two from the Spanish corpus and three from the Mexican samples were found to have exactly the same gamut as the Cora song. Thus, the Cora song obviously is composed from a basic set of tones that is used only rarely in Spanish and Mexican traditions.

INTERVALLIC CHOICE AND DISTRIBUTION

Underlying the analytical models used in this study is the hypothesis that cultures having related traditions use specific melodic intervals in specifically similar ways; that is, given an identical gamut, cultures of similar traditions form similar sets of intervals on each degree of the gamut but cultures of dissimilar traditions use the same gamut in differing ways. For example, culture A's melodies might have only ascending major thirds generated off the lowest two tones of the gamut whereas culture B generates only ascending major seconds off the same two tones in its melodies. To make the analysis, a paradigmatic grid can be constructed to show the relative distribution of ascending and descending intervals on each degree of the gamut used in the songs selected for this study.

With respect to the intervals used in the examples chosen for this experiment in comparative analysis, the gamut of tones permits forty-nine different intervals to be generated; these are shown in table 1. Notation conventions used in table 1 have been selected because they are compatible with several European languages and

TABLE 1. Tabulation of all possible intervals that can be permuted from the gamut of tones used in the Cora, Spanish, and Mexican examples

Gamut degree	Primes	Ascending intervals						Descending intervals					
0	P	3MA	4JA	5JA	6MA	7NA	8JA						
4	P	2NA	3NA	4JA	5TA	6NA		3MD					
5	P	2MA	3MA	4JA	5JA			2ND	4JD				
7	P	2MA	3NA	4JA				2MD	3ND	5JD			
9	P	2NA	3NA					2MD	3MD	4JD	6MD		
10	P	2MA						2ND	3ND	4JD	5TD	7ND	
12	P							2MD	3ND	4JD	5JD	6ND	8JD

NOTE: In tables 1-2 and 11-14 alphabetic symbols are read according to position: A and D on the right signify <u>ascending</u> and <u>descending</u>; in the middle position, M = major, N = minor, J = perfect or <u>juste</u>, and T = tritone. Numerical symbols in the left position signify class of interval.

facilitate transfer of this information – and that of other paradigms – to computer cards. Each interval is notated with three symbols: the first is numerical, indicating the interval class; the second is alphabetic, indicating the quality class; and the third is alphabetic, indicating the direction of movement. Thus 2MA is an ascending major second. Not used in this paper is the sign 'OPØ' designating primes, in which 'O' (zero) is the numerical distance of interval movement, 'P' is the quality class of <u>prime</u>, and 'Ø' is the null direction of movement; for the present purposes, primes are designated by 'P.' Of the forty-nine intervals shown in table 1, the Cora song employs twenty-eight; Spain A, fifteen; Spain B, nineteen; Mexico A, seventeen; Mexico B, twenty-three;

and Mexico C, nineteen. From these facts alone, it is apparent that cultural selectivity is operative at least in the number of intervals used and that some significant differences are probably present in the structural system of the melodies.

Intervals used in the Cora melody are listed in table 2. This paradigm shows which of the Cora intervals are found on the same gamut degree as those in the Spanish and Mexican songs; intervals

TABLE 2. Affinity of melodic-interval distribution, comparing the Cora-Indian melody with Spanish and Mexican examples

Culture	Primes and ascending intervals															
	Gamut degree:															
	0	0	0	0	4	4	5	5	5	5	5	7	9	9	10	12
Cora	P	3M	4J	8J	2N	3N	P	2M	3M	4J	5J	P	P	3N	P	P
Spain A		X			X	X	X	X								
Spain B	X			X		X	X					X	X	X	X	X
Mexico A		X		X		X	X						X		X	
Mexico B	X	X			X	X	X	X				X	X	X		X
Mexico C	X				X	X				X		X	X	X		X

Culture	Descending intervals										
	Gamut degree:										
	4	5	5	7	7	9	9	9	10	10	12	12
Cora	3M	2N	4J	2M	3N	2M	3N	4J	2N	4J	2M	3N
Spain A	X	X	X	X	X				X			
Spain B	X	X	X		X	X			X			
Mexico A| X		X		X	X		X	X			
Mexico B|	X	X	X				X	X	X		
Mexico C| X	X			X		X	X				

NOTE: Correspondences of Spanish and Mexican intervals with those of the Cora are as follows: Spain A = 39%, Spain B = 53%, Mexico A = 42%, Mexico B = 60%, Mexico C = 45%.

in the latter songs that are not found in the Cora example are not shown here. The results demonstrated in table 2 show that there is a high degree of correspondence although, on the average, the Cora and Mexican songs have a greater affinity than the Cora and Spanish specimens. Four of the Cora intervals do not appear in any of the other songs: an ascending octave on the zero degree of the gamut; an ascending perfect fifth on the fifth degree; a descending major third on the fourth degree; and a descending perfect fourth on the ninth degree. There are three examples of 100 per cent correspondence: a prime and an ascending major third on the fifth degree, and a descending major second on the seventh degree.

62 Charles Lafayette Boilès

Differences of interval use can be illustrated even more dramatically if the paradigmatic emphasis is shifted from that of affinity to that of interval class and percentage of incidence. Tables 3 to 8 show the melodic-interval distribution as found in each song. It should be remembered at this point that a statistical listing of intervals is not 'melodic' unless it is known where the intervals occur in relationship to various tones of the gamut; thus the paradigm must be structured so that such relationships are manifest. Some major differences of interval use are immediately noticeable when a comparison is made of the interval distribution shown in these tables. To obtain a notion of a culture's overall use of

TABLE 3. Melodic-interval distribution of the Cora-Indian melody as transcribed by von Hornbostel (example 1). The gamut is expressed in semitones from 0 to 12 degrees, which encompasses the ambit of one octave.

Gamut degree	Interval class and percentage of incidence						
	Prime	2nd	3rd	4th	5th	6th	8ve
				ascending			
0	P 1.7		3M 1.1	4J 2.3			8J 1.7
1							
2							
3							
4		2N 6.9	3N 1.7	4J 0.57	5J 0.57		
5	P 18.4	2M 6.9	3M 2.3	4J 0.57	5J 0.57		
6							
7	P 15.0						
8							
9	P 1.7		3N 1.1				
10	P 11.1						
11							
12	P 6.9						
				descending			
0							
1							
2							
3							
4			3M 3.4				
5		2N 1.7		4J 1.7			
6							
7		2M 2.8	3N 7.5				
8							
9		2M 2.3	3M 2.3	4J 1.1			
10		2N 1.7		4J 0.57			
11							
12		2M 1.7	3N 1.7				

NOTE: In tables 3-10, J = perfect or *juste* interval, M = major, N = minor, and the numerical symbol to the left of the alphabetical symbol signifies the class of interval.

63 A Paradigmatic Test of Acculturation

intervals, however, it is necessary to make the composite data shown in tables 9 and 10; for these the incidence of each corpus is averaged. Now that the composites have been obtained, the information can be transferred to the graphs shown in figures 1 to 7.

These graphs illustrate a profile of the relative use of each type of interval in relationship to the various points of the gamut, for it seems that these cultures have a tendency to favour certain degrees over others for the production of specific types of intervals.

In figure 1 the Spanish and Mexican uses of primes are seen to be somewhat parallel, the major difference being that, on the zero degree, the Spanish alone use 4.2 per cent primes and, on the fifth degree, Mexicans use 1.2 per cent primes as compared to the Spanish incidence of 7.73 per cent; but Cora use of primes contrasts totally with the other cultures, although showing an oblique similarity to the Mexican songs with regard to the tenth and twelfth

TABLE 4. Melodic-interval distribution of example Spain A 'El sagrado nacimiento' (example 2)

Gamut degree	Interval class and percentage of incidence						
	Prime	2nd	3rd	4th	5th	6th	8ve
	------------------------ ascending------------------------						
0				4J 5.1			
1							
2							
3							
4			3N 7.6				
5	P 10.2	2M 5.1	3M 7.6				
6							
7		2M 10.2					
8							
9		2N 2.5					
10		2M 2.5					
	------------------------descending------------------------						
0							
1							
2							
3							
4							
5		2N 5.1		4J 2.5			
6							
7		2M 17.9	3N 2.5				
8							
9		2M 15.3					
10			3N 2.5				
11							
12		2M 2.5					

TABLE 5. Melodic-interval distribution of example Spain B 'Los reyes de la baraja' (example 3)

Gamut degree	Interval class and percentage of incidence						
	Prime	2nd	3rd	4th	5th	6th	8ve
	---------------------------ascending------------------------						
0	P 8.4					6M 5.0	
1							
2							
3							
4		2N 3.3					
5	P 5.0	2M 3.3					
6							
7	P 3.3	2M 11.8					
8							
9	P 18.6	2N 5.0	3N 5.0				
10	P 8.4						
11							
12	P 8.4						
	---------------------------descending------------------------						
0							
1							
2							
3							
4							
5		2N 3.3		4J 3.3			
6							
7		2M 1.6					
8							
9		2M 8.4	3M 5.0				
10			3N 5.0				
11							
12			3N 5.0				

TABLE 6. Melodic-interval distribution of example Mexico A 'Orlachia' (example 4)

Gamut degree	Interval class and percentage of incidence						
	Prime	2nd	3rd	4th	5th	6th	8ve
	----------ascending----------						
0				4J 3.2			
1							
2							
3							
4		2N 6.45					
5	P 9.6	2M 16.1					
6							
7		2M 9.6	3N 3.2				
8							
9	P 6.45	2N 6.45					
10	P 3.2	2M 3.2					
11							
12							
	----------descending----------						
0							
1							
2							
3							
4							
5		2N 6.45					
6							
7		2M 9.6					
8							
9		2M 3.2	3M 3.2				
10		2N 3.2		4J 3.2			
11							
12				4J 3.2			

TABLE 7. Melodic-interval distribution of example Mexico B, 'Los tulisanes' (example 5)

Gamut degree	Interval class and percentage of incidence						
	Prime	2nd	3rd	4th	5th	6th	8ve
	------------------------ascending------------------------						
0			3M 3.6	4J 3.6			
1							
2							
3							
4	P 3.6		3N 3.6				
5	P 10.9	2M 1.8	3M 5.4				
6							
7	P 5.4		3N 3.6	4J 3.6			
8							
9	P 1.8	2N 7.2	3N 3.6				
10							
11							
12	P 3.6						
	------------------------descending------------------------						
0							
1							
2							
3							
4							
5				4J 1.8			
6							
7		2M 5.45			5J 3.6		
8							
9		2M 3.6					
10		2N 7.2	3N 5.4	4J 1.8			
11							
12		2M 5.4	3N 3.6				

TABLE 8. Melodic-interval distribution of example Mexico C
'Lucrecia' (example 6)

Gamut degree	Interval class and percentage of incidence						
	Prime	2nd	3rd	4th	5th	6th	8ve
	---------ascending---------						
0				4J 5.5			
1							
2							
3							
4						6N 2.7	
5	P 2.7	2M 5.4		4J 2.7			
6							
7	P 5.4	2M 8.1					
8							
9	P 16.2	2N 8.1	3N 2.7				
10							
11							
12	P 8.1						
	---------descending---------						
0							
1							
2							
3							
4							
5		2N 2.7					
6							
7		2M 5.4					
8							
9			3M 2.7			6M 2.7	
10		2N 8.1	3N 5.4				
11							
12		2M 2.7		4J 2.7			

TABLE 9. Composite melodic-interval distribution chart of the Spanish songs (examples 2 and 3). Intervals found in both songs have been placed here and their percentages of incidence have been averaged.

Gamut degree	Interval class and percentage of incidence						
	Prime	2nd	3rd	4th	5th	6th	8ve
	------------------------------ascending------------------------						
0	P 4.2			4J 2.55		6M 2.5	
1							
2							
3							
4		2N 1.65	3N 3.8				
5	P 7.6	2M 4.2	3M 3.8				
6							
7	P 1.65	2M 11.0					
8							
9	P 9.3	2N 3.75	3N 2.5				
10	P 4.2						
11							
12	P 4.2						
	------------------------------descending-----------------------						
0							
1							
2							
3							
4							
5		2N 4.2		4J 1.65			
6							
7		2M 9.7					
8							
9		2M 11.85	3M 2.5				
10			3N 3.75				
11							
12		2M 1.25	3N 2.5				

69 A Paradigmatic Test of Acculturation

TABLE 10. Composite melodic-interval distribution chart of the Mexican songs (examples 4,5, and 6). Intervals found in all three songs have been placed here and their percentages of incidence have been averaged.

Gamut degree	Interval class and percentage of incidence						
	Prime	2nd	3rd	4th	5th	6th	8ve
	------------------------------ascending------------------------						
0			3M 1.2	4J 4.06			
1							
2							
3							
4	P 1.2	2N 2.15	3N 1.2				
5	P 7.73	2M 7.76	3M 1.8	4J 0.9			
6							
7	P 3.6	2M 5.9	3N 2.26	4J 1.2			
8							
9	P 8.15	2N 7.25	3N 2.1				
10	P 1.06						
11							
12	P 3.9						
	------------------------------descending-----------------------						
0							
1							
2							
3							
4							
5		2N 3.05		4J 0.6			
6							
7		2M 6.81			5J 1.2		
8							
9		2M 2.26	3M 1.96			6M 0.9	
10		2N 6.16	3N 3.6	4J 1.6			
11							
12		2M 2.7	3N 1.2	4J 1.96			

degrees. Figure 2 demonstrates the unique characteristics of each culture with regard to use of ascending seconds: the Cora have a fairly high incidence located only on the fourth and fifth degrees; Spanish and Mexican songs show similarity at the fourth degree, and diverge on the fifth degree; and from that point the songs of the two cultures show a complete contrast. Use of ascending thirds,

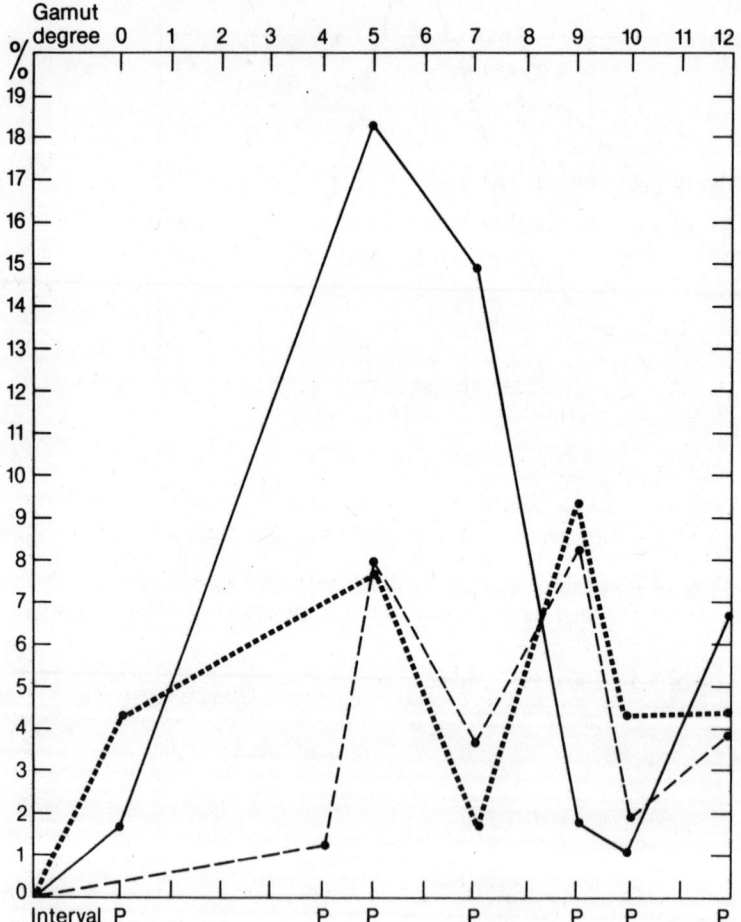

Figure 1. Comparative profiles of the use of primes according to the percentage of incidence on the various degrees of the gamut. In figures 1-7 the unbroken line represents the Cora; the dotted line, the Spanish; and the broken line, the Mexican mestizo.

71 A Paradigmatic Test of Acculturation

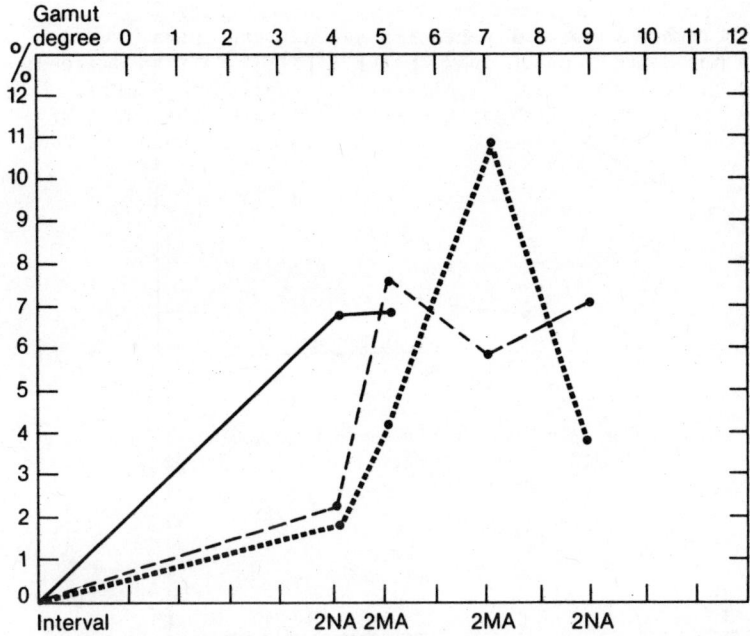

Figure 2. Comparative profiles of the use of ascending seconds according to the percentage of incidence on the various degrees of the gamut. In figures 2-7, J = perfect or _juste_ interval, M = major intervals, N = minor, A = ascending, D = descending, and the numerical symbol to the left of the alphabetical symbol signifies the class of interval.

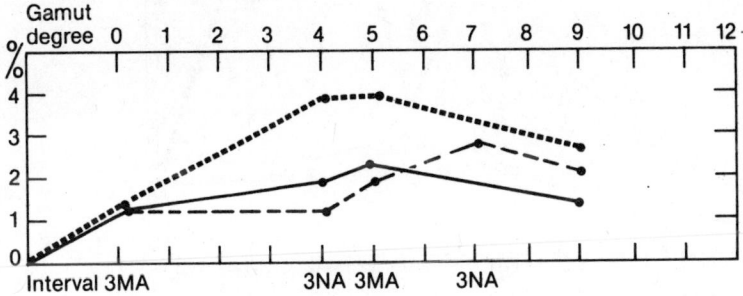

Figure 3. Comparative profiles of the use of ascending thirds according to the percentage of incidence on the various degrees of the gamut.

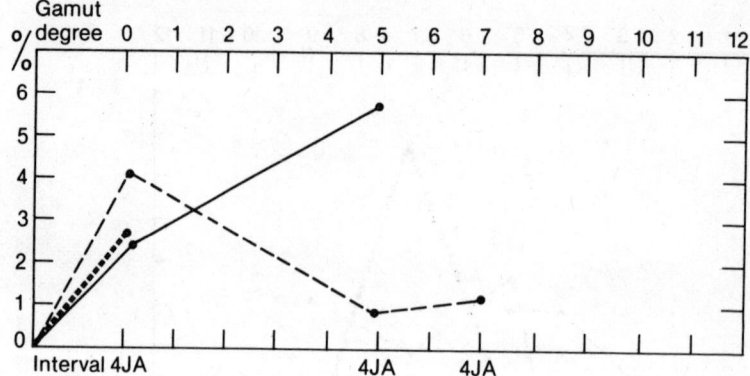

Figure 4. Comparative profiles of the use of ascending perfect fourths according to the percentage of incidence on the various degrees of the gamut.

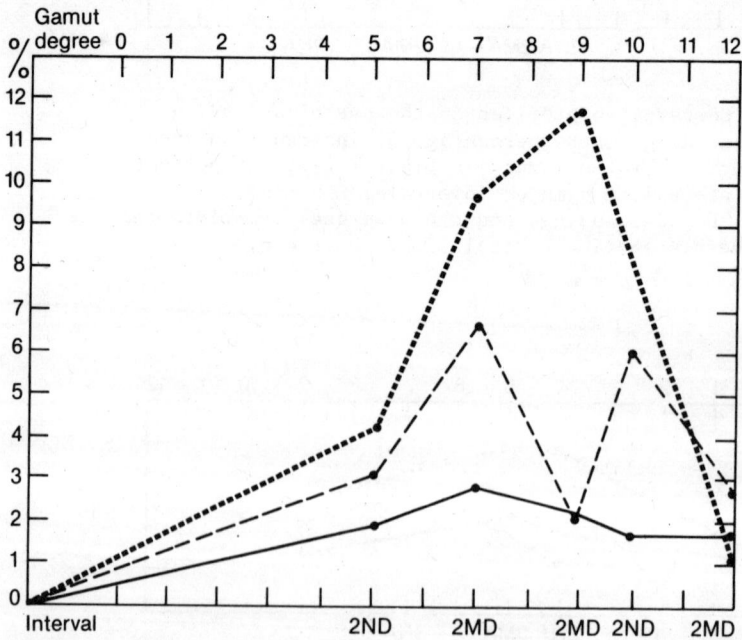

Figure 5. Comparative profiles of the use of descending seconds according to the percentage of incidence on the various degrees of the gamut.

73 A Paradigmatic Test of Acculturation

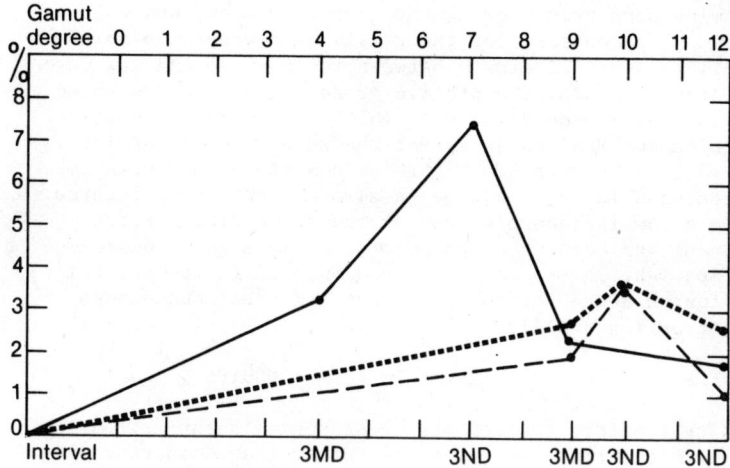

Figure 6. Comparative profiles of the use of descending thirds according to the percentage of incidence on the various degrees of the gamut.

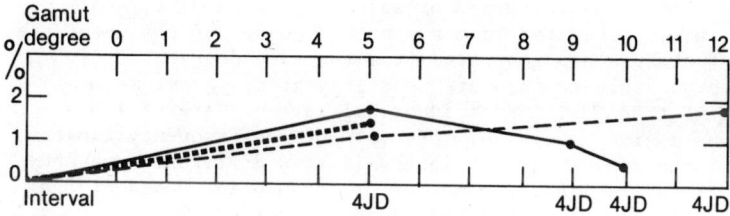

Figure 7. Comparative profiles of the use of descending perfect fourths according to the percentage of incidence on the various degrees of the gamut.

shown in figure 3, is similar on the lower degrees of the Cora and Mexican examples, whereas the Spanish songs have a higher incidence at the fourth and fifth degrees. The major difference is that on the fifth and ninth degrees, none of the cultures has or uses the same interval in the same way. Figure 4 shows that Mexicans and Cora use more ascending perfect fourths than do the Spanish, but the relative importance of gamut degrees used contrasts greatly between the two New-World cultures.

Graphs illustrating the use of descending intervals are confined to intervals of the second, third, and fourth because only the Mexican examples have descending intervals larger than these (which is, of course, another point of contrast). Figure 5 shows an oblique similarity with respect to descending minor seconds on the fifth degree, becoming more pronounced on the seventh degree, and the profiles show sharp contrast for the remaining degrees. In this graph the Mexican songs alternate between the Spanish and the Cora use of descending seconds. The profile of descending thirds shown in figure 6 indicates wide divergence in the Cora song as compared with the Spanish and Mexican examples; the same sort of parallelism seen in figure 1 is apparent in figure 6, and the higher Cora emphasis of intervals in the midrange is also noticeable. All three cultures have a low incidence of use of the descending perfect fourth; Mexicans and Cora, however, use it on more gamut degrees than do the Spanish. In figure 7 Cora and Spanish incidences coincide at the fourth degree of the gamut but all other incidences present a contrasting profile.

HOMOLOGOUS VERSUS ANALOGOUS INTERVALLIC RELATIONSHIPS

Paramount in this effort to evaluate these songs is the methodological restraint of isolating like elements rather than comparing elements that seem to be alike. From this point of view, the paradigms concerned with interval distribution were based on the principle of discovering homologous intervals and avoiding those that were analogous. Confusion creeps into our analyses when any major third is accepted as being like any other. This is not only logically an anomaly, but also a contravention of scientific method; for only those major thirds generated from a specific degree of the gamut are like those of other songs generated from the same degree. It is none the less possible to encounter homology at different degrees of the gamut if transposition of identical sets of intervals has occurred. Thus a given series of intervals at one frequency can be homologous to the same series of intervals at a different frequency level. In terms of reality, the number of frequencies heard at one level is not the same as the number heard at another, but - because we hear intervals logarithmically - if the two series have intervals existing in identical relationships with each other, they are homologous.

In order to establish that two intervals are homologous, they must be found in similar environments. The sound 3MA at varying levels of pitches in differing combinations is an analogous phenomenon: it sounds similar in isolation but is not the same in context. To illustrate, the sound 2MD-3MA-2NA as compared with the sound P-3MA-2ND might be perceived as having a homologous major third, but in actual fact, the one does not function in the same way as the other. To discover if an interval of any musical system exists in a homologous relationship with an interval of another system, the same aural environment - that is, the intervals surrounding the interval in question - must exist in both systems. In other words, the sound X, when compared with any other sound called X is homologous if both Xs are bounded by the same set of entities, as in the example of Y-X-Z when compared with Y-X-Z. The concept seems simple enough, but it is one of the principles most frequently ignored by humanists involved with the comparative sciences.

75 A Paradigmatic Test of Acculturation

Mutually exclusive sets of environments exist among musical systems of different cultures, and sometimes also among subsystems of a given culture. This is demonstrated effectively in tables 11, 12, and 13 corresponding respectively to Cora, Spanish, and Mexican melodic environments. Comparative analysis produces the results listed in table 14: there are seven correspondences from Cora to Spanish, ten from Cora to Mexican, twelve from Mexican to Spanish, but only three in common among all three cultures. That there is so little in common among the three cultures indicates two things: the uniqueness of each culture's musical system, and the possibility of coincidences in the correspondences merely because of circumstances of a mutually shared diatonicism. Without entirely ruling out the possibility of acculturation, it is none the less significant to note that 9.5 per cent Cora environments correspond to those of the Spanish, whereas Cora-to-Mexican correspondences are 12.3 per cent and Mexican-to-Spanish are 11.6 per cent.

CONCLUSION

It is not necessary to dwell at length on the evidence presented in these paradigms. It is clear that Spanish and Cora uses of intervals are more unlike than they are similar, and Mexican uses of intervals are similar sometimes to the one, sometimes to the other, and sometimes to neither. The greater correspondences of Mexican to Spanish as compared with Cora to Spanish are even reflected in Kolinski's melodic level formula (1957: 3; 1976: 3) as applied to

TABLE 11. Cora melodic-interval environments

Primes

P-P-#	2MD-P-P	2NA-P-P	3ND-P-P	
P-P-P	2MD-P-2MA	2ND-P-2MD	4JA-P-P	
P-P-2MD	2MD-P-2MD	3MA-P-2MD	4JA-P-3MA	
P-P-3ND	2MA-P-2MD	3MD-P-P	4JD-P-8JA	
P-P-4JD	2MA-P-3ND	3NA-P-P	5JA-P-P	
P-P-5JA	2NA-P-#	3NA-P-3ND	8JA-P-P	

Seconds

P-2MA-P	4JD-2MA-P	P-2MD-2ND	2ND-2NA-#	4JD-2NA-2MA
2NA-2MA-P	P-2MD-#	2NA-2MD-3ND	3MA-2NA-3MA	4JD-2NA-2MD
3MD-2MA-3ND	P-2MD-P	3ND-2MD-P	3ND-2NA-P	2MD-2ND-P
4JA-2MA-P	P-2MD-2NA	2MD-2NA-P	3ND-2NA-2MA	2MD-2ND-2NA
				2MD-2ND-3NA

Thirds, fourths, fifths, and eights

P-3MA-3MD	3ND-3MD-3MA	P-3ND-3NA	3MD-4JA-3MA
2NA-3MA-4JD	3ND-3MD-4JA	P-3ND-4JD	P-4JD-P
3MD-3MA-2NA	2ND-3NA-P	2MA-3ND-2NA	P-4JD-2MA
4JA-3MA-P	3ND-3NA-P	2MD-3ND-P	3MA-4JD-2NA
#-3MD-P	P-3ND-2MD	#-4JA-P	3ND-4JD-2NA
3MA-3MD-P	P-3ND-2NA	3MD-4JA-P	P-5JA-P
3ND-3MD-2MA	P-3ND-3MD	3MD-4JA-2MA	P-8JA-P

76 Charles Lafayette Boilès

TABLE 12. Spanish melodic-interval environments

Primes

#-P-6MA	P-P-3MD	2NA-P-P	3ND-P-2MD	6MA-P-2MD
P-P-P	P-P-3ND	3MD-P-2ND	4JA-P-P	
P-P-2MA	2MA-P-P	3NA-P-3ND	4JD-P-6MA	

Seconds

P-2MA-2MA	2MD-2MA-2NA	2MA-2MD-3MA	3MA-2MD-2MA	2NA-2NA-4JD
2MA-2MA-P	2MD-2MA-3NA	2MA-2MD-3ND	3NA-2MD-3MA	P-2ND-2NA
2MA-2MA-2MD	2NA-2MA-2MD	2MD-2MD-3MA	3NA-2MD-4JA	2MD-2ND-3NA
2MD-2MA-2MA	P-2MD-2MA	2MD-2MD-2ND	2MA-2NA-P	
2MD-2MA-2MD	2MA-2MD-2MD	3NA-2MD-#	3MA-2NA-2MA	

Thirds, fourths, and sixths

2MD-3MA-2MD	2MA-3NA-P	2MD-3ND-3ND	#-4JA-P	2NA-4JD-P
2MD-3MA-2NA	2ND-3NA-2MD	3ND-3ND-3NA	2MD-4JA-P	P-6MA-P
P-3MD-P	P-3ND-P			

TABLE 13. Mexican melodic-interval environments

Primes

P-P-P	2MA-P-P	2NA-P-2MA	3NA-P-P	4JD-P-2MA
P-P-2MD	2MA-P-3MD	2NA-P-3ND	3ND-P-2MD	6NA-P-P
P-P-2NA	2MA-P-5JD	2NA-P-4JD	3ND-P-4JA	
P-P-3MA	2MD-P-2ND	2ND-P-P	4JA-P-P	
P-P-6MD	2MD-P-3MA	3MA-P-3NA	4JA-P-2MA	

Seconds

P-2MA-2MA	2NA-2MA-4JD	P-2NA-4JD	3ND-2MD-4JD	P-2ND-6NA
P-2MA-2MD	4JA-2MA-2MA	P-2MD-5JD	4JA-2MD-2ND	2MD-2ND-2NA
P-2MA-2NA	4JA-2MA-2MD	2MA-2MD-2MA	P-2NA-2ND	2MD-2ND-3ND
2MA-2MA-P	4JD-2MA-P	2MA-2MD-2ND	2MA-2NA-P	2NA-2ND-3NA
2MA-2MA-2NA	P-2MD-P	2MD-2MD-P	2MA-2NA-2MA	3NA-2ND-3MA
2MD-2MA-2MD	P-2MD-2MA	3MA-2MD-2MD	2ND-2NA-P	3NA-2ND-2NA
2MD-2MA-2NA	P-2MD-2ND	3ND-2MD-#	2ND-2NA-3ND	4JA-2ND-P

Thirds, fourths, fifths, and sixths

P-3MA-2MD	3MA-3NA-P	2ND-3ND-2MD	3MD-4JA-2ND	2MD-4JD-4JA
2ND-3MA-#	3MA-3NA-3ND	3NA-3ND-P	4JD-4JA-P	3NA-4JD-P
5JD-3MA-P	4JD-3NA-2ND	3NA-3NA-2ND	6MD-4JA-2MA	P-5JD-3MA
P-3MD-4JA	P-3ND-P	#-4JA-P	P-4JD-2MA	P-6MD-4JA
P-3NA-3NA	2NA-3ND-P	#-4JA-2MA	2MA-4JD-3NA	2ND-6NA-P
2ND-3NA-4JD	2NA-3ND-2MD	P-4JA-2MD	2MD-4JD-2MA	

A Paradigmatic Test of Acculturation

TABLE 14. Correspondences in melodic-interval environments

A. Cora to Spanish correspondences (7)
Primes
P-P-P   2NA-P-P   P-P-3ND   3NA-P-3ND   4JA-P-P

Seconds
2MD-2ND-3NA

Thirds, fourths, fifths, and sixths
#-4JA-P

B. Cora to Mexican correspondences (10)
Primes
P-P-P   P-P-2MD   3NA-P-P   4JA-P-P

Seconds
4JD-2MA-P   P-2MD-P   P-2MD-2ND   2MD-2ND-2NA

Thirds, fourths, fifths, and sixths
#-4JA-P   P-4JD-2MA

C. Mexican to Spanish correspondences (12)
Primes
P-P-P   2MA-P-P   3ND-P-2MD   4JA-P-P

Seconds
P-2MA-2MA   2MA-2MA-P   2MD-2MA-2MD   2MD-2MA-2NA   P-2MD-2MA   2MA-2NA-P

Thirds, fourths, fifths, and sixths
P-3ND-P   #-4JA-P

D. Correspondences among all three cultures (3)
P-P-P   4JA-P-P   #-4JA-P

---

the study of these songs. In all the Spanish and Mexican examples, the song starts on zero and ends on the fifth degree (0° : 47°), giving a level shift of +47°, whereas the Cora song starts on the ninth degree and ends on the fifth degree (75° : 47°), giving a level shift of -28°. From all the data presented here, it may be concluded that the Cora might have adopted the tuning style of European and Euro-American diatonicism, but the process of acculturation does not seem to have extended to the nomology of their musical system as reflected in the Cora song, and the Cora do not generate intervals in the same way as the dominant cultures with which they have had contact for about four hundred years.

My conclusions are that one should not abdicate the historian's responsibility, as Stevenson (1968: 149) so admirably put it, by refusing to recognize all the existing conditions for effecting acculturation, and one should also seek to complement this excellent attitude by accepting the musicologist's responsibility for developing procedures that discern exactly how and to what extent acculturation may have occurred. To accept such a challenge is, indeed, in the spirit and tradition of Mieczyslaw Kolinski.

NOTE

1 Investigation for this paper was sponsored in part by a research grant from Indiana University, Bloomington.

REFERENCES

Aguila, J. Juan del 1959 Villancicos tradicionales (Barcelona, Editorial Alas)
- 1960 Las canciones del pueblo español (Madrid, Unión Musical Española)
- 1966 Lo que canta el pueblo español (Madrid, Unión Musical Española)

Densmore, Frances 1910 Chippewa Music Bulletin 45 of the Bureau of American Ethnology (Washington, Government Printing Office)
- 1913 Chippewa Music - II Bulletin 53 of the Bureau of American Ethnology (Washington, Government Printing Office)
- 1918 Teton Sioux Music Bulletin 61 of the Bureau of American Ethnology (Washington, Government Printing Office)
- 1929 Papago Music Bulletin 90 of the Bureau of American Ethnology (Washington, Government Printing Office)
- 1932 Yuman and Yaqui Music Bulletin 110 of the Bureau of American Ethnology (Washington, Government Printing Office)

Kolinski, Mieczyslaw 1957 'Ethnomusicology, Its Problems and Methods' Ethnomusicology 1 (10): 1-7
- 1961 'Classification of Tonal Structures' Studies in Ethnomusicology 1: 38-76
- 1972 'An Apache Rabbit Dance Song Cycle as Sung by the Iroquois' Ethnomusicology 16 (3): 451-64
- 1976 'Herndon's Verdict on Analysis: tabula rasa' Ethnomusicology 20 (1): 1-22

Kurath, Gertrude Prokosch 1968 Dance and Song Rituals of Six Nations Reserve, Ontario Bulletin 220 of the National Museum of Canada (Ottawa, Queen's Printer)

Mendoza, Vicente T. 1964 Lírica narrativa de Mexico (Mexico, Universidad nacional autonoma de México)

Nettl, Bruno with Blum, Stephen 1968 'Studies in Blackfoot Indian Musical Culture, part III: Three Genres of Song' Ethnomusicology 12 (1): 11-48

Stevenson, Robert 1968 Music in Aztec and Inca Territory (Berkeley, University of California Press

TIMOTHY J. McGEE
Eastern Influences in Medieval European Dances

The fifteen monophonic dances in the Ms British Library Additional 29987 constitute the largest single extant collection of medieval dances. Indeed, it is not until such publications as those of Pierre Attaingnant and Claude Gervaise in the sixteenth century that one can again find any sizable collection of dances. It was apparently the practice of professional musicians during the Middle Ages and Renaissance to improvise the music performed for dances, which explains why so few examples survive. The total number of extant dances from before 1425 is fewer than forty, and the attention the British Museum Ms dances have received from scholars and performers is at least in part a result of the paucity of the repertory. These dances have been described and analysed in several publications, and transcribed by Wolf in the early years of the present century and by two different editors in recent years (Gennrich 1932; Handschin 1929; Moser 1920; Wolf 1919; Bokum 1967; McGee). It has been noticed by several writers that the dances have some unusual traits, but no one has adequately described them or accounted for the degree to which they differ from the rest of the repertory.

British Library Additional 29987 is dated circa 1400 (von Fischer 1956). It contains 120 compositions from the fourteenth century, including polyphonic ballate, madrigale, caccie, three Mass sections, a hymn, four monophonic chançonete tedesche, and the fifteen monophonic dances. Eighty of the vocal compositions have been identified as works by Francesco Landini, Nicolò da Perugia, Jacopo da Bologna, and various lesser-known trecento composers (Reaney 1958, 1965). Of the fifteen dances, eight are usually referred to as estampies (although the word 'istampitta' appears at the head of only the first of them), four are labelled 'salterello' [sic], one a 'Trotto,' and two dance pairs are labelled 'Lamento di Tristano' and 'La Manfredina,' both with rottas appended.

The dance items that are the particular focus of this paper are the eight estampies and one saltarello. They differ from all other known medieval and Renaissance dances in form, length, and melodic style.[1] Whereas most medieval dances are composed of relatively short partes of approximately equal length (seven to fourteen measures), the dances under consideration have partes more than 100

measures long with a difference of as much as fifty measures between
partes of the same dance. The two formal plots in table 1 indicate
the variety of formal constructions, lengths, and complexities of

TABLE 1. In the plots for these two dances, capital
letters signify melodic sections; x = first, or open,
ending; y = second, or closed, ending; and numerals in
parentheses indicate number of measures.

'Tre Fontane'   Total

A (6)   B (51)   C (28)   D (5)   x (14)   y (14)   (118)
E (23)   B (51)   C (28)   D (5)   x (14)   y (14)   (135)
F (51)   C (28)   D (5)   x (14)   y (14)   (112)
G (60)   D (5)   x (14)   y (14)   (93)

'Belicha'

A (10)   B (36)   x (8)   y (20)   (74)
C (26)   B (36)   x (8)   y (20)   (90)
D (13)   B (36)   x (8)   y (20)   (77)
E (27)   F (16)   B (36)   x (8)   y (20)   (107)
G (31)   F (16)   B (36)   x (8)   y (20)   (111)

the dances. For comparison, following is the plot[2] of a representa-
tive dance from Ms Paris, Bibliothèque Nationale, fr. 844, the
second-largest collection of medieval dances:

'La Tierche estampie rial'
A (10)   x (6)   y (7)
B (8)   x/y
C (8)   x/y
D (8)   x/y
E (8)   x/y
F (7)   x/y

The complex forms, the widely varying lengths of the individual
sections, and the extreme overall lengths set the dances in Ms
29987 apart from much of the rest of the dance repertory. Some
writers in the past have mentioned these features, but their
melodic structure is also unusual and suggests a style not found
in the rest of the fourteenth-century European repertory. Analyses
of two of the nine dances can serve as examples of all.
    The formal plot of 'Ghaetta' (example 1), the first dance in the
collection, can be described by the following outline:

ABC   x/y
DEC   x/y
FEC   x/y
GBC   x/y

Eastern Influences in Medieval European Dances

Example 1. 'Ghaetta'

83 Eastern Influences in Medieval European Dances

Common to each of the four partes are the open and closed endings preceded by section C, which serves as a refrain. Each pars has a new opening section, and in each there is one of two middle sections which links the opening section to the refrain. The phrases are of unequal length: opening sections D and F are each only five measures long and thus constitute nothing more than two different introductions to middle section E, while the first and last opening sections A and G, are twenty-two and forty-seven measures long, respectively, and are thus independent sections by themselves. Middle sections B

Eastern Influences in Medieval European Dances

and E have thirteen and thirty-four measures; they too can be considered independent sections.

The various sections of 'Ghaetta' have uncommon melodic shapes. Rather than presenting the clearly marked phrases with melodic-rhythmic motives that would be expected in a European dance, the opening eight measures appear to be various melodic and rhythmic decorations of the note d. In fact, the rhythm and melody of the entire piece seem to be the consequence of a melodic line constructed to affirm or decorate particular notes.

Following the emphasis on d in the first eight measures, the melody stresses c for two measures, and e combined with c for five. In measure sixteen f is introduced, and for seven measures all four notes, c, d, e, and f, are given equal stress. For the twenty-three measures of section A therefore, the melodic intention appears to be the introduction and methodical stressing of each of four notes in the ascending tetrachord from c to f, with the heaviest stress placed upon the note d that opens the section.

In a similar manner the descending tetrachord b-flat, a, g, and f-sharp is introduced in section B from measures twenty-four to thirty-five, which also emphasizes d from the tetrachord found in the first section. The refrain, C, beginning in measure thirty-six and including both endings, explores the relationship of the various notes of the two tetrachords previously stated (avoiding high f) and the character of the lower tetrachord with both a b and b-flat. In the *prima pars* the two notes that seem to be singled out as principal structural notes are d - which opens the work and is constantly reinforced by repetition and by the implication of the c-sharp in the endings - and g, which is the modal final.

Section E, the middle of both the *secunda* and *tercia partes*, uses the entire scale of sections A and B, with the addition of a low f, where the *prima pars* uses only high f and (probably) low f-sharp, and a b rather than both the b and b-flat of the *prima pars*. Combined with the opening melodic sections for the *secunda* and *tercia partes*, section E achieves a melodic goal similar to that of the *prima pars*; that is, the systematic elucidation of each note of the scale. The *secunda pars* opens in the same way as the *prima pars* with an emphasis on d, which, together with middle section E, makes a fairly straightforward scale from f to high f with an occasional c-sharp. This scalar stability stands out when juxtaposed with the refrain C, where the emphasis is upon the variety in the qualities of the tetrachords.

The *tercia pars* also presents contrasts because of its opening on b-flat as opposed to the b of middle section E. The *quarta pars* returns the emphasis to d and again contrasts the variety of tetrachords with and without b-flat and with and without c-sharp. The dance is rounded off by the return of sections B and C, which dwell on the same contrasts and add f and f-sharp.

Throughout 'Ghaetta' the chromatic alterations of c and c-sharp, f and f-sharp appear to have two functions: in certain situations they emphasize the tonic and dominant, as in measures fifty-one and eighty-six, but in certain other situations where they do not go

86 Timothy J. McGee

directly to d̲ and g̲, such as in measure thirty-five, they may be considered to function like the b̲-flat, creating contrasting tetrachords for melodic variety. There would seem to be little other explanation for the use of the sharped notes in some places, such as those cited above, and their absence in many other places where emphasis on the tonic and dominant would seem to be important.

In summary, 'Ghaetta' appears to consist of melodic-rhythmic elaborations of a scale from f̲-sharp to high f̲ that has a final on g̲, avoids the tonic octave, and includes d̲ in a dominant function. The prima pars establishes the basic scale in two tetrachords, and during the remainder of the piece these tetrachords are first changed by chromatic alteration or tonal emphasis and finally re-affirmed.

The second dance in the collection, 'Chominciamento di gioia' (example 2), illustrates the same kind of melodic construction.

Example 2. 'Chominciamento di gioia'

87 Eastern Influences in Medieval European Dances

89 Eastern Influences in Medieval European Dances

This dance is in five partes, with the following form:

ABC   x/y
DBC   x/y
EBC   x/y
FGC   x/y
HGC   x/y

Again section C, with the open and closed endings, functions as a refrain, the opening of each pars presents new material, and two different middle sections link the opening material to the refrain. The prima pars begins on d, which is also the final and therefore the tonic. In the first section, A, the emphasis throughout the six measures is on d and its dominant a. Middle section B is divided into emphasis of the notes of an ascending pentachord a, b-flat, c, d, and e from measures eight to thirteen, and the descending tetrachord g, f-sharp, e, and d and introducing the lower semitone on c-sharp from measures fourteen to twenty-one. The refrain, C, moves from one end of the scale to the other but eliminates the chromatic alterations on b and f, thereby establishing tonal contrast similar to the kind established by contrasting tetrachords in 'Ghaetta.'

The opening of the secunda pars, D, introduces the upper neighbour e and emphasizes the upper tonic and dominant of the scale. The tercia pars offers another contrast by emphasizing lower f natural, a note not in the original scale.

The quarta and quinta partes both begin by emphasizing lower ranges in contrast to the upper range in the first two partes. In both quarta and quinta the emphasis revolves around the tonic note d before moving off to use the entire scale. In G the upper pentachord is explored first and then, in the second section, the lower tetrachord, followed by descent to the lower dominant on a. Section G therefore appears to have two sets of contrasts - the high and low sections of the d scale, and the high and low sections of the a scale - before returning to the original d scale in the refrain at the end of the dance.

The melodic style of the two dances described above is different from that of the remainder of the fourteenth-century European repertory. It is based on emphasis of certain pitches and on juxtaposition of different tetrachords. In each new pars a new emphasis or a new tetrachord is selected, after which the original scale returns in a common refrain.[3] A large number of rhythmic motives are used, which provide variety for the melodic emphasis of particular notes and tetrachords. The melodic curve is the result of

Eastern Influences in Medieval European Dances

this emphasis, and each change of tetrachord brings a change of phrase. Because no attempt is made to treat each tetrachord or each note equally, the phrase lengths are irregular.

All other European music of the period, both monophonic and polyphonic, is composed according to a different set of principles that causes the rhythms, melodies, and phrases to function in a manner different from those found in these dances. Broadly stated, the basic elements usually found in Western music of that time are short melodic-rhythmic motives, which are varied, expanded, and contracted to form phrases; only a small number of motives are chosen for a single composition. They are shaped in such a way that a feeling of forward motion is given to each phrase; that is, the motives and phrase shapes are made to seem increasingly restless until relaxation is achieved when the end of each phrase is reached. A feeling of tension and relaxation results from the combination of the melodic curve, rhythmic motion, and scalar polarity. (Scalar polarity is also found in the dances described above, but it is used for contrast rather than melodic direction.) Each composition, of course, requires an individual analysis, but perhaps the differences between the usual European melodic practice and that found in the dances may be exemplified by a comparison with an anonymous monophonic Italian ballata from the first half of the fourteenth century (example 3). This was chosen to resemble as closely as possible the melodic style found in the dances.[4]

Example 3. 'Per tropo fede'

'Per tropo fede' superficially resembles 'Ghaetta' in that it has the same tonic and dominant and begins by emphasizing the dominant. It also emphasizes the various notes of its scale as do all compositions, but at that point the similarity ceases. 'Per tropo fede' employs only a small amount of melodic-rhythmic material. There are two basic melodic-rhythmic motives: one consists of a pair of notes as found at the beginning of the second measure, and the other of

three notes as found at the end of the same measure. Throughout
the composition these two motives are combined and varied to form
the individual melodic curve of each subphrase. The notes d and g
are established as dominant and tonic in the first three-measure
phrase, and g is again affirmed as the tonic in the last (eleventh)
measure of the refrain.

The composition proceeds as a succession of subphrases, all consisting of variations of the two motives, each moving rhythmically
towards the long note at the end of the subphrase. This rhythmic
tension-relaxation is coupled with a tonal tension-relaxation as
each phrase-end is directed towards the final g. The motives and
melodic curve of each short phrase impart a feeling of direction
towards the end of the phrase, and the tonal relationships direct
each phrase-end towards the tonic. The small amount of basic motivic
material and the consistent tension-relaxation of each short phrase
are characteristic of western-European compositional technique of
the time.

If we look back at 'Ghaetta' we will see that different techniques are employed to achieve different objectives: a relatively
larger number of melodic-rhythmic motives are used in order to produce variations on the notes of the scales, and the phrase lengths
are determined by the elaboration and contrast of the tetrachords
rather than by the tension of the phrase shape and motives. In
'Ghaetta' a far greater emphasis is placed on elaboration, variation,
and contrast of notes and scales than in 'Per tropo fede,' where
motivic variation and phrase direction are of primary concern.

It is obvious, therefore, that the compositional style, both
formal and melodic, of the dances in Ms 29987 is not typical of
western Europe, and we must look elsewhere for possible models.
One possibility is the music of the eastern Mediterranean countries,
where forms and techniques very similar to those found in the dances
are known.

Jacques Handschin has noted that there is a similarity between
medieval dance forms and the eastern-Mediterranean instrumental
form known as peşrev, a traditional composition found in several
eastern-Mediterranean countries, including Turkey and the Arab
countries (Handschin 1929, 1954). Handschin limits his observations
to the formal similarities and suggests a common link involving
the sequence by way of the 'Joculator.' As he observed, a peşrev
usually has four partes, a common refrain for all partes, and new
material at the beginning of each pars, producing a form similar
to the dances we have seen.

The points at which the peşrev form differs from the overall
formal plot of the dances are in the refrain and the ending. Whereas
the European dances have the same refrain at the end of each pars,
the peşrev endings are basically similar but are sometimes varied
and the individual partes are not always repeated. The similarity
between the two types of compositions - the peşrev and the Italian
dances in question - goes much further than Handschin realized,
however, as can be shown by an analysis of Eastern melodic structure.

Eastern Influences in Medieval European Dances

In his book on the Turkish makam system, Karl Signell (1977) presents a clear picture of Eastern melodic practice. I believe the melodic style of the Italian dances can be better understood in terms of this theory than of Western practice, and therefore I will briefly summarize information given in Signell's monograph (see also Manik 1969).

The basic tonal organization of Turkish music is the makam system, scales that are similar in structure to the Greek modes. There are thirteen 'basic' makam scales, each made up of a tetrachord and a pentachord and thus producing a complete octave. The scales differ from their Western counterparts, however, in that there are five possible sizes for each interval: the small half-tone (roughly ninety cents); the large half-tone (114 cents); the small whole tone (180 cents); the large whole tone (204 cents); and the augmented second (271 cents). In addition, the music of Turkey commonly included the 'natural third,' which is the interval produced by a whole tone, and a 'flat' whole tone (the small and large whole tones). The makams are differentiated from one another by their seyir, an abstraction of melodic progression. Each makam has its distinctive final (karar), dominant (güclü), entry (giriş), and temporary stops (muvakkat kalışlar). All of these tones bring comparative rest to the melodic line. The tonic is the last note in the progression, and there is also an 'upper tonic' (tiz durak) an octave above the tonic. The dominant is usually located a fourth or a fifth above the tonic, though in some makams it may be a third. The entry note may be the tonic, dominant, or upper tonic, and is the note around which the first phrase revolves.

The activity in any makam is created by using the leading tone (which may be a half tone or whole tone below the tonic) and by dwelling on certain active tones, that is, tones other than tonic, dominant, and temporary stops. Some makams have a specific note on which this must happen while in others there is a choice of active tones.

Classification of makams is by direction, of which there are three main types: ascending, in which the melody enters on or near the tonic and gradually rises to the dominant and returns to the tonic; descending, in which the melody begins near the upper tonic and descends to the dominant and finally to the tonic; and ascending-descending, which begins near the dominant and remains in that area before finally descending to the tonic. Thus, although several makams share the same scale notes, their melodic directions distinguish them from one another.

A simple example from Signell's study will illustrate the construction of a Turkish composition in the makam sabâ. Example 4 is not an actual composition but a seyir, a musical description of a makam (Signell 1977: 64).[5]

The scale of sabâ is given in example 5, and its direction is ascending, that is, beginning near the tonic (a), rising to the dominant (c), and ending on the tonic.

Example 4 begins and ends on the tonic (a) and cadences on the dominant (c) at the end of the first phrase. Characteristic of sabâ

Example 4. Sabâ

Example 5. Sabâ scale

are its secondary emphasis on f, the active tone b♮, and the appearance of the leading tone g in the final phrase. It will also be noted that in the upper octave the tonic a becomes a♭, another characteristic of sabâ.

The seyir above is a model for the progression of any composition in the makam sabâ. It outlines the important notes and the general activities of any melody in this particular makam.

As in Western music, modulation occurs only when intervals change over a period sufficiently large to change the tonal centre or the mode. Notes from another makam may be borrowed for temporary colour or function (such as heightening of the dominant by raising the note below it) but do not cause modulation (Signell 1977: chap. VI). It is also a practice to introduce phrases, tetrachords, and pentachords from other makams during the exposition before the makam of the particular piece is completely established (Signell 1977: 77). The system is further complicated by the fact that many compositions have more than a single makam.

In a typical instrumental four-part peşrev, the first part (hane) and refrain (teslim) function as exposition and recapitulation. The development takes place in the second hane, which modulates away from and then returns to the principal makam. The return of the

95 Eastern Influences in Medieval European Dances

refrain following each hane constitutes the recapitulation. Each hane in turn modulates to a new area, makam, or range, and thus the makam form of a peşrev could be stated as:

A (first hane, principal makam)   A (refrain)
B (second hane, first modulation)   A (refrain)
C (third hane, second modulation)   A (refrain)
D (fourth hane, third modulation)   A (refrain)

Like chant modes, each makam has particular phrases and motives that are stereotyped and appear in compositions of only that particular makam. Some of these phrases and motives are melodic, others consist of a particular sequence of stressed notes that can take various melodic shapes, and others are melodic-rhythmic motives, such as the two cadential phrases in the makam segâh shown in example 6 (Signell 1977: 129-30). The characteristic phrases are included in nearly all compositions and improvisations because without these recognizable phrases 'the listener would feel something lacking' (Signell 1977: 131).

Example 6. Segâh cadences

Similarities between the Turkish compositional practice and the first of the Italian dances, 'Ghaetta,' can now be noted. Although its scale cannot be definitely associated with the intervals of the Turkish scale, the dance can still be analysed in terms of Eastern practices.

The 'Ghaetta' scale is of the ascending-descending variety. It begins on the dominant, remains in that area, and finally descends to the tonic. Thus, as with Turkish music, 'Ghaetta' in its prima pars identifies its makam by stating its scale and following an ascending-descending direction. The makam of 'Ghaetta' could be identified in Turkish music as rast or in Arabic theory as mutlaq fi majra al-wusta (Farmer 1954; Manik 1969; Wright 1966), assuming that the b-natural in the prima pars of 'Ghaetta' is an accidental.

The form of 'Ghaetta' also follows the Turkish practice. The original makam identified in the prima pars is restated each time in the refrain, and each of the other partes introduces either tetrachordal or range differences before returning to the original makam in the refrain. 'Chominciamento di gioia' exhibits the same formal outline although its scale is a descending one and from its range and seyir could possibly be identified as the Turkish makam uzzal or zengüle (transposed), or the Arabic khinsir fi majra al-binsir (Farmer 1954: 181).

Another of the Turkish instrumental forms is saz semaisi, which is identical with the peşrev in terms of form but in place of a new makam in the fourth hane there is a change of metre. Two of our dances exhibit this feature ('Isabella' and 'Tre fontane'), and a third, 'Belicha,' changes to a different metre at the beginning of the tercia pars and during the middle sections of the quarta and quinta partes.

As can be seen, in matters of form and melodic-rhythmic style, the nine dances in Ms 29987 match the description of the Eastern peşrev far more closely than they match the compositional practices of the West. The only identifiable Western element in the dances is the repetition of each pars with open and closed endings.

The major difference between the Turkish melodic system and that of the Italian dances is the variety of intervals. Should some evidence be found to assign to the dances intervals larger and smaller than the step and half-step, a nearly airtight case could be made for their identification with Eastern style.

No direct evidence survives attesting to the existence of such intervals in European music of the late Middle Ages, but at least one fourteenth-century Italian theorist, Marchettus of Padua, was aware of an unusual interval. Marie Louise Martinez-Göllner (1969) has described Marchettus's theory of the division of the whole tone into five parts, which may have some bearing on monophonic music although in the treatise the theory is clearly presented in relation to polyphony. Marchettus put forward a theory of three semitones, based on the model of the Greek tetrachords, named semitonium enarmonicum, semitonium diatonicum, and semitonium chromaticum. The three tones are the small semitone, equivalent to our half-step and signified by the b molle; the middle size signified by the b quadratum (♮) and equal to our whole step; and the new interval, the chromaticum, signified by the sharp sign, which is larger than our whole step. Marchettus explained that the new interval's form was derived from a lengthening of the vertical lines of the quadratum (ibid.: 190).

Martinez-Göllner has pointed out that the theory is derived from neither logic nor conventional theory, and her explanation is a reasonable one - that it comes from Marchettus's astute observation of actual polyphonic performance practice in which the leading tone is slightly raised in intervals of a third and a sixth in order to form perfect consonances and also, as Marchettus said, 'in order to embellish a dissonance such as the third, sixth or tenth, tending towards resolution in the nearest consonance' (ibid.: 189). Since they were used in polyphony, it is quite possible that the variable intervals were also present in monophonic music as well. That there was some Eastern influence in Italy during the late Middle Ages is a fact, and it is probable that Marchettus and other Italian musicians had heard Eastern music and attempted to use some of the Eastern techniques in their own performances.

Eastern Influences in Medieval European Dances

There is no way for us to know how much of the Eastern practice may have been adopted by the Italian musicians, but consideration of Marchettus's large whole step may help explain some of the unusual characteristics of the Italian dances. In addition, the unusual interval f-sharp - b-flat in measure thirty-six of 'Ghaetta' may indicate the 'natural third' described earlier in reference to Turkish music.[6] If the music in Ms 29987 follows Marchettus's theory, the sharps used for embellishment would be raised and therefore the curious intervallic relationship in measures seven, eight, and nine of 'Chominciamento di gioia' might be explained as a very slight embellishment on either side of the note a in which the sharp signifies accurately the very high g-sharp, which would imply that the b-flat is very flat. Application of Marchettus's chromatic interval, therefore, makes possible an even closer association between fourteenth-century Italian music and Eastern music.

It should not be surprising that Eastern influences can be found in Western music, for it was present in many other aspects of European civilization in the late Middle Ages. The Arabs controlled the Kingdom of the Two Sicilies from the early ninth to the middle of the eleventh century and were in control of much of Spain from the eighth to the thirteenth centuries. The works of Islamic scholars in all fields were translated into Latin from the tenth century onward, in part because of the interaction of Moors and Spaniards on the Iberian Peninsula. Commerce with the Near and Far East, which increased throughout the late Middle Ages, was always dependent upon Eastern ports and often upon Islamic ships so that the merchants and the citizens of European coastal cities were in constant contact with people from Asia Minor.

The Crusades were for Europe a source of very practical knowledge about the culture of the eastern Mediterranean. It is recorded that during breaks in the siege of Acre by Richard the Lion-hearted in 1189-91, the opposing armies danced and sang together (Grousset 1936: III, 28), and such musical instruments as the rebec, lute, and shawm, originally from the Islamic world, were introduced into Europe by the returning Crusaders (Ursprung 1934; Shiloah 1962; Perkuhn 1976). It is not improbable that the musicians who were so impressed by Eastern instruments were also impressed by the music played on them, and that, as a result, Eastern-style music flourished to some extent in European centres.

Although the existence of Eastern influence on European music must remain in the realm of speculation, the influence of the East on European painting and other arts is well documented. Even the paintings of Jan Vermeer and various objects in the works of Rembrandt and other artists show Eastern influence, and the inventories of European noblemen, such as Cosimo de' Medici, attest to a strong interest in Islamic art objects (Ettinghausen 1974).

The last bit of circumstantial evidence may be found in the fanciful titles of some of these nine dances. Six of the titles are Italian words or phrases, referring perhaps to some long-lost song, literary stimulus, or occasion that inspired the dance: 'Chominciamento di gioia,' 'Isabella,' 'Tre fontane,' 'Parlamento,' 'In pro,' 'Principio di virtu.' The other two titles, 'Ghaetta' and 'Belicha,' however, are not Italian. Ghaetta is the Arabic word for shawm, the etymon of the Spanish word for bagpipe (and perhaps for shawm),[7] and the name of a city, Gaeta, on the Tyrrhenian Sea, between Rome and Naples. Gaeta was ruled by the Arabs in the ninth century and is only a few kilometres north of the continental half of the Kingdom of the Two Sicilies and, as a result, was close to both Arabic and Spanish influence from the ninth to the fourteenth centuries. The name 'Ghaetta' for the first dance in the collection may therefore refer to the city of Gaeta as the source of the dances, or possibly to the instrument on which the dance was once played. 'Belicha' may be derived from the Arabic billīq, meaning 'popular comic and licentious poem.'[8]

Even the title 'Istampitta' at the beginning of this collection of dances is open to suspicion. Both Helene Waganaar-Nolthenius (1969) and Lloyd Hibberd (1944: 226) confirm that istampitta is a borrowed word and therefore may not have had a specific meaning for the Italians. It has been generally assumed until now that these dances are estampies, but given their variable formal properties, their Eastern orientation, and their vast contrasts with the French estampies, the word istampitta may well have had a more general meaning. The use of this borrowed word as a heading for the unusual dances described here may have signified only that the material to follow was dance music rather than vocal and that they were not traditional Italian dances. In other words, it may have meant only 'non-Italian dances.'

The first nine dances in Ms 29987 exhibit a very strong Eastern influence, although we shall probably never know whether they were composed by Easterners or by Italians attempting to write in the Eastern style. It would be difficult, however, to deny the style characteristics that show very close links with the East. During the Middle Ages most dance music was improvised and therefore never written down, and it may well be that the preservation of these dances is due to their unfamiliar Eastern characteristics.

NOTES

1 Some similarities do exist with the dances in London, BL Add. 28550 (Robertsbridge Codex) and Faenza Bibl. Com. 117. See discussion in McGee (in preparation).
2 In all formal plots capital letters refer to melodic sections and lower-case letters (i.e., x/y) refer to open and closed endings. Numbers in parentheses show the length of each section in measures.
3 Two of the dances, 'In pro' and 'Parlamento,' are slightly different in that the final two partes have a refrain and endings different from those of the other partes.
4 From Vatican, Biblioteca Ap. Vat. Codex Rossi 215, after transcription in N. Pirrotta Music of Fourteenth-Century Italy (Rome, American Institute of Musicology) 2: 36.

99 Eastern Influences in Medieval European Dances

5 In the Turkish examples the following symbols are used: ↓, lower one comma; ⩘, lower four commas; ♭, lower five commas (similar to the same symbol in Western music.
6 The appearance in example 1, measure 6, of both flat and sharp as editorial additions is in need of explanation. B-flat appears in the Ms in measure 32 and is not cancelled until measure 41. The f-sharp is given in the Ms for the note preceding the f in measure 36 without any visible reason to change back to natural. The reader's attention is directed to a similar b-flat - f-sharp juxtaposition in measures 49-51, which tends to strengthen the editorial markings in measure 36.
7 For a discussion of variable references to instruments see this author's forthcoming article, 'Instrument Information in Florentine Carnival Songs.'
8 R. Dozy Supplément aux dictionnaires arabes, vol. 1, 3d. ed. (Lyde, 1976). I am indebted to George Sawa for this fact and other information concerning Arabic music.

REFERENCES

ten Bokum, J. 1967 De dansen van het trecento. Scripta musicologica Utrajectina 1 (Utrecht, Instituut voor muziekwetenschap der Rijkumiversitaet)

Ettinghausen, R. 1974 'The Impact of Muslim Decorative Arts and Painting on the Arts of Europe' in Joseph Schacht and C.E. Bosworth, ed. The Legacy of Islam 2d ed., (London, Oxford University Press)

Farmer, H.G. 1954 'Arabian Music' Grove's Dictionary of Music and Musicians 5th ed., (London, Macmillan)

von Fischer, K. 1956 Studien zur italienischen Musik des Trecento und frühen Quattrocento, Publikationen der schweizerischen musikforschenden Gesellschaft, series 2, no. 5 (Bern, P. Haupt)

Gennrich, F. 1932 Grundriss einer Formenlehre des mittelalterlichen Liedes (Halle, Max Niemeyer)

Grousset, R. 1936 Histoire des croïsades (Paris, Presses universitaires de France)

Handschin, J. 1929 'Über Estampie und Sequenz' Zeitschrift für Musikwissenschaft 12: 1-20; 13: 113-32

- 1954 'Estampie' Die Musik in Geschichte und Gegenwart 3: cols. 1459-1561

Hibberd, L. 1944 'Estampie and Stantipes' Speculum 19: 222-49

Manik, L. 1969 Das arabische Tonsystem im Mittelalter (Leiden, E.J. Brill)

Martinez-Göllner, M.L. 1969 'Marchettus of Padua and Chromaticism' in F. Alberto Gallo, ed. L'Ars nova italiana del trecento 3 (Certaldo, Centro di studi sull'ars nova italiana del trecento) 187-202

McGee, T. In preparation. 'Medieval Dances'

Moser, H.J. 1920 'Stantipes und Ductia' Zeitschrift für Musikwissenschaft 2: 194-206

Perkuhn, E.R. 1976 Die Theorien zum arabischen Einfluss auf die europäische Musik des Mittelalters (Walldorf-Hessen, Verlag für Orientkunde)
Reaney, G. 1958 'The Ms London B.M. Add. 29987' Musica Disciplina 12: 67-91
- 1965 The Ms London B.M. Add. 29987: Musicological Studies and Documents (Rome, American Institute of Musicology)
Shiloah, A. 1962 'Réflexions sur la danse artistique musulmane au moyen âge,' Cahiers de civilisation médievale X^e-XIIe siècles 5: 463-74
Signell, K. 1977 Makam: Modal Practice in Turkish Art Music (Providence, Asian Music Publications)
Ursprung, O. 1934 'Um die Frage nach dem arabischen bzw. maurischen Einfluss auf die abendländische Musik des Mittelalters' Zeitschrift für Musikwissenschaft 16: 129-41
Wagenaar-Nolthenius, H. 1969 'Estampie/Stantipes/Stampita' in F. Alberto Gallo, ed. L'Ars nova italiana del trecento 3 (Certaldo, Centro di studi sull'ars nova italiana del trecento) 399-409
Wolf, J. 1919 'Die Tänze des Mittelalters' Archiv für Musikwissenschaft 1: 10-42
Wright, O. 1966 'Ibn al Munajjim and the Early Arabian Modes' Galpin Society Journal 19: 27-48

SONG BANG-SONG
Sanjo versus *Rāga*: A Preliminary Study

Over the past decade, Korean musicians and scholars have been bringing their musical traditions to the West, performing and teaching their music, and trying to provide Westerners with a better understanding of the Korean cultural heritage. As a result of their activities, many reference materials - including discs and books - dealing with the many genres of Korean traditional music have been produced in recent years. Among the genres sanjo, perhaps one of the most attractive, is quite fascinating to Western audiences because of the diversity and subtlety of its melodic and rhythmic configurations.

Ethnomusicologists sometimes tend to identify unfamiliar sounds from another country with more familiar sounds from their own experience. For example, the resemblance in instrumental performances of Korean sanjo and Indian rāga has been mentioned to me repeatedly. Barbara Smith, an American ethnomusicologist, states that 'the formal structure [of sanjo] may be understood more easily by comparison with the classical music of India than with that of the West, for sanjo is an aural tradition in which variants of the basic melodic structure are played within a series of basic rhythmic patterns' (1965: 5). This view has frequently been expressed in Korean publications. Hwang Byong-ki, for example, states in his essay 'Sanjo':

> Solo instrumental music in forms like sanjo does not occur in the traditional music of neighboring China and Japan, but it is possible to make comparisons with the rāgas of distant India. Points of similarity include: (1) Both begin in free rhythm, without accompaniment, later coming to have a fixed rhythmic pattern with an accompanying percussion instrument; (2) They both begin with a slow tempo and gradually increase speed, taking a long period of time and reaching a climax; (3) They both use complicated ornamental tones, subtle tone colors, and dramatic vibrato; [and] (4) They both display performing skills by means of powerful and abundant melodies and rhythms.
> (National Academy of Arts 1974: 297)

To find solid evidence in support of this statement is not an easy
task. First of all, the musical structure of sanjo is not derived
from that of Indian classical music. Furthermore, the comparison
between the two distinct traditions would appear misleading without
a careful study of the specific traditions and cultures of each
country.

Although there are a number of substantial differences between
the two musical heritages, the overall impression of a sanjo performance invites a comparison with that of a rāga performance.
This is mainly because the musical systems of both sanjo and rāga
are based primarily upon melody and rhythm, without any features
comparable to Western harmony and counterpoint. The fundamental
element of melody in Korean and Indian music is complemented by
the essential metro-rhythmic patterns (compare Kolinski 1973) of
changdan in Korea and tāla in India. The oral tradition of the two
countries also shows a common ground in their performance practices
with regard to improvisation.

In order to contribute to a better understanding of Korean music,
I will compare four main structural aspects of sanjo (melody, rhythm,
form, and performance practice) with those of North-Indian rāga.[1]
I believe that this comparative approach can help to explain the
ways in which Korean music, using sanjo as an example, differs from
music of other parts of Northeast Asia.[2]

MELODY

The music of both Korea and India is based on an interpenetration
of melody and rhythm. In neither of the two musical traditions is
there the polyphony or harmony that is found in Western classical
music. Rather, Korean sanjo and Indian rāga are built on a highly
sophisticated development of one monophonic melody line with an
accompaniment. Indeed, the core of their performances lies in
melody that has been refined to a very high degree with a variety
of subtleties never equalled in Western music.

A consistent use of microtones, combined with grace notes and
embellishments, produces the characteristic qualities of both
Korean and Indian music. Just as there are no straight lines in
Korean architecture (for example, the elegant curve of the palace
roof contour) so Korean music is characterized by gentle curves or
oscillations and controlled grace notes. As in the Indian gamaka
('the ornaments of the notes'), the system of ornamentation called
nonghyŏnbŏp (literally 'rules for vibrating strings') is the primary
device that creates the delicate shadings and nuances of a tone or
a melodic pattern.[3] In instrumental music, both Korean nonghyŏn and
Indian gamaka can be considered synonymous with left-hand technique,
involving methods of attacking or ornamenting notes. As a rule the
nonghyŏn techniques are found predominantly in slow movements of sanjo.

The well-known seven gamakas of North-Indian music are given in
example 1. In sanjo one can distinguish at least ten kinds of ornamentations used in the chinyangjo movement of kŏmun'go sanjo. They
can be classified in two categories: one type that ornaments before

103 Sanjo versus Rāga

Example 1. The seven gamakas of North-Indian music (after Danielou 1969)

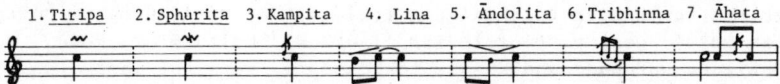
1. Tiripa   2. Sphurita   3. Kampita   4. Lina   5. Āndolita   6. Tribhinna   7. Āhata

the main tone as a sort of 'pre-appoggiatura,' and the other type, a kind of 'post-appoggiatura,' that ornaments after the main tone, as in example 2. The sliding down-up ornament and the vibrating

Example 2. A melodic phrase of chinyangjo by kŏmun'go

note e are typical instances of 'post-appoggiatura,' whereas the sliding-down note b denotes a 'pre-appgogiatura.' The vibrating e and sliding-down b are important in determining the modal structure of the A mode, just as Indian gamaka occurs as a functional feature in certain rāgas. The sliding down-up ornament (\ /) can be compared with the Indian gamaka āndolita (example 1), and the sliding-down ornament (\ ) with kampita (example 1). In sanjo the ornaments are not superficially attached to a melody but seem to grow out of it, like Indian gamakas. Generally speaking, the Korean nonghyŏn and the Indian gamaka are just as essential to Korean and Indian music as harmony and counterpoint are to Western classical music.

As each rāga has its own psychological temperament related to its tempo or speed, so the relationship of speed to the predominant musical expression also exists in sanjo. A joyful or exuberant expression would be executed, not in the very slow chinyangjo movement, but in such fast movements as chajinmori, hwimori, and tanmori. Throughout the slow movements (chinyangjo and chungmori) of a sanjo performance, the dominant mood of the music is in general pathetic and tearful, expressing extreme loneliness, which represents an idiosyncratic characteristic of Korean music. The sorrowful mood can be compared with the concept of karuna rasa, one of the nine sentiments (nava rasa) of North-Indian classical music.

Besides the tonic sa, each rāga has one prominent note called vadi, which is emphasized most strongly, and another important note, samvadī, at the interval of a fourth or fifth from the vadi. In the tonal structure of sanjo, too, apart from the tonal centre, two predominant notes are stressed in the course of melodic progressions and cadential patterns. They are the vibrating notes a fourth below the tonal centre and the sliding-down note, a flexible, sometimes compressed, major second above the tonal centre (see example 2). The vibrating note has the function of a dominant in the context of melodic progressions and cadential patterns, and the sliding tone functions as a leading note. As already mentioned, the two notes play a significant role in determining the modal character of sanjo. As

the emphasis on the vadi and samvadi is one of the most effective
means of setting the mood for the entire rāga, so the device of
vibrating and sliding notes is crucial for establishing the modal
structure of an entire sanjo composition.

By far the largest part of Indian classical music is based on
vocal styles. Dhrupada and khyāl, for example, were the most distinctive singing styles of Hindustani music and served as models
for the development of later intrumental music. It is still common
in India for every instrumental musician to take voice training,
learn fixed song compositions, and thus improve his musical sensitivity. As a result, there is no considerable difference between
the vocal and instrumental versions of a particular rāga performance. Sanjo, although basically a genre of instrumental solo music
today, is believed to have been strongly influenced by the vocal
genre of p'ansori in the early stage of its historical development.
In fact, certain musical features of sanjo are thought to be the
instrumental counterpart of the melodic patterns of the p'ansori
aria. At first, instrumentalists closely followed the vocal model,
but gradually developed an idiomatic and distinctive playing style
in accordance with the nature and techniques of their instruments.
Today there are many kinds of sanjo, not only for string instruments
- such as the twelve-stringed zither (kayagŭm),[4] the six-stringed
zither (kŏmun'go),[5] the two-stringed fiddle (haegŭm),[6] and the
bowed seven-stringed zither (ajaeng)[7] - but also for such wind
instruments as the transverse flute (taegŭm), the cylindrical oboe
(p'iri), and the conical oboe (hojŏk or t'aep'yŏngso).[8]

In spite of these common elements, there are a number of theoretical and practical features that make Korean sanjo melody distinct
from that of Indian rāga. First of all, the octave of the Indian
tone system is theoretically divided into twenty-two units called
shrutis (see Kolinski 1961; Jairazbhoy 1975), whereas the octave
of the Korean system comprises the twelve semitones based on the
Chinese san-fên sun-i (sambun sonik in Sino-Korean) theory (see
Sŏng 1968: 21a-6; Pian 1967: 154; Kaufmann 1967: 17-18), which
represents the Pythagorean principle in which all tones are derived
from the cycle of fifths.

The rāgas comprise three types of scales: the heptatonic scale
(sampūrna), the hexatonic scale (shādava), and the pentatonic scale
(audava). However, the main Indian scale is heptatonic and consists
of the seven notes (svara), like the Western diatonic scale. By
contrast, the anhemitonic-pentatonic scale is most common in Korean
music. Although this pentatonic scale forms the tonal basis of a
sanjo composition, the sensitive listener perceives the appearance
of a number of other scales, such as hemitonic-pentatonic, tetratonic, and even tritonic ones with microtonal embellishment.

Another difference is the sanjo technique of employing the 'tonic
shift,' that is, a kind of modulation, which changes the tonal
centre within a given sanjo performance. The tonic shift from the
A mode to the E mode is common throughout Sin's kŏmun'go sanjo
(example 3) because both the A and E modes share such common notes
as e, a, and b. Thus, in order to change the tonal centre from a to

105 Sanjo versus Rāga

Example 3. Tonic shift from A mode to E mode in Sin's kŏmun'go sanjo

e, the musician has simply to transfer the position of vibrating and sliding-down notes according to the oral tradition transmitted from his master. In example 3 the A mode has been established by the vibrating note e (measures one and two) but the E mode is newly formed by changing the position of the vibrating note from e to b (measure three). In contrast to sanjo masters, Indian musicians do not change the fundamental note, the tonic, within a given rāga performance.

A prominent feature of Indian music is the use of a drone instrument in any vocal or instrumental rāga performance. The tonic must sound continuously for the musician and listener to experience the relationship between the tonic and other scale notes. This is the principal reason why a tambura (sometimes replaced by a hand-pumped harmonium, or surpeti) is indispensable for any performance of Indian classical music. Throughout the entire performance of a rāga, the drone instrument provides the tonic sa and the next important note, usually the dominant pa, for both the performer and the audience. The sound of the tambura forms the framework and foundation of any rāga performance. In sanjo performances, on the other hand, there is no exact parallel to the role of the Indian drone instrument. It should be noted, however, that in the course of a sanjo performance musicians sometimes emphasize a certain note by plucking other strings simultaneously: kayagŭm players pluck the string at the interval of an octave from the melody string, and kŏmun'go musicians strum the first drone string or sweep the fourth, fifth, and sixth open strings in connection with the main melody string.

Furthermore, there are no Korean sanjo counterparts to the following essentials of the Indian rāga. First, every rāga has a specific ascending and descending arrangement in which the individual notes may sometimes be flattened in the descent but kept natural in the ascent, or vice versa. Second, the emotional effect of a certain rāga is created not only through the important tones (vadi and samvādī) and the embellishments (gamaka), but also through the presentation of a particular mood characteristic of each rāga. Each rāga may be associated with a certain time of the day or season of the year. These are specific characteristics of North-Indian classical music not found in Korean sanjo.

RHYTHM

Changdan is the essential element of rhythm in Korean music just as tāla is the fundamental constituent of rhythm in Indian music. In a sanjo performance the changdan is played on an hourglass drum, or changgo, which can be viewed as the Korean counterpart of tabla in North-Indian music. Tradition has it that the word changdan originated from the syllables chang ('long') and dan ('short'), and that rhythm is called changdan because it is based on a combination of long and short durational values. The changdan also denotes organized temporal units, that is, a rhythmic cycle, composed of various rhythmic patterns just as the Indian tāla, perhaps best translated as 'time-measure,' is conceived as a cycle.

Korean master drummers have developed an extremely sophisticated system of rhythm. An ordinary sanjo performance consists of five or six movements based on as many different rhythmic cycles. The rhythmic cycle of chinyangjo is composed of twenty-four triple beats, groups 6 + 6 + 6 + 6 (18/8 + 18/8 + 18/8 + 18/8 metre), in a very slow tempo; the chungmori of twelve beats, grouped 3 + 3 + 3 + 3 (12/4 metre), in a moderate tempo; the chungjungmori of twelve beats, grouped 3 + 3 + 3 + 3 (12/8 metre), in a moderately fast tempo; the ŏnmori of ten beats, grouped 2 + 3 + 2 + 3 (10/8 metre), in a fast tempo; the chajinmori of four triple beats, grouped 3 + 3 + 3 + 3 (12/8 metre), in a fast tempo; and the hwimori and tanmori of four duple beats, grouped 2 + 2 + 2 + 2 (4/4 metre), in a very fast tempo. The appearance of many rhythmic cycles in a sanjo composition is a prominent feature that differentiates sanjo from the persistence of one tāla throughout a given rāga performance.

Although an ordinary sanjo performance comprises as many as five or six different changdan in various tempi, the major tempi are slow chanyangjo, moderate chungmori, and fast chajinmori, corresponding the the three main speeds used in Indian classical music: vilambita (slow), madhya (moderate), and druta (fast). There is no strictly consistent speed concept for sanjo performance, since the tempo mainly depends on the temperament of the instrumentalist. Generally speaking, however, in sanjo the speed chosen for wind instruments is slower than that chosen for string instruments. Each movement usually begins very slowly and the tempo gradually increases towards the end. This tendency of gradual acceleration throughout the entire movement tends to link smoothly the consecutive movements in terms of tempo feeling.

The basic sanjo rhythm can be classified as commetric or contrametric (see Kolinski 1973). Commetric rhythm is predominant in slow and moderate movements, and contrametric rhythm is found in fast movements. The latter includes such devices as syncopation, hemiola, and rubato. When an instrumentalist performs a melody in 6/4 metre in the chajinmori movement (see example 4, measures two to four) and a drummer simultaneously keeps a steady rhythmic cycle of 12/8 metre, the effect upon the audience is that of tension resulting from the conflicting rhythmic configurations (see also Yi 1968). The climax of tension is abated as soon as the soloist returns to the normal

107 Sanjo versus Rāga

Example 4. Excerpt from the chajinmori movement using hemiola technique

rhythmic patterns of the chajinmori in the fifth measure. Periods of
tension and relaxation between the soloist and drummer occur several
times in a given sanjo performance, particularly in the fast
chajinmori movement. The audience expects and enjoys the exciting
dialogue between the performers. A similar dialogue between a soloist
and drummer can be found in North-Indian music when the drum accompaniment, known as sath sangat is used.

One of the unique features of the Indian tāla counting is a combination of hand clapping, waving, and finger counting by both
musicians and audiences. In sanjo, the drummer is the only person
who indicates the beats of a rhythmic cycle with his left hand and
a bamboo stick (changgo ch'ae) in his right hand. The use of the
bamboo stick, a characteristic feature of this Korean drum accompaniment, distinguishes the changgo player from the Indian drummer who
uses both hands. Each changdan contains beats of different degrees
of importance. The most vigorously stressed is usually the first
beat in every changdan. It is played by beating the left side of
the drum with the palm of the left hand and the other side with the
bamboo stick in the right hand. Second in importance are the seven-
teenth beat of the rhythmic cycle of chinyangjo (see example 5)
and the ninth beat of the rhythmic cycles of chungmori and chajinmori
(see example 5). These beats are struck strongly by the bamboo stick
in the right hand. The other beats are distributed between the hands.

The drum accompaniment plays an extremely important role in both
vocal and instrumental music of India. In a given rāga performance
the drummer employs various types of accompaniment. For instance,
perhaps the most popular type of drum accompaniment is the jawabi
sangat of North-Indian music, in which the tabla player imitates a
rhythmic phrase executed by the other instrumentalist. Another drum
accompaniment is the sath sangat of North-Indian music, in which the
tabla musician tries to follow very closely - playing almost simultaneously - the rhythmic patterns played by the main instrumentalist,
and the two players must end a phrase together on the important beat,
sam. This active participation of the drummer in any rāga performance
represents a significant aspect of Indian classical music.

In a sanjo performance there is no exact counterpart to the Indian
drummer's active participation. Nevertheless, the changgo player
occupies an important position and constitutes an integral part of

Example 5. Basic rhythmic patterns on changgo

♩ or ♪ indicates to strike the right-side rim of the drum with the changgo ch'ae; ┌ or ┌ to strike the left side of the drum with the palm of the left hand.

a sanjo performance. In fact, a successful sanjo performance is inconceivable without a drum accompaniment. The drummer's participation may be either passive or active. The passive type of drum accompaniment consists of the drummer's playing of the basic rhythmic pattern of a changdan, frequently adding various variants of the basic pattern, while the main instrumentalist performs his fixed pieces or improvisations within the strict rhythmic framework of a particular changdan. In the passive type of drum accompaniment, the prime role of the drummer is to keep time with a rhythmic drum cycle.

By contrast, in performances of both sanjo and p'ansori, the active drummer inserts calls of encouragement, or ch'uimsae, to the main instrumentalist at appropriate moments, usually at the end of a rhythmic cycle. The ch'uimsae include several specific short words, usually praising the soloist's skill and artistry: for instance, choch'i ('Nice!'), kŭroch'i ('Right on!'), chot'a ('Excellent!'), or ŏlsigu ('Bravo!'). An effective presentation of the ch'uimsae creates a very exhilarating and exciting mood for both the instrumental soloist and the audience, provided there is a satisfactory mutual understanding. The changgo player's encouragement of the soloist can be compared with the mutual satisfaction shared through visual communication between instrumentalist and drummer in the course of an Indian rāga performance. Sometimes the ch'uimsae originate from the audience at a moment of musical excitement. A similar situation can be observed at a performance of Indian classical music: sometimes Indian audiences sigh at an exciting moment when the drummer and instrumentalist arrive together dramatically on the important beat, sam. Audiences have come to expect such spirited dialogue between the drummer and the soloist in both Korean sanjo and Indian rāga performances.

The Korean changgo kuŭm (literally meaning 'mouth sound of hourglass drum') can also be compared with the Indian theka in terms

109 Sanjo versus Rāga

of its function in drumming practice. In North-Indian drumming the theka is a set of mnemonic syllables representing the strokes on the tabla, as in example 6. The changgo kuŭm, a sequence of drum

Example 6. The thekas of tintāl on tablas (Kaufmann 1967: 248)

1	2	3	4	5	6	7	8	9	10	11	12
Dha	dhin	dhin	dha	dha	dhin	dhin	dha	dha	tin	tin	ta
X				2				0			

13	14	15	16
ta	dhin	dhin	dha
3			

syllables, is actually a series of imitations of the changgo sound produced on both sides of the drum, and serves as the basic framework of changgo notation. While I was learning drum patterns, however, I found that the changgo kuŭm is not now demonstrated by traditional musicians when they teach drum patterns. On the basis of traditional drumming syllables, the rhythmic patterns of chungmori and chajinmori (compare example 5) may be notated as in example 7.

Example 7. The kuŭm of chungmori and chajinmori on changgo

Chungmori

1	2	3	4	5	6	7	8	9
Tŏng	-	kidŏk	k'ung	kidŏk	kidŏk	kugung	k'ung	ttak

10	11	12
k'ung	-	k'ung

Chajinmori

1	2	3	4	5	6	7	8	9
Tŏng	-	tŏk	k'ung	tta	k'ung	k'ung	-	ttak

10	11	12
k'ung	-	k'ung

In both Korean and North-Indian classical music, the instrumental soloist is traditionally the leader of the ensemble and the drummer is merely an accompanist. In recent times, however, some North-Indian instrumentalists do allow their accompanists much licence, and thus the drummer has been getting an increasing share of improvisation. This tendency, however, has not been practised in sanjo performance: the soloist still prefers his changgo player to serve merely as an accompanist and does not permit him to participate in the improvisation of sanjo.

FORM

Most of the vocal and instrumental pieces in North-Indian classical music open with an ālāpa, a solo exposition without drum accompaniment. The very slow and serene beginning of the ālāpa section states the essential features of the rāga and emphasizes its tonal centre. After gradually unfolding the whole range of the rāga, the ālāpa leads into the sthāyi section, in which the musician presents specific melodic themes within the framework of a steady tāla rhythm. In this section, the first main part of the composition, the musician concentrates on exploiting the low and middle ranges of the rāga and emphasizing the most prominent note (vadi). The tempo of the sthāyi section ranges between slow and moderate. Then follows the second main section, the antarā; there the music rises to the upper range of the scale, emphasizing the note (samvādī) that is second in importance. As variation and development of the basic rāga are built up, the rāga gains speed and the melodic patterns become more intricate. The improvisations become most daring in the third main section, or sanchāri, and the last section, the ābhoga, and end with an exciting climax.

A traditional Korean musician used to begin an instrumental performance with the tasŭrŭm[9] section, which is a counterpart of the tan'ga ('short song') preceding a vocal p'ansori presentation. Like the Indian ālāpa section, the tasŭrŭm is a kind of rhapsodic and free-rhythmic instrumental introduction. In accordance with the term tasŭrŭm (which means 'to govern or to manage' in a general sense and 'to tune' in its musical sense), the musician checks the tuning of his instrument by unfolding the whole range of the instrument. There is no changgo accompaniment in the tasŭrŭm section as the musician delineates the principal expressive phrases in a very slow and relaxed tempo, warming himself up to perform the sanjo proper. Nowadays this tasŭrŭm section is rarely performed by sanjo or other traditional instrumentalists. As a result, there are no discs manufactured in Korea or abroad that include the tasŭrŭm section, except for a tape recording of the kayagŭm sanjo performed by Madam Ham Tongjŏngwŏl[10] and now kept in the Music Archive of Seoul National University.[11]

Apart from the tasŭrŭm section, a sanjo performance is made up of five or six movements. As in the sections of North-Indian music, the tempo of the movements proceeds from slow to fast: the slowest chinyangjo; the moderate chungmori; the slightly fast chungjungmori; the fast ŏnmori and chajinmori; and the very fast hwimori and tanmori. The title of each movement is identical with that of the changdan it uses. Of these movements, the chinyangjo, the chungmori, and the chajinmori are the most essential. These three movements must be included in any sanjo performance,[12] chiefly because they are indispensable in maintaining the identity of the sanjo proper and also because, as pointed out earlier, they comprise the three basic tempi. Besides the basic movements, others can be added depending on the instrument played, the occasion, and the individual sanjo master.

In the slow chinyangjo movement, which is the most important one, the element of strict rhythm (changdan) appears for the first time. Within a relatively calm and very slow rhythmic cycle the movement exposes the characteristic features of the particular sanjo melody, decorating it with dexterous and rich ornamentations. The general mood of the whole movement is sometimes serene but mostly pathetic and tearful, comparable to the karuna rasa of Indian music. After unfolding the expressive content of the sanjo melody and accelerating towards the end of the movement, the chinyangjo leads into the moderate chungmori movement. This movement exploits complicated melodic configurations with a rather lively changgo accompaniment and may be compared to the antarā section of the North-Indian music. In the chajinmori movement the instrumental soloist demonstrates his virtuosity in rapid passage work to a fast and exciting drum accompaniment. As in the sanchāri and ābhoga sections of North-Indian rāga performance, the chajinmori movement displays more intricate melodic and rhythmic patterns characterized by increasing speed and excitement leading to a climactic ending.

Just as a North-Indian musician performs a complete rāga without interruption, so the sanjo proper is played without any break between the movements, although there is a change in the rhythmic cycle (changdan) between the movements and the increases of tempo. A complete sanjo performance normally takes about forty minutes but can take from thirty minutes to an hour, depending upon the individual player. A full-length sanjo performance would be given privately or on informal occasions for a sanjo connoisseur and occasionally at ordinary concerts and for tape recordings. At the request of television or radio programmers, however, short sanjo compositions, lasting five to fifteen minutes, are frequently heard at the present time. But these are simplified arrangements and not authentic in terms of sanjo style and character. The recent tendency to present short versions of rāga performances is a parallel development in India.

PERFORMANCE PRACTICE

In both Korean sanjo and Indian rāga, the arts of performance and creation merge into one, that is, improvisation. Sanjo represents indeed an improvisatory process unique in the performing arts of Northeast Asia. I use the term improvisation in the sense of a type of composition, because improvisation cannot be regarded as a concept separate from composition, at least in the sanjo tradition. A sanjo musician believes that his performance re-creates the traditional sanjo and he may perform his music not very differently from the model provided by his teacher's sanjo. Nevertheless, the musician improvises to some extent in the course of his sanjo presentation.

With regard to improvisation in Indian music, it may suffice to quote the following statements: 'An Indian musician does not "improvise," ... His aim is to build the structural character of a particular modal form which is called a Rāga' (Datta and Lath 1967: 27); and 'A musician sets himself a general plan and follows it, yet at each step he puts in his own creative interpretation in formulating, enriching and giving meaning to the patterns he employs ... an artist's individual imagination and the rigid laws to which he has to conform are like the two wheels of a chariot, both of them being equally indispensable for its movement' (ibid.: 34).

I hold substantially the same view, namely, that improvisation is a kind of creative process or composition involving a musician's insight and imagination while still adhering to the tradition handed down orally to the musician by his teacher. Thus improvisation in both Korean and Indian classical music assumes a similar meaning. In this respect, I agree with Nettl's conclusion when he says: 'perhaps we must abandon the idea of improvisation as a process separate from composition and adopt the view that all performers improvise to some extent. What the pianist playing Bach and Beethoven does with his models - the scores and the accumulated tradition of performance practice - is only in degree, not in nature, different from what the Indian playing an alap in Rag Yaman and the Persian singing the Dastgah of Shur do with theirs' (1974: 19).

In contrast with many Western musicians who spend several years studying the history and background of their musical traditions at institutes, Korean and Indian students (chejas and shishyas, respectively) learn from their masters (sŏnsaengs and gurus, respectively) and concentrate primarily on practical music, memorizing traditions handed down to them by their masters.

In the oral tradition of sanjo, the student has to rely completely on the guidance of his teacher, who transmits everything individually and directly. The student gradually learns to play his teacher's basic patterns in a strictly imitative way. At this stage of training the student normally conforms to certain more or less fixed melodies and to the sequence in which basic patterns of elaboration are used. He also constantly works at adapting many other techniques of style and ornamentation until he himself feels free and confident to improvise. As his musicianship grows, he acquires a high degree of technical proficiency in playing his instrument. At this stage of maturity his technique and knowledge have become sufficiently developed to enable him to render his own versions of sanjo on the spur of the moment. After the student has achieved a fair degree of proficiency as a sanjo performer, he will handle various flexible and spontaneous techniques and finally shape his own musical personality. All in all, it will take him at least ten years of constant work and practice to reach maturity and a high standard of achievement in sanjo music. Today all outstanding sanjo masters were once students of former master musicians. The teaching method of Indian musicians seems to be quite similar to that of sanjo players, especially as described by the eminent sitar player Ravi Shankar.

Three factors contribute to the establishment of a personal style of sanjo: preservation, elaboration, and creation. By 'preservation' I mean retention of the original and fixed melodies or compositions that form the present framework of sanjo; by 'elaboration' I mean an extensive variation and modification or embellishment of the original melody or composition; and by 'creation' I mean an extemporizing or improvisatory process for new musical ideas apart from the previous composition or model.

The preservation of a previous model is the most essential component of sanjo composition since no sanjo can be improvised without a traditional framework. In this phase the musician has to present basic patterns learned from his teacher and cannot make a major contribution to sanjo improvisation.

113 Sanjo versus Rāga

Example 8. Comparison of melodic phrases in Paek's and Sin's chungmori movement

As we can see in example 8, the sanjo master, Sin K'we-dong, has tried to preserve as closely as possible the original melody of his teacher, Paek Nak-chun, although Sin's ornamentations are added to Paek's melody.

The second phase, elaboration, allows the musician to invent a certain degree of variation and modification of the original melody and rhythm by means of various ornamentational techniques and slight alterations. Example 9 shows Sin's variation of his teacher's melody and rhythm, from normal rhythm to syncopated rhythm in 12/8 metre, and a slight modification of melodic progressions in Sin's performance in accordance with his rhythmic alteration. Since Sin is still restrained by the traditional model in the second phase, he

Example 9. Rhythmic and melodic variations of Sin's sanjo

can proceed only cautiously towards improvisation. It is during the third phase, creation, that the musician learns to improvise new musical ideas on the basis of temporal units, that is, rhythmic cycles (changdan). Of course, the extemporaneous creation of a new musical composition must be built upon the basic musical elements of a traditional model, such as cadential formulae, rhythmic structure, or modal progressions. In other words, the creation of a new composition is the musician's new interpretation or imitation of an existing sanjo model according to his creative imagination and knowledge. The more a sanjo musician is talented and creative, the more his composition may be integrated within the tradtional framework of his teacher's sanjo. Apart from the traditional models by the great masters of the past, sometimes the musician imitates or borrows fixed melodies of a sanjo crystallized by his contemporaries and then adds them to the traditional body of his teacher's sanjo (see Cho 1969). Through these improvisatory processes, sanjo musicians are able to refine their new compositions and eventually to establish a distinctive personal style of sanjo. After the achievement of his own mature musical style, a sanjo master tends to consolidate the personal character of his sanjo and thus to distinguish his style from those of his contemporaries. The musician would then teach his students the individual brand of composition of his own sanjo.

CONCLUSION

The continuity of tradition handed down from master to disciples is gradually disappearing today with the rapid social, economic, and cultural changes in both countries under discussion. Indian classical music, however, seems to be in a better position than Korean music, as Jairazbhoy predicted: 'This is once again a period of exploration and change, and it will certainly influence the form of Indian music in years to come. At the present time, however, there is no reason to believe that the basic fundamentals of Indian music are in any danger of distortion in the foreseeable future' (1971: 26). In Korea the creative tradition of sanjo has gradually become the musical legacy of the older generations, particularly because of urgent demands for modernization in music education. Since the establishment of the Department of Traditional Music at Seoul National University in 1959, young students have been able to learn several schools of sanjo with the aid of transcribed scores. As a result, a line of demarcation between performer and composer has firmly emerged among younger musicians, gradually restricting the creative ability in the improvisational sanjo style. University-educated students of this generation have not developed the improvisational art of the great sanjo masters of the past, although they are able to learn several sanjo schools cultivated and refined by the life-work of outstanding masters. However, the younger musicians may be able to create new styles of composition for instrumental solo music based upon some of the traditional values of a bygone generation.

NOTES

1 My statements about North-Indian rāga are based on Kaufmann (1967), Jairazbhoy (1971), and Shankar (1968) unless otherwise noted.
2 More detail on sanjo can be found in my dissertation, Song (1975).
3 For intensive studies of the topic, see Chang 1966: 453-8; 1975: 173-217; Pace 1970.
4 For kayagŭm sanjo performances see Smith (1965), Side I performed by Hwang Byong-ki; Philips (n.d.), Side II, Band 5 (hereafter II/5) by Seung Keum-Ryun [Sŏng Kŭm-yŏn]; and Lewiston (1972), I/3 by Sung Keum-yun [Sŏng Kŭm-yŏn].
5 Ibid., II/2 by Kim Yoon-duk [Kim Yun-dŏk]; and Levy (n.d.), I/1 by Sin K'we-dong.
6 Lewiston (1972), II/1 by Chi Young-hee [Chi Yŏng-hŭi]. In the record jacket notes, the term shinawi (sinawi) has been used instead of the word sanjo. Today the term sinawi denotes

115 Sanjo versus Rāga

shamanistic dance music rather than solo instrumental music, but the old generations of folk musicians use the term in the same sense as sanjo; for example, taegŭm or chŏttae sinawi for taegŭm sanjo, and haegŭm sinawi for haegŭm sanjo. For a historical relationship between sinawi and sanjo, see Song 1975: 138-48.
7 Levy (n.d.), I/2 by Han Ilsup [Han Il-sŏp].
8 Ibid., I/3 by Han Il-sŏp.
9 The tasŭrŭm, or tasŭrim, is referred to in Sino-Korean as choŭm, 'tuning sound (of strings).' The choŭm is found in old kŏmun'go handbooks; for instance, the Yanggum sinbo 1601 Reprinted, Seoul, T'ongmun'gwan, 1959, 43-6. For a transcription of tasŭrim melodies practised around the early 1930s, see Chang Sa-hun Kugakki yŏnjubŏp (Seoul, Korean Musicological Society, 1963) 93-6; and Kugak ch'ongnon (Seoul, Chŏngŭm sa, 1976) 312-18.
10 This is her art name; her real name is Ham Kŭm-dŏk (b. 1917). For a short biography, see Yi Po-hyŏng Kayagŭm sanjo (Seoul, Munhawjae kwalliguk, 1972) 47-8.
11 The recording date is unknown, but I had a copy of her performance made in 1974 from the original tape in the Music Archive, Seoul National University.
12 In reality, however, there are many discs showing different and even wrong arrangements of sanjo performance. Take Levy (n.d.) as an example: I/1 comprises only the chinyangjo movement, omitting the other movements with an excuse: 'It is not possible to give it all here.' It must be stressed that the chinyangjo movement alone is not sufficient to illustrate the sanjo proper, so that the editor should have included even short pieces of the other movements, for example, Ajaeng sanjo in I/2 of the same disc. Other wrong presentations are Haegŭm sinawi in Lewiston 1972, I/1, and Kayagŭm sanjo in Philips II/5. Both performances lack the chinyangjo movement, probably to save time in their limited spaces. For a critical review of the latter, particularly II/5, see Song Bang-song 'Record Review' Asian Music 7 (1): 84-5. For a transcription of many sanjo compositions of different schools, see Kim Ki-su et al. (transcribed by) Han'guk ŭmak (Anthology of Korean Traditional Music) (Seoul, National Classical Music Institute, 1969) 9-23 (Kayagŭm sanjo of Pak Sang-gun ryu); 24-38 (Kayagŭm sanjo of Sin K'we-dong ryu); 41-68 (Kŏmun'go sanjo of Sin K'we-dong ryu); 71-115 (Taegŭm sanjo of P'yŏn Chae-jun, Yi Ch'ung-sŏn, Han Pŏm-su, and Han Chu-hwan ryu); 118-25 (P'iri sanjo of Yi Ch'ung-sŏn ryu); 129-36 (Haegŭm sanjo of Han Pŏm-su ryu).

REFERENCES

Chang Sa-hun 1966 Kugak non'go (Studies in Korean Music) (Seoul, Seoul National University Press)
- 1975 Han'guk chŏn-t'ong ŭmak ŭi yŏn-gu (Seoul, Pojinjae)
Cho Wi-min 1969 'Hyŏn'gŭm sanjo ŭi wŏnhyŏng kaw hyŏn haenghyŏng' (Kommun'go Sanjo: Its Past and Present Form), in Essays on Ethnomusicology: A Birthday Offering for Lee Hye-ku (Seoul, Korean Musicological Society)

Datta, Vivek and Lath Mukund 1967 'Improvisation in Indian Music' The World of Music 11 (1): 27-34
Danielou, Alain 1969 North Indian Music (New York, Frederick A. Praeger)
Jairazbhoy, Nazir A. 1971 The Rāgs of North Indian Music (Middletown, Conn., Wesleyan University Press)
- 1975 'An Interpretation of the 22 Srutis' Asian Music 6 (1/2): 38-59
Kaufmann, Walter 1965 'Rasa, Raga-Mala and Performance Times in North India' Ethnomusicology 9 (2): 272-91
- 1967 Musical Notations of the Orient (Bloomington, Indiana University Press)
Kolinski, Mieczyslaw 1961 'The Origin of the Indian 22-Tone System' Studies in Ethnomusicology 1 (1): 3-18
- 1973 'A Cross-cultural Approach to Metro-rhythmic Patterns' Ethnomusicology 17 (3): 494-506
Levy, John n.d. Korean Social and Folk Music (New York, Lyrichord Discs LLST 7211)
Lewiston, David [1972] P'ansori: Korean Epic Vocal Arts and Instrumental Music (New York, Nonesuch Records H 72049)
National Academy of Arts 1973 Survey of Korean Arts: Traditional Music (Seoul, National Academy of Arts)
- 1974 Survey of Korean Arts: Folk Arts (Seoul, National Academy of Arts)
Nettl, Bruno 1974 'Thoughts on Improvisation: A Comparative Approach' The Musical Quarterly 60 (1): 1-19
Park Chong-gil 1970 'Ornamentation in Korean Music' MA thesis, University of Washington, Seattle
Philips n.d. Korean Music UNESCO Collection of Musical Sources: Art Music of the Far East, VIII-1. Philips 6586011
Pian, Rulan C. 1969 'China: II. Theory' Harvard Dictionary of Music, 2d. ed. (Cambridge, Harvard University Press)
Shankar, Ravi 1968 My Music, My Life (Delhi, Vikas Publications)
Smith, Barbara, ed., 1965 Music from Korea, vol. I: The Kayakeum Recording performed by Hwang Byong-ki (Honolulu, East-West Center Press EWS 1001)
Song Bang-song 1971 An Annotated Bibliography of Korean Music. (Providence, Asian Music Publications, Brown University)
- 1975 'Kŏmun'go Sanjo: An Analytical Study of a Style of Korean Folk Instrumental Music,' PhD dissertation, Wesleyan University, Middletown, Conn.
Sŏng Hyŏn 1968 Akhak kwebŏm [1493], Seoul, Yonse University Press
Yi Chae-suk 1968 'Chajinmori ŭi rhythm hyŏngt'ae yŏn'gu' (A Study of the Chajinmori Rhythm in Sanjo Music) Ŭmdae hakpo 4: 29-38

GEORGE D. SAWA
Bridging One Millennium:
Melodic Movement in al-Fārābī and Kolinski

The object of this article is to compare the outlooks towards melodic movement of two men separated from one another by a thousand years: the famous tenth-century Muslim philosopher and music theorist al-Fārābī, and the twentieth-century scholar Mieczyslaw Kolinski. The comparison will be to most readers a somewhat surprising one, but each man was among the greatest music theorists of his time and both developed terminology and other methods for the analysis of melody and specifically of melodic movement.

Al-Fārābī's name in full was Abū Nasr Muhammad ibn Muhammad ibn Tarkhān ibn Awzalagh al-Fārābī (d. 950). Of Turkish orign, he studied the sciences of the Greeks in Baghdad and later was patronized in Aleppo by Sayf al-Dawlah, the founder of the Hamdānid dynasty in northern Syria. Al-Fārābī was one of the foremost Muslim philosophers and was given the title of 'Second Master,' the first being Aristotle. He wrote books not only on music but on logic, ethics, mathematics, politics, and alchemy as well (d'Erlanger 1930: xix-xx; Farmer 1929: 175-7). His Kitāb al-mūsīqá al-kabīr ('Great Book of Music'), like all his works, is permeated with Greek models and Greek logical thinking and gives an articulate and concise presentation of contemporary musical practices which, in his view, were inherited from the traditions of the Near East and ancient Greece.

In those portions of his work with which we will be concerned here, al-Fārābī aimed not at developing an analytical system but at offering guidance on the proper construction of melodies according to then acceptable standards. In common with other scholars of his time, he did not concern himself with music outside his own cultural sphere. According to von Grunebaum (1953: 7), 'man in the Middle Ages made, on the whole, little or no effort to comprehend the outsider whose status as an infidel disqualitied him as an object of dispassionate inquiry.' Thus, in al-Fārābī's view, the world's peoples were divided into those having 'normal' sensory perception and those having 'abnormal' perception. Those with normal perception were people living within the boundaries of the then Islamic world, as well as Greece and Byzantium, during the period from roughly the founding of the library in Alexandria in the latter part of the third century BC to al-Fārābī's own lifetime. Those with abnormal perception were the

Negroes, Ethiopians, and Sudanese living to the south, the Turkish
nomads to the northeast, and the Slavs to the northwest. 'Especially
abnormal,' in his eyes, were the people living still farther north
(d'Erlanger 1930: 38-9; al-Fārābī 1967: 108-10).

The precise extent of his influence on composers of the time is
difficult to assess, since little music from that period has been
preserved in written form. We do know, however, that al-Fārābī's
influence on subsequent theorists was considerable, and that al-
Fārābī himself, unlike many other medieval theorists, was a proficient performer on the ᶜūd and was generally conversant with a
full range of music-related sciences. In short, he, like Kolinski,
was a practitioner of the art and not merely a theorist.

Our comparison, then, is really between the prescriptions of a
consciously 'ethnocentric' medieval writer and the cross-cultural
analytic approach of a modern ethnomusicologist. In this comparison
a search will be made for the two theorists' meeting ground, which
may constitute basic principles on which later researchers can build
evolving theories. The comparison will bring to the attention of
ethnomusicologists a medieval theorist who dealt a millennium ago
with melodic movement - an important methodological problem that
is still relevant. It will also show that 'historical ethnomusicology,' an often neglected aspect of the discipline, can make a useful contribution to modern ethnomusicology.

KITĀB AL-MŪSĪQÁ AL-KABĪR

The 'Great Book of Music' originally comprised two books, of which
the second is now lost. (This study is based on four versions of
the original: d'Erlanger 1930, 1935; al-Fārābī 1347, 1461, 1967.)
The first book is divided into an introduction and three parts.
Part I is concerned with music theory, Part II with musical instruments, and Part III with musical composition. There are two sections
dealing specifically with melodic movement: one in the second discourse of Part I, the other in the first discourse of Part III
(d'Erlanger 1930: 145-9, 1935: 18-26; al-Fārābī 1347: 74a-6b, 154a-7b;
1461: 46b-8b, 72a-5a; 1967: 418-34, 959-83). The division of material
on this one topic is difficult to explain. One would have expected
the material to be united, probably in Part III, in which al-Fārābī
considers the process of composition. All one can say is that, in
his virtually encyclopaedic discussion of the many facets of music,
al-Fārābī more than once places aspects of the same topic in different sections of the treatise.

The purpose of al-Fārābī's treatment of melodic movement in these
two sections is to guide the composer rather than to analyse a given
melody. This purpose is restated in Part III. Al-Fārābī says that
after the composer has chosen the melodic elements he will consult
the tables of consonance and melodic movement, choosing examples
that fit the melodic elements (regarding range and consonance) and
fitting them within the framework of a rhythmic mode (d'Erlanger
1935: 49-50; al-Fārābī 1967: 1056-8).

119 Melodic Movement in al-Fārābī and Kolinski

AL-FĀRĀBĪ: SOME PRELIMINARY DEFINITIONS

Al-Fārābī's treatment of melodic movement is closely tied to his concept of consonance and dissonance and to the modal system. For a transition to occur between two notes, for example, they must be consonant with each other. Following the example of Ptolemy, in the second century AD, al-Fārābī divided the consonances into three classes: (1) the greater consonances, like the octave and its multiples (whether sounded together or in succession); (2) the medium consonances, like the fifth, fourth, octave-and-fifth, and the octave-and-fourth (whether sounded together or in succession); and (3) the small consonances, like the major second (9/8) and the other intervals with superparticular ratios smaller than the fourth (d'Erlanger 1930: 100-1; 1935: 269-70; al-Fārābī 1967: 269-70).

Melody is defined as 'a definite number of notes, all or almost all consonant with one another, arranged in a definite group, in which a definite genus (tetrachord) is used; its intervals are definite and are in a definite tonality; a definite movement occurs through the notes within a definite rhythmic mode' (d'Erlanger 1930: 160; al-Fārābī 1967: 487). The group is a succession of notes composed of at least one tetrachord plus one whole tone. As such the five notes of a fifth constitute the smallest group possible. Groups are 'incomplete' when their range is less than an octave, 'complete' when their range is an octave, and 'complete absolute' when their range is two octaves. The different intervals constituting the group (or for that matter the group itself) are on a certain pitch level (tonality) within the two-octave ambitus (d'Erlanger 1930: 117; 1935: 4; al-Fārābī 1967: 324, 882). Melodic movement (al-intiqal, literally, 'moving from one point to another') is defined as 'the transition that may occur from note to note, from interval to interval, from genus to genus if the group is made up of different tetrachords, from group to group, and from tonality to tonality' (d'Erlanger 1930: 145; al-Fārābī 1967: 418). For al-Fārābī, then, melodic movement is more than merely the transition from note to note, which is only the nucleus; it is, in fact, closely bound up with the entire modal system. Kolinski (1968: 218) is opposed to the mixing of tone system and melodic movements. In his analysis he states that 'tonal and melodic structure are necessarily correlated; however, a consistent investigation of these two aspects of pitch and tint organization requires opposite approaches: while the analysis of tonal structure hardly touches upon matters concerning melodic shape, the analysis of melodic structure deals with tonal construction only on the lowest level of a classification of melodic shapes' (Kolinski 1968: 218).

In al-Fārābī's system, the preferred ranges for a melody (within his two-octave ambitus) are the octave, the perfect fifth, and the perfect fourth. A good melody uses all the notes contained within these ranges, that is, eight notes, five notes, and four notes, respectively (d'Erlanger 1930: 118; 1935: 18; al-Fārābī 1967: 327, 960). Al-Fārābī uses the octave as the basis for his tables of melodic movements, since a movement using an octave constitutes a model that can be applied to a movement using less than an octave, the latter being merely a fraction of the whole. His model can also be applied to a melodic movement exceeding an octave, since the notes beyond the octave range are a repetition of those contained in the lower octave (d'Erlanger 1935: 20-5; al-Fārābī 1967: 964-83). In Kolinski's terms this is because the octaves have an identical tint. Moreover, what applies to one group also applies to another, provided, of course, that the law of consonance is observed. (Category 3, by the way, uses two octaves instead of one because, by definition, it encompasses both octaves.)

Al-Fārābī makes one further and extremely important distinction between notes that are 'essential' to a melody and those that 'give the melody perfection' (d'Erlanger 1935: 50; al-Fārābī 1967: 1058). The notes that give the melody perfection are not only ornaments in the Western sense but also notes sounded together with a note of the melody.

AL-FĀRĀBĪ'S CATEGORIES OF MELODIC MOVEMENT

In Section II, al-Fārābī gives tables in which he divides melodic movement into four categories:

1 Al-nuqlah 'alá istiqāmah
  Translation: straight, direct, rectilinear movement
  Meaning: non-returning movement
2 Al-nuqlah 'alá in'iṭāf
  Translation: folding, turning, curving, surrounding movement
  Meaning: movement returning to the starting note. By returning to the starting note, the movement 'surrounds' the intermediary notes. Compared to the next movement, it might be termed semi-circular. D'Erlanger's 'combinaisons comportant des retours au point de départ' gives the meaning without translating the phrase.
3 Al-nuqlah 'alá istidārah
  Translation: circular movement
  Meaning: movement returning to the starting note, then returning again from the reverse direction
4 Al-nuqlah 'alá in'irāj
  Translation: deviating movement
  Meaning: movement returning but not as far as the starting point

Section I mentioned some of the above categories and two additional ones:

5 'Aṭf bi-dawr
  Translation: a circular motion
  Meaning: a descent from, followed by a descent to, the starting note without touching any other note already played
6 Al-nuqlah bi-in'irāj
  Translation: deviating movement
  Meaning: an ever-widening up-and-down movement without touching any note already played

Melodic Movement in al-Fārābī and Kolinski

Among the tables given by al-Fārābī are three basic divisions. Category 1 does not return to the starting note. Categories 2, 3, and 5 return to the starting note. Categories 4 and 6 return, but not to the starting note.

After presenting his tables, al-Fārābī says that they include most of the 'simple' forms of melodic movement; the compound ones are simply a mixture of the simple forms, derivable by the reader. Likewise, it is left to the reader to derive the remaining 'simple' forms according to the principles of the tables. (The derivation of both the remaining simple forms and the compound forms is beyond the scope of this paper, however.) His tables, therefore, unlike Kolinski's, are not exhaustive. Al-Fārābī adds that in any melodic movement it is possible to repeat any note any number of times without changing the essential nature of the movement. In this he agrees with Kolinski's notion of tone reiteration.

There are, finally, three basic concepts behind al-Fārābī's first four categories. The first concept is what I term the basic pattern, which is derivable from al-Fārābī's definition of each category. The second is the subdivision of the basic pattern according to its extensions, for example, by returning after every note or by returning after every two notes. The third is the application of the pattern to the range of an octave (or two octaves, in category 3).

AL-FĀRĀBĪ COMPARED TO KOLINSKI

Before beginning this comparison, it is important to note that al-Fārābī's examples are theoretical models which apply a basic pattern to various notes of the octave in succession, resulting in what scientists would call a 'general formula.' This particular general formula is a practical tool which can apply to melodic movements whose ranges are either less or more than an octave. Such applications result in what Kolinski terms 'complexes of recurrent movements' or 'non-recurrent multimember movements.' To facilitate comparison of the two methods, al-Fārābī's examples, given in letter notation in the original manuscripts, are here transcribed in Western notation and analysed in their entirety according to Kolinski's system.

It will also be helpful to show the most basic features of Kolinski's method. There are two fundamental categories: recurrent movements and non-recurrent movements. The subdivisions of these two categories are shown below, together with a graphic representation. (See Kolinski 1965 and 1976 for a more detailed account of the basic movements and for their merging into complexes.)

RECURRENT MOVEMENTS

Flexure

Pendulum

returning pendulum   progressing pendulum

122 George D. Sawa

NON-RECURRENT MOVEMENTS

One-member movement   step   line

Two-member movement   hook

Multimember movement   zigzag

Category 1[1]
The basic pattern of category 1, that is, a non-returning one-directional movement, is what Kolinski terms a step movement.

Example 1. Category 1, al-nuqlah 'alá istiqāmah, a movement that does not return to notes already touched. This definition is misleading unless one adds 'and does not change direction.'

A. Without skipping notes

B. Skipping notes

1. Skipping every one note

2. Skipping every two notes

3. Skipping every three notes

4. Skipping every four notes

5. Skipping every five notes or more

123 Melodic Movement in al-Fārābī and Kolinski

Al-Fārābī names the subdivisions of the category according to the number of notes 'skipped' during the course of the movement, that is, those skipping no notes, one, two, three, four, or five notes (see example 1). Kolinski disregards such isolated direct ascents or descents, stating that at least two 'steps' or 'lines' of changing direction are needed to form a true melodic movement. It would therefore misrepresent Kolinski's method to analyse al-Fārābī's category 1.

Category 2

According to al-Fārābī, there are three basic patterns in this category: (A) a return directly to the starting note without touching intermediary notes (see example 2); (B-a) a return by means of notes already used (see example 3); and (B-b) a return by means of notes not already used (see example 4). Although Kolinski uses different criteria for classification and consequently arrives at a different hierarchy, the resulting patterns show a close similarity: al-Fārābī' pattern 2A (example 2) is analogous to the flexure, that is, to the recurrent step movements or mixed recurrent movements combining line and step. Pattern 2B-a (example 3) is analogous to homogeneous recurrent movements, and pattern 2B-b (example 4) is analogous to mixed recurrent movements combining step and line. Within this category, al-Fārābī's basic patterns develop through the octave into what Kolinski would describe as a widening standing (or hanging) complex of the first degree nexus. According to Kolinski, this complex consists of recurrent movements; for al-Fārābī, however, it is no more than a 'simple' movement, since the extension of a basic pattern still generates the same simple movement.

Example 2. Category 2A, al-nuqlah 'alá in'iṭāf, a movement that returns to the starting note without touching intermediary notes

1. After every note = Kolinski's recurrent step movements

Widening-standing six-movement complex in first-degree nexus, composed of step up-flexures

Widening-hanging six-movement complex, composed of step down-flexures

124 George D. Sawa

2. After every two notes = mixed recurrent movements (line
and step) in three-pitch areas

Widening-standing three-movement complex composed of mixed
up-flexures (line and step) in the major-third area gab, the
quintal area gcd, and the minor-seventh area gef; three-
pitch areas

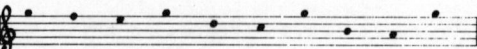

Widening-hanging three-movement complex composed of mixed
down-flexures (line and step) in the minor-third area efg,
the quintal area cdg, and the minor-seventh area abg; three-
pitch areas

3. After every three notes = in four-pitch areas

Widening-standing two-movement complex composed of mixed up-
flexures (line and step) in the tetrachordal area gabc and
the minor-seventh area gdef; four pitch-areas

Widening-hanging two-movement complex composed of mixed down-
flexures (line and step) in the tetrachordal area defg and
the minor-seventh area abcg; four-pitch areas

4. After every four notes = in a five-pitch area

Mixed up-flexure (line and step) in the pentachordal area
gabcd

Mixed down-flexures (line and step) in the pentachordal
area cdefg

125 Melodic Movement in al-Fārābī and Kolinski

5. After every five notes or more = in a six-pitch area or more

Mixed up-flexure (line and step) in the hexachordal area gabcde

Mixed down-flexure (line and step) in the hexachordal area bcdefg

Example 3. Category 2B-a, a movement that returns to the starting note by means of notes already touched = homogenous recurrent movements

1

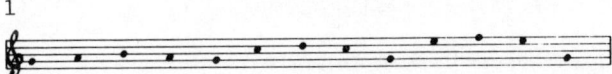

Widening-standing three-movement complex composed of homogeneous up-flexures in the major-third area gab, the quintal area gcd, and the minor-seventh area gef; three-pitch areas

Widening-hanging three-movement complex composed of homogeneous down-flexures in the minor-thrid area efg, the quintal area cdg, and the minor-seventh area abg; three-pitch areas

2

Widening-standing two-movement complex composed of homogeneous up-flexures in the tetrachordal area gabc and the minor-seventh area gdef; four-pitch areas

Widening-hanging two-movement complex composed of homogeneous down-flexures in the tetrachordal area defg and the minor-seventh area abcg; four-pitch areas

3

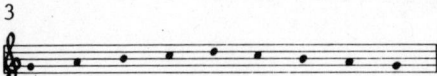

Homogeneous up-flexure in the pentachordal area gabcd

Homogeneous down-flexure in the pentachordal area cdefg

Example 4. Category 2B-b, a movement that returns to the starting note by means of notes not touched = mixed recurrent movements (step and line)

1

Widening-standing three-movement complex composed of mixed up-flexures (step and line) in the major-third area gab, the quintal area gcd, and the minor-seventh area gef; three-pitch areas

Widening-hanging three-movement complex composed of mixed down-flexures (step and line) in the minor-third area efg, the quintal area cdg, and the minor-seventh area abg; three-pitch areas

2

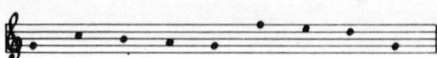

Widening-standing two-movement complex composed of mixed up-flexures (step and line) in the tetrachordal area gabc and the minor-seventh area gdef; four-pitch areas

Widening-hanging two-movement complex composed of mixed down-flexures (step and line) in the tetrachordal area defg and the minor-seventh area abcg; four-pitch areas

3

Mixed up-flexure (step and line) in the pentachordal area
<u>gabcd</u>

Mixed down-flexure (step and line) in the pentachordal area
<u>cdefg</u>

Category 3
The basic pattern of this category is, in Kolinski's terminology, a falling tangential complex of the first degree nexus (see example 5). The basic pattern develops into tangential multimember complexes.

Example 5. Category 3, <u>al-nuqlah 'alá istidārah</u>, a movement that returns to the starting note, then proceeds to the lower octave in a contrary motion along the starting note, twice or more = a falling tangential complex of recurrent movements gradually widening to the two-octave range. The diamond-shaped notes are additions to d'Erlanger's rendition in order to comply with the definition. The other sources also contain inconsistencies and scribal errors.

1. After every note = composed of step movements

Tangential fourteen-member complex composed of gradually widening pairs of step up- and down-flexures

2. After every two notes = composed of mixed movements (line and step) in three-pitch areas

Tangential eight-movement complex composed of gradually widening pairs of mixed up- and down-flexures (line and step) followed by a step up- and down-flexure

128 George D. Sawa

3. After every three notes = composed of mixed movements
(line and step) in four-pitch areas

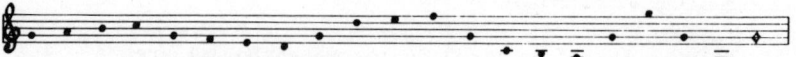

Tangential six-movement complex composed of two widening
pairs of mixed up- and down-flexures (line and step) in
four-pitch areas followed by a step up- and down-flexure

4. After every four notes = in five-pitch areas

Tangential four-movement complex composed of two widening
pairs of mixed up- and down-flexures (line and step) in
five-pitch and four-pitch areas, respectively

5. After five notes or more = in six-pitch areas or more

Tangential four-movement complex composed of two widening
pairs of mixed up- and down-flexures (line and step) in six-
and three-pitch areas, respectively

Kolinski would interpret both the basic pattern and the complete
example as a complex of recurrent movements. Al-Fārābī probably felt
that this pattern was a 'simple' movement because it is composed of
symmetrical subpatterns in succession; in fact, it is a 2B-a pattern
in two opposite directions. The reverse of category 3, which is not
given (for example, g-f-g-a-g), gives a rising tangential complex
as a basic pattern.

Category 4
Category 4 is different from category 2B only in that it does not
return to the starting note. The basic pattern in category 4A is,
according to Kolinski, a flexure preceded by a prefix, that is, two
movements: a recurrent movement preceded by a non-recurrent movement
(see example 6). The example as a whole is a rising or falling
distant complex in a broken linear nexus. The basic pattern in
category 4B is a rising-up or falling-down hook, while the example
as a whole is a zigzag (see example 7). For al-Fārābī, 4B differs
from 4A only because the return is not effected by using notes
already touched. Kolinski places the two subdividons in very different categories. In Kolinski's terms, this difference makes pattern
4A a flexure preceded by a prefix and pattern 4B a hook, and the
whole example changes from an indirect complex of recurrent movement

129 Melodic Movement in al-Fārābī and Kolinski

to a non-recurrent movement (zigzag). This difference between the systems of al-Fārābī and Kolinski is very important.

Example 6. Category 4A, <u>al-nuqlah 'alā in'irāj</u>, a movement that returns by means of notes already touched = distant complex preceded by a prefix

1

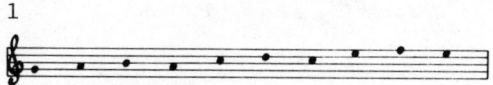

Rising-distant three-movement complex comprising three step up-flexures connected in broken-linear nexus by two ascending step infixes and preceded by an ascending linear step prefix. An indirect three-trend ascent leads from the lowest to the highest tone.

Falling-distant three-movement complex comprising three step down-flexures connected in broken-linear nexus by two descending step infixes and preceded by a descending linear step infix. An indirect three-trend descent leads from the highest to the lowest tone.

2

Rising-distant two-movement complex comprising two homogeneous up-flexures connected in broken-linear nexus by an ascending step infix and preceded by an ascending linear step prefix. An indirect ascent leads from the lowest to the highest tone.

Falling-distant two-movement complex comprising two homogeneous down-flexures connected in broken-linear nexus by a descending step infix and preceded by a descending linear step prefix. An indirect descent leads from the highest to the lowest tone. Manuscripts have scribal errors, and the two editions' renditions are incomplete. I have followed here the general line of the preceding example.

Example 7. Category 4B, al-nuqlah 'alá in'irāj, a movement that returns by means of notes not already touched = zigzag

1

Rising six-member step up-zigzag comprising seven pitches

Falling six-member step-down zigzag comprising seven pitches

2

Rising mixed four-member zigzag composed of alternating up-steps and down-lines; comprises seven pitches

Falling mixed four-member zigzag composed of alternating down-steps and up-lines; comprises seven pitches

Category 5
The movement called 'aṭf bi-dawr involves a return to the starting note through a circular motion, but it is quite different from that in category 3 because it returns to the starting note only once and involves no contrary motion (see example 8). The difference in Kolinski's terms is between a falling tangential complex (category 3) and a balanced zigzag (category 5). Al-Fārābī was aware of the difference but called both movements circular simply because they have the form of a circle.

Example 8. Category 5, 'aṭf bi-dawr = balanced zigzag[2]

Balanced wide-centred down-zigzag composed of an inner up-step and connecting two outer down-lines

131 Melodic Movement in al-Fārābī and Kolinski

Category 6
This movement is a different kind of zigzag - a widening down-zigzag (see example 9).

Example 9. Category 6, al-nuqlah bi-in'irāj = widening zigzag

Widening seven-member step down-zigzag

CONCLUSION

The obvious difficulties of comparing the thought of two men so widely separated in time, culture, and purpose make mandatory the exercise of considerable caution in the statement of any conclusion. In many ways, the methods of the two scholars are quite different: al-Fārābī's is synthetic, whereas Kolinski's is analytical; al-Fārābī's is consciously 'ethnocentric,' whereas Kolinski's is cross-cultural; al-Fārābī's method is totally linked to the modal system, whereas Kolinski's deals with pure melodic analysis.

However, al-Fārābī's basic patterns correspond to all of Kolinski's recurrent and non-recurrent movements, except for the pendulum. Al-Fārābī's examples include a large number of direct and indirect complexes, such as standing, hanging, tangential, and distant. If his sytem is not as exhaustive as Kolinski's, it is simply because al-Fārābī left its exhaustiveness to the student.

The discrepancy between the two systems, in regard to simple versus complex movements, is only superficial. To Kolinski, application of the same basic pattern to the octave - al-Fārābī's obsession - engenders a complex movement, but not to al-Fārābī, who sees the unchanged pattern unfolding and engendering the same simple movement. A curious example of the reverse situation is the pendulum, which Kolinski does not consider a complex movement but which al-Fārābī would have had to deal with as a complex movement.

A serious discrepancy occurs only in category 4. It is neither a returning nor a non-returning movement, but an incomplete return. Since Kolinski has only two basic movements, recurrent and non-recurrent, category 4 translates into a mixture of recurrent and non-recurrent movements. Thus the basic pattern of 4A is, according to Kolinski, a combination of a recurrent and a non-recurrent movement, while 4B is a non-recurrent movement. Whereas al-Fārābī regards the two subdivisions as in one category, to Kolinski they definitely belong to different classifications.

Despite the differences of intention and approach, there remains one important basic principle that is common to the two methods. Both men recognize as fundamental the related concepts of recurrence/non-recurrence (Kolinski) and returning/non-returning (al-Fārābī) in melodic movement. Al-Fārābī based all his tables on these concepts, and Kolinski has noted the 'far-reaching impact' and 'worldwide distribution' of the concept of melodic recurrence. In view of the importance of this concept in the work of these two men separated by a thousand years, it seems reasonable to suggest that they may well be on the right track in making this principle the basis of their analysis of melodic movement.

NOTES

1 The tables encompassing these four categories are given in letter notation in the original; I have transcribed them here from a g scale. The ratios of the scale are given by al-Fārābī (1967: 968-9) as follows:

9/8	10/9	16/15	9/8	10/9	21/20	24/21
g	a	b(11/10)	c(12/11)	d	e(11/10)	f(12/11) g

The two readings for c are in order to have the law of consonance enforced in figure 1, categories 1A and 1B; similarly those for f for figure 1, category 1A. Al-Fārābī allows in his tables the melodic intervals g-e and g-f, although he considers them dissonant. He probably considered such dissonances to be of the type that is not noticed (d'Erlanger 1930: 145; al-Fārābī 1967: 421) or expected the composer to add an intermediary note consonant with both (d'Erlanger 1930: 149; al-Fārābī 1967: 434).

2 This example, as well as the following one, is taken from a scale whose ratios are as follows:

16/15	9/8	10/9	16/15	9/8	9/8	10/9
c	d	e	f	g	a	b c

REFERENCES

d'Erlanger, Baron Rodolphe 1930 La Musique arabe I. al-Fārābī. Grand Traité de la musique. Kitāb al-mūsīqā al-kabīr 1 (2), traduction française (Paris, Paul Geuthner)
- 1935 La Musique arabe II. al-Fārābī. Kitāb al-mūsīqā al-kabīr 3, traduction française (Paris, Paul Geuthner)
al-Fārābī 1347 Kitāb al-mūsīqā al-kabīr MS No. 289, Milan Ambrosian Library, dated 748 AH
- 1461 Kitāb al-mūsīqā al-kabīr MS No. 220B, Garrett Arabic MS, Princeton University Library, dated 866 AH
- 1967 Kitāb al-mūsīqā al-kabīr Gh. Khashabah, ed., revised with an introduction by M. Al-Ḥifnī (Cairo, Dār al-Kātib al-'Arabī lil-Ṭibā'ah wa al-Nashr)

Farmer, H.G. 1929 <u>A History of Arabian Music to the 13th Century</u> (London, Luzac and Co.)
von Grunebaum, G.G. 1953 <u>Medieval Islam</u> 2d ed. (Chicago, University of Chicago Press)
Kolinski, Mieczyslaw 1965 'The Structure of Melodic Movement: A New Method of Analysis (Revised Version)' <u>Studies in Ethnomusicology</u> 2: 95-120
- 1968 '"Barbara Allen": Tonal versus Melodic Structure' part 1 <u>Ethnomusicology</u> 12 (2): 208-18
- 1976 'Herndon's Verdict on Analysis: <u>tabula rasa</u>' <u>Ethnomusicology</u> 20 (1): 1-22

JEAN-JACQUES NATTIEZ
Comparisons within a Culture:
The Example of the *Katajjaq* of the Inuit

The problems raised by the comparative method in ethnomusicology are not concerned only with the similarities and differences between distinct cultures. Although it is possible to consider at a very general level the musical culture of the Inuit as a homogeneous entity comparable to that of such other peoples as Indians, Ainu, and Lapps, it cannot be denied that a comparative study of the different cultural groups constituting the Inuit ensemble (for example, the Alaska Inuit from Mackenzie, the Copper Inuit, Caribou, Netsilik, Igloolik) may be both legitimate and necessary.

All ethnomusicologists have at one time or another been confronted with the diversity of, or contradictions within, the data obtained for a given musical genre. The objective of this article[1] is to propose an analytical grid, inspired by certain concepts of musical semiology, that can be used to attempt to explain these discrepancies by establishing a link between the contradictory information and the different groups. The grid also traces the evolution of the genre within these groups through its transmission from a group of one area to that of another. It will not resolve all the discrepancies, but it will at least classify them so that they may be better understood.[2]

Many kinds of katajjait ('throat-games') exist but for the present purpose a brief description will suffice. A katajjaq is performed, in most cases, by two women facing each other; it is constructed from the repetition of motifs, organized in groups, and may contain several groups. The motifs, often metrically dephased between the voices, are characterized by specific rhythmic patterns. Any combination of inspiratory and expiratory, and voiced and voiceless sounds may be used. In certain katajjait, paralinguistic sounds predominate; in others, more or less recognizable vocables (such as hamma, udlu, hahe) are predominant; in still others, melodies borrowed from other traditional songs attract attention. There are different names for katajjaq according to geographical area. Although the term is restricted mostly to northern Quebec and southern Baffin Island, katajjaq will be used in this paper as a designation for all throat-games.

I have briefly described what one hears during a katajjaq and

135 The Katajjaq of the Inuit

what it is possible to transcribe and analyse. But if one tries to discover and understand the meaning of a katajjaq to the Inuit of all the different Arctic cultural areas, the information that one obtains is of great variety. This extent of the variety may be illustrated with a partial list (numerous other examples could be added) of my informants' comments, together with descriptions or definitions reported by collaborators and colleagues (for the katajjaq of Povungnituq, see Montpetit and Veillet 1977). This anomalous collection of information has been organized by grouping the data under three headings: (a) statements pertaining to the creation circumstances of the game, and more precisely, to the ideas associated with the game in the minds of those who play it; (b) performance circumstances, or what Norma McLeod has termed 'musical occasions'; (c) sound structures of the game as such.

DEFINITIONS OF KATAJJAQ

Creation Circumstances
1 A katajjaq tells a story: 'the words are suggestive of meaning but not explicit. This helps to develop the imagination and reasoning powers of the child' (Cavanagh 1976: 46-7).
2 A katajjaq serves educative purposes since proper breathing is learned in difficult physical circumstances. This has been encountered only in Pond Inlet, in northern Baffin Island.
3 Katajjaq word creation can be based on actual happenings in the community. This is reported in the Belcher Islands in Hudson Bay, where women made up a new katajjaq using the word 'beard' to laugh at the bearded collector, my collaborator Claude Charron.

Performance Circumstances
1 A katajjaq is a game played for the fun of it. This is stated in most regions.
2 A katajjaq is performed by a mother while rocking a baby on her back with the movements of her body. This custom occurs in many regions.
3 Katajjait are played during spring feasts, along with other games. This information was obtained in Pond Inlet.
4 Katajjaq are played in teams during inter-camp visits. This was found in Cape Dorset, in southwestern Baffin Island.

Sound Structure
1 The words of a katajjaq have no meaning; they must sound good. This is reported in northern Quebec.
2 In most places one can use imitations of the cries of geese as material for a katajjaq. In the opinion of the informants in Pond Inlet, dogs and mosquitoes are also imitated at Cape Dorset, although this practice has not been corroborated by any of our Cape Dorset informants.
3 In playing a katajjaq the object is to outlast the performance of the other person; the first person to stop loses. This is true in most places.

136 Jean-Jacques Nattiez

4 The discrete number of elements in a given katajjaq tends to be reduced in each successive generation. This was reported in Igloolik.
5 A katajjaq can be constructed by putting together as many motifs as desired. This is true in Pond Inlet and on Belcher Island.

In figure 1, the three headings are shown as links in a series of entities involved with musical communication. To them is added a fourth factor: the listeners. Figure 2 illustrates that the women, who at some time or other performed katajjaq, also become listeners. Data provided by these women come, either partially or totally, under the first, second, or third headings and, as may be expected, there are lacunae because of lapses in memory. What might be forgotten most easily? On the one hand, there is loss of the underlying story or event related to the invention of a katajjaq, especially

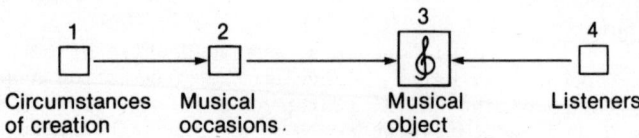

Figure 1

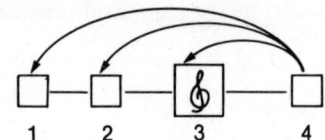

Figure 2

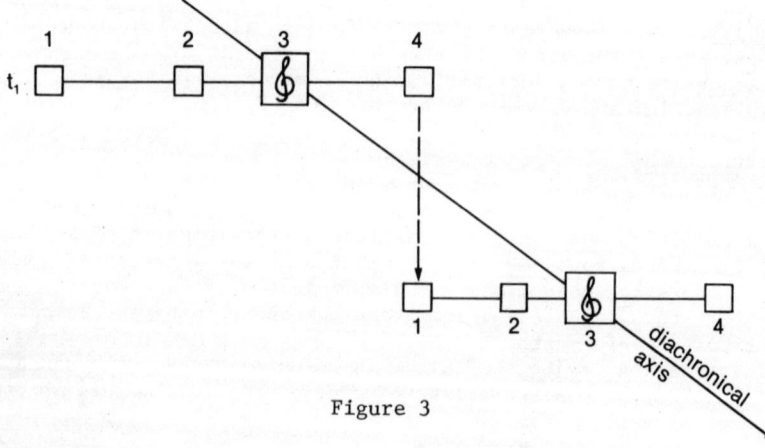

Figure 3

when not present in the surface structure of the text. On the other hand, one might easily forget traditional festival occasions that are no longer celebrated, although daily occasions for performance continue to exist.

In a katajjaq recorded in Pond Inlet, some players affirmed they use cries of geese and that it was the only kind performed in this area; they offered no other qualifying information. Another informant of the same village confirms these facts but adds that these katajjait concern male and female geese. He does not, however, remember the underlying story, although he is aware that there was one. It is possible to date his information as having originated before 1930, whereas the players learned this katajjaq only after 1940. The diachronic situation is described in figure 3. A katajjaq is repeated at period t_2 but the circumstances of period t_1 have been forgotten. Another example is characteristic: according to the testimony of an informant, one might remember a katajjaq by recognizing its sounds, even without remembering their meaning. Syllables of a katajjaq, transformed by vocal manipulations specific to this genre and isolated from their original circumstances, understandably lose their meaning and are henceforth considered as sounds chosen for their musical qualities proper.

Another example concerns a katajjaq based on the morpheme 'marmartuq' recorded in Igloolik, a settlement on a small island off northwestern Baffin Island. The informant, Eqatliôq, does not know the story underlying this katajjaq but is quite conscious of how it should be played. But a story does exist for it: according to an informant from Pond Inlet, it is about a woman, with a baby on her back, who picks blueberries. This is precisely the situation illustrated by figure 3, but here the gap in the information is filled by data from another source. The same piece among the Netsilik - recorded by Beverley Cavanagh in Gjoa Haven, on King William Island, in the central Arctic - is much longer. Passing from the Netsilik to the Igloolik area, the informant has, no doubt, lost some of the pieces. The layout in figure 3 must therefore be completed as shown in figure 4.

This example demonstrates not only diachronic evolution but also a process of diffusion. Eqatliôq, who learned the katajjaq from her Netsilik mother and aunt, is typical of what von Sydow (1965) describes as a 'bearer of culture.' For Igloolik Inuit, only katajjait with the cries of geese are recognized as local, whereas all others such as marmartuq are recognized as being of Netsilik origin. Our informant has taught both her daughters the katajjait she knows. I have filmed them and now other Igloolik school children may witness them and learn the game. Perhaps, with transformations brought about by Eqatliôq, these katajjait may become widespread in Igloolik.

It is necessary to have a diachronic track for each cultural group. There is no doubt in my mind that, if investigation circumstances were to yield more detailed observations, there would be a track for each camp or for each extended family forming the camp. The juxtaposition of these tracks would explain how, within the same period in two distinct areas, a katajjaq exists according to different

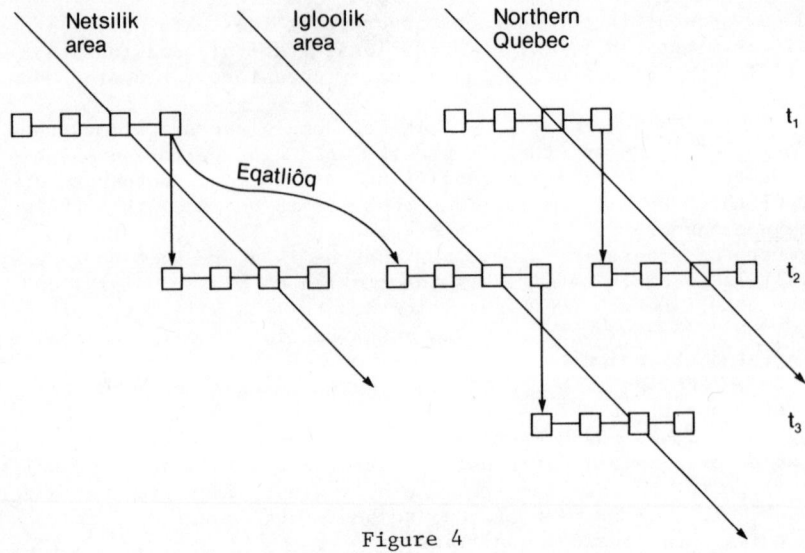

Figure 4

modalities and follows diachronic evolutions that are not necessarily parallel.

In northern Quebec, for example, it seems that the longest katajjaq would not necessarily be the oldest. A member of our group, Nicole Beaudry (1978), has studied the characteristics of games in the central Arctic. She notes that existing games are frequently combined to form new games. In northern Quebec, katajjait could be formed in this way: instead of attributional elements, as reported in Igloolik, the throat-games would result from the concatenation of katajjaq motifs chosen from the 'stock' existant in the informant's culture.

Why should we refer to semiotic concepts for the construction of our grid? Because different diagrams show that, whether synchronically or diachronically, there is great diversity in the significant elements - what Peirce would name 'interpretants' - that are affixed to the sound of a katajjaq. The invention, execution, and perception of a katajjaq cause this genre to become - to use Mauss's expression - a total musical and 'ludique'[3] fact. The data given by the informants constitute, in fact, the verbal expression of the significant elements through which each actor establishes a relation with the katajjaq as a sign, which he considers from any of various standpoints: circumstances of creation, musical occasions, the sonic object itself or his personal projection upon it. Indeed, for the last, it is necessary to be reminded that perception is not a passive phenomenon but a veritable re-creation, a symbolic reconstruction: if the original semantic associations of the occasions are forgotten, it is possible for anyone to project new associations on the sound substance. This explains why the essential elements of the circumstances of creation and the actual playing of a katajjaq, its sonic

139 The Katajjaq of the Inuit

material, and the perceptual behaviour it provokes may appear mutually heterogeneous, contradictory, or dissonant. It is my hypothesis that the semiotic discrepancy can explain, in certain cases, the changes in the Inuit conception of katajjaq.

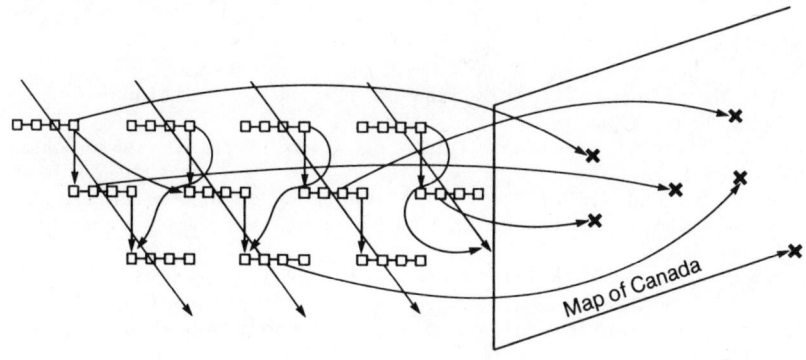

Figure 5

Thus, it is clear that observations collected within a relatively short period of investigation (1974-77) are only traces of historically and semiotically complex processes. The investigatory conditions make the traces appear artificially synchronic. Figure 5 represents this situation. To the right, there is a positional map indicating the locations in northern Canada where the data were collected. To the left are the historical and semiotic processes underlying the data. I do not mean that this grid should impel the reader to reconstitute all the stages in the symbolic transformation and diffusion of a musical genre. Objective conditions of inquiry do not allow such a procedure. However, it seems necessary to relocate isolated data in a diagram that both encompasses and explains them to better advantage. After all, an archaeologist uses rigorous methods to date the monuments he unearths and to complete missing pieces of pottery with dotted lines. These 'dotted lines' are found in the proposed grid and allow the construction of hypotheses. Within ethnomusicology, obviously, there is a place for this kind of musical archaeology.

NOTES

1 This article is a revision of a paper given at the annual meeting of the Society for Ethnomusicology at the University of Texas at Austin in November 1977. I wish to express my thanks to Nicole Beaudry, who translated it, and to Charles Boilès and Sid McLauchlan, who aided me in its revision.
2 The construction of this model represents a portion of the work done by the Groupe de Recherches en Sémiologie Musicale de Montréal. Since 1974, this group has concentrated on the study of katajjait (singular, katajjaq), or throat-games, of the Canadian Inuit.

This research project is sponsored by the Social Sciences and Humanities Research Council of Canada and by the University of Montreal.
3 We have used this neologism based on its French connotation of game organization.

REFERENCES

Beaudry, Nicole 1978 'Le Katajjaq: un jeu inuit traditionnel' Etudes Inuit Studies 2 (1): 35-54
Cavanagh, Beverley 1976 'Some Throat-games of Netsilik Eskimo Women' Canadian Folk Music Journal 4: 46-7
Montpetit, C. and C. Veillet 1977 'Recherches en ethnomusicologie: les katajjait chez les Inuit du Nouveau-Québec' Etudes Inuit Studies 1 (1): 154-64
von Sydow, C.W. 1965 'Folklore Studies and Philology: Some Points of View' in Alan Dundes, ed. The Study of Folklore (Englewood Cliffs, NJ, Prentice-Hall) 219-42. (The paper appeared originally in 1945.)

III/PROBLEMS AND PROSPECTS

PANDORA HOPKINS
Aural Thinking

> I shall never be able to dance to the playing of my husband; for he was born and brought up in Hallingdal, while I am from Telemark.
> Dagne Groven Myhren, Norwegian dancer and singer

Certain characteristics of the Hardanger fiddle tradition, including the physical make-up of the instrument, reflect general European culture, whereas others are particularly Norwegian.[1] The rhythmic structure of the music is not only fundamentally Norwegian, it even changes from one locality to another. One Norwegian dance, the springar (literally, 'to jump'), has three sometimes uneven beats whose durations are interpreted differently in the various regions of hardingfele[2] territory. Magne Myhren, a hardingfele player and folklore scholar, agreed with the implications of Dagne Groven Myhren's remark. The correct perception of a springar's three-beat cyclic structure is necessary to both animate the dancers and form a constant background against which the ebb and flow of cross-rhythmic tension in the music may be felt.

THE PROBLEM

The extremely esoteric nature of the hardingfele tradition demonstrates the necessity of having specialized knowledge (and that acquired early in life) in order to perceive this music as it is meant to be perceived. In more general terms, it highlights the problems involved in approaching any unfamiliar music. To what extent will our understanding be impeded or enhanced by previous knowledge and experience? Our attention is thus drawn to the cognitive component in music perception, which is crucially important in understanding the nature of the difficulties involved in attempting to acquire what Mantle Hood has called 'bi-musicality.'

   Perhaps it is not necessary to remind the reader that we are speaking of the world of music, that training in basic musicianship of one order or another is characteristic of cultivated music wherever it is found and to some extent is unconsciously present in the practice of ingenuous music. It may be of some

comfort to the music student of the West to realize that the
Chinese, Javanese or Indian student also must jump through a
series of musical hoops. But if this kind of training is indeed
essential, the Western musician who wishes to study Eastern
music faces the challenge of 'bi-musicality.' (Hood 1960: 55)

<u>Hardingfele</u> playing was developed by farmers in the southern
mountainous regions of Norway; aurally transmitted and unattached
to any formalized theoretical system, it is undoubtedly the kind
of tradition that Hood had in mind when he referred to 'ingenuous
music.' Just how much, and what kind of, training (unconscious or
not) is necessary for an intelligent understanding of this kind of
music is an important (and so far unanswered) question. The attitude
expressed in Dagne Myhren's comment indeed indicates the presence
of a strong cognitive component in this Norwegian folk tradition.
Yet many have refused to acknowledge the existence of thinking without a verbal manifestation:

The writer, for one, is strongly of the opinion that the feeling
entertained by so many that they can think, or even reason without language is an illusion ... Once more, language, as a structure, is on its inner face the mold of thought ... It is doubtful
if any other cultural asset of man, be it the art of drilling for
fire or of chipping stone, may lay claim to a greater age. I am
inclined to believe that it antedated even the lowliest developments of material culture, that these developments in fact were
not strictly possible until language, the tool of significant
expression, had taken shape. (Sapir 1921: 15, 21 ff.)

More recently, however, Lévi-Strauss claimed that music is one of
the prime manifestations of thinking (1971: 577, 581 ff.), and John
Blacking defined music, whether improvised or not, as 'humanly
organized sound' and further suggested 'that a perception of sonic
order, whether it be innate or learned, or both, must be in the mind
before it emerges as music' (1974: 11). Thus, a detailed study of
how skilled musicians from outside the Norwegain <u>hardingfele</u> tradition initially perceive, and then try to understand, the esoteric
rhythmic component described above may give us insight into the
nature of this music. By extension, it may also tell us something
about the cognitive element in aurally transmitted music in general.
The musical feature chosen for this study seems especially well
suited to the subject, for it happens to be a feature that, as we
shall see, defies notation of any kind.

Linguists, aided by the development of information theory, have
done interesting work on the influence of phonological systems upon
the perception of speech patterns (see Fry 1970 and Fudge 1970).
However, it is the perception of non-verbal patterns of communication
in which we are interested. The art historian and psychologist Rudolf
Arnheim has drawn an analogy between abstract art and music: 'In a
successful piece of abstract art or music, a pattern of forces
transmits its particular blend of calmness and tenseness, lightness

and heaviness – a complete transubstantiation of form into meaningful expression' (Arnheim 1966: 10). In another work, the same author made a detailed study of what he termed 'visual thinking,' an interest that stemmed from his extreme dissatisfaction with the status of the arts in academic institutions:

> The arts are neglected because they are based on perception, and perception is disdained because it is not assumed to involve thought. In fact, educators and administrators cannot justify giving the arts an important position in the curriculum unless they understand that the arts are the most powerful means of strengthening the perceptual component without which productive thinking is impossible in any field of endeavor. The neglect of the arts is only the most tangible symptom of the widespread unemployment of the senses in every field of academic study. What is most needed is not more aesthetics or more esoteric manuals of art education but a convincing case made for visual thinking quite in general. (1969: 3)

Arnheim has compared the historically 'high esteem of music' with 'the disdain of the fine arts' (1969: 2), but, as Charles Seeger pointed out: 'It was communication in speech about music, not communication in music itself that had a place in the quadrivium' (1961: 78).

Arnheim examined – indeed built a powerful case for – the intellectual component in the visual arts, and certain of the conceptual tools he used have proved useful in my somewhat analogous study of aural perception. I am going to describe the method I used to obtain the reactions of skilled musicians, trained in different musical cultures, when they were presented for the first time with a sample of music from the totally unfamiliar – to them – Hardanger fiddle tradition. For the particular musical component to be tested, I chose the rhythmic structure of the springar.

THE RHYTHMIC STRUCTURE OF THE SPRINGAR

The springar – which may be thought of as the essence of hardingfele music – has a special significance to the spelemann ('player'), and a student of this tradition is considered to have reached a milestone when he is ready to learn his first springar. It may be danced to a lively tempo in triple metre, or it may occur as a lydarslått ('listening slått') – not intended for dancing at all. It is with the normal, danced springar, with its recurrent, three-beat cycle, that we shall be concerned in this study. The rhythmic composition of this dance is extremely complex and may be characterized as consisting of the following features:

1 Several large sections, usually of contrasting tonalties that result from the utilization of different open strings as tonal centres.
2 A number of phrases of equal length within each section. Each

phrase, which often may be repeated more or less literally, usually contains two or more occurrences of the basic three-beat pattern.
3 The beat pattern, which differs according to locality, in both stress and duration. In several regions the beats are of the unequal variety more commonly associated with Bulgarian dance music.
4 The subdivisions of the beat, which are characteristically uneven (usually of the short-long variety).
5 Ornaments, containing odd numbers of little notes. They are usually accented and consequently must take time from the first of the uneven units.

   is performed close to:

6 The bowing style, which involves a characteristic slurring across the beat - a factor that produces syncopated articulations in the drones and polyphony of the lower voices.

Abrupt shifts from one phrase or one section to another may be superimposed on all the above features, the result sometimes of elision (the last beat of one phrase coinciding with the first beat of the next phrase), and sometimes of cross-rhythms in the melodic line.

Fundamental to this rhythmic edifice is the three-beat pattern, which is of such structural importance to the totality that not only the fiddler but also the audience foot-beats while the music is being played (much in the spirit of the Indian audience keeping the tāla.) Indeed, the full effect of deliberately contrasting accentual patterns in the melodic line of a particular section (and their resolution) can best be felt by the listener who is experiencing this foot-beating. I limited the scope of my experiment to this element in the Telemark and Hallingdal versions of the springar. In Telemark, the second of the three beats receives the accent and the last is somewhat shorter than the other two. In contrast, the Hallingspringar has a short, accented first beat and longer second and third beats, which are nearly equal in length and stress.

THE EXPERIMENT

Record companies have not understood the inherent importance of the foot-beaten pattern and have taken care to dub out this sound from their commercial recordings. I was able to take advantage of this omission and chose five springars from RCA Norsk Folkemusikk discs for my taped examples:

'Jon Vestafe' played by Kjetil Løndal of Tuddal, Telemark (FEP 46)
  - composed by Knut Dahle, played in form of Svein Løndal

'Hallingstuga' played by Odd Bakkerud of Nes, Hallingdal (FEP 32)
    - after To-ingen (Knut Tuen, Nes)
'Rjukanfossen' played by Johannes Dahle of Tinn, Telemark (FEP 22)
    - composed by Knut Dahle, Tinn
'Igletveiten' played by Kjetil Løndal of Tuddal, Telemark (FEP 46)
    - after Leiv Sandsdalen
'Vrengja' played by Odd Bakkerud of Nes, Hallingdal (FEP 32)
    - after To-ingen (Knut Tuen, Nes)

The demonstration tape contains lengthy portions from the beginnings of the examples (in the order listed above). Each of the selections is long enough to include several sections and represents more than half the entire <u>slått</u>. The three musicians consulted in this project were:

Lakshminarayan Shankar, who is a well-known virtuoso in both his native India and the United States. He has made numerous recordings, has taught Indian violin playing at Wesleyan University, and has written a doctoral dissertation on Indian violin playing. He holds a PhD in world music.
Michael Kaloyanides, who plays the bouzouki, <u>lyra</u>, guitar, and percussion instruments. He has performed in rock and Greek bands, has made field trips to Greece and Turkey for ethnomusicological research, and learned to play the <u>lyra</u> while living in Crete. Kaloyanides also holds a PhD in world music and has written a dissertation on Cretan music. He is now on the faculty of the University of New Haven.
Blanche Blitstein, who majored in violin and in music education for her Bachelor and Master of Music degrees. She has done orchestral work under such conductors as Jonel Perlea and Leon Barzin and is at present a string specialist in the Long Island (New York) school system.

It will be noticed that the musicians participating in this project were players of fiddle-type instruments, had extensive applied and theoretical training in music, and have functioned professionally as both teachers and performers. In the interviews, each of the three musicians recorded his or her perceptions of the basic structure during a work session lasting from an hour to an hour and a half. They were informed beforehand that there was a regularly recurrent cycle of beats and that the beating of this pattern would be audible in a live performance of the music.

In studying the response of these musicians to previously unknown music, I was interested in ascertaining to what extent their perceptions constituted passive reception of the material, and to what extent perception was dependent upon active cognitive operations. To this end, I asked five basic questions:

1 Was the meaningfully transmitted immediately? (the <u>initial perception</u>)

2 How did the perceptions of the three musicians compare with those of one another? (three different perceptions)
3 Upon finding their original perceptions of the music to be unreliable, how did the musicians proceed? (search for appropriateness)
4 What features came to light during the restructuring process? (aural concepts)
5 How did the musicians themselves sum up their experience? (judgments)

In evaluating the responses of the musicians, I have made use of a number of terms and concepts derived from the work of Rudolf Arnheim. These include active exploration, focusing, selection, completion, correction, synthesis, combining, separating, simplification, memory, comparison, abstraction, concept formation, putting into context, learning, reappraisal, confirmation, deepening of understanding (Arnheim 1969).

The role of the consulted musicians (as will become evident) is one of active participation in the project. This study is essentially a collaborative enterprise. The original ideas grew out of my own experience with the hardingfele, especially in striving to play the instrument idiomatically from instructions of the spelemenn in Norway.

During the working out of the project itself, I benefited from an active correspondence with Norwegian musicians and scholars. At each stage of my work, they provided me with intellectual information and other assistance, including tapes made expressly for the project.[3]

MECHANICAL MEASUREMENT OF THE BEAT PATTERN

In order to obtain a machine's-eye view of the beat pattern, I worked with equipment in the Mason Laboratory at Yale University.[4] To produce a graphic representation, I used a variable band-pass filter to screen out all high frequencies and a level chart recorder to produce a visual pattern on paper (see figure 1). I used this method to analyse the foot-beating on a re-recording, specially prepared for this purpose in Norway, of the five springars represented on the demonstration tapes.

The wave pattern pictured in example 1 provides impressive proof of the regularity of the uneven-beat cycle. This design was produced at the beginning of 'Jon Vestafe' (the first example on the demonstration tape). The ratio 18/15/10 is maintained at a lively tempo. Eivind Groven, who some years ago analysed foot-beating structures of the hardingfele music by hand pricking rolls of moving paper, similarly found examples of astonishing consistency (Groven 1971: 99 ff.). The existence of such consistency is important evidence of the purposefulness and control of musical execution in this tradition. Perhaps even more important to the theme of this paper, however, was the large area in which mechancial representation of the beat structure did not convey the intentions of the musicians. The individual expression of a particular performance

149 Aural Thinking

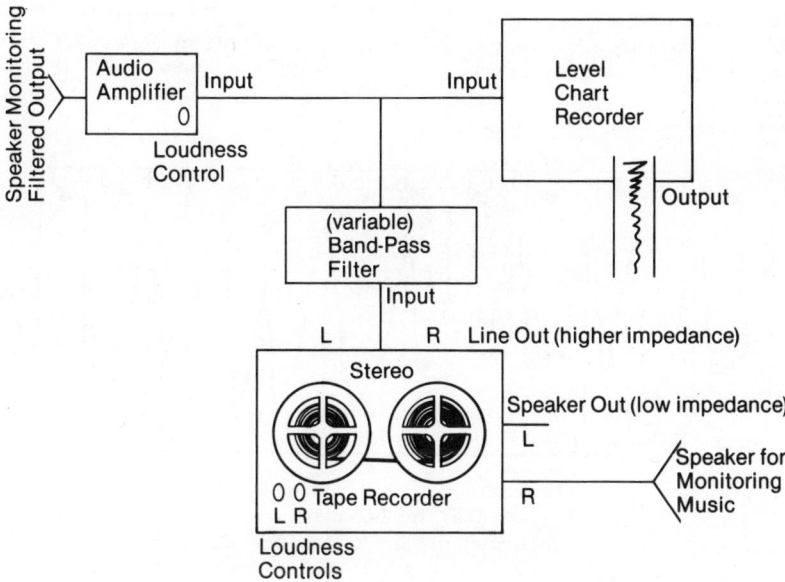

Figure 1. Apparatus used for analysis of foot-beaten patterns.

must include the special inflections, ritardandos, and accelerandos that result from the articulations of personal communication. Even more difficult to deduce from the mechanical record was a perceived beginning or ending. Indeed, no slått would actually be performed so rigidly that a ratio like the one in our first example would be maintained throughout. It is interesting to note the findings of the psychologist Carl Seashore regarding this matter. Not understanding the important area of interpretive licence (which has to exist in any musical tradition that includes performance), he expressed amazement that the measurements of sound-wave patterns made by famous pianists, violinists, and singers showed great areas of divergence from musical notation. He found, for example, that 'in a very real sense, a singer never sings on pitch,' and 'the violinists deviated over 80% of the time from exact note values' (Seashore 1938: 288). Thus, it turned out that the machine, although extraordinarily useful for analytical purposes, was - in respect to significant communication - a completely uninitiated observer.

THE TAPED INTERVIEWS

1 The Initial Perception
All three musicians listened silently to the five taped examples and then requested at least three additional hearings of example 2 before offering any comment. It was clear that, in each case, the

Example 1. Mechanical representation of the actual foot-beating (comparative distance = comparative time) of the first phrase of 'Jon Vestafe': level chart recorder 10 mm/s (paper speed half of recorded speed). Frequency range of information let through by band-pass filter: 20-100 hertz.

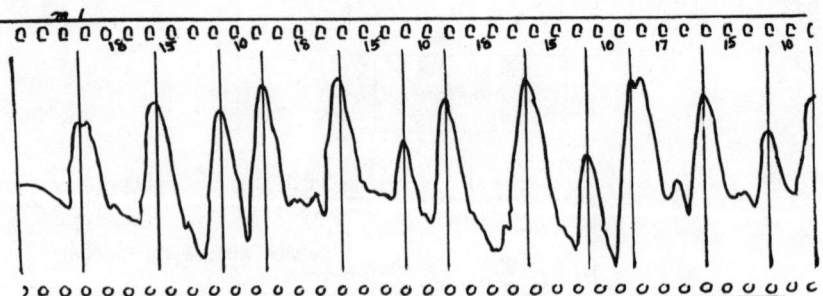

initial perception of the music did not include a recurrent beat cycle. This is especially noteworthy, because (as mentioned above) the listeners had been informed of the existence of such a structure at the outset of the interview and their attention was focused on this matter. The musicians, like the machine, were uninitiated observers.

2 Three Different Perceptions

A second phase of the investigation began when the musicians sought to uncover what was not readily apparent. Shankar continued for some time to express scepticism that there was, in fact, a rhythmic cycle.

Shankar: Well, I don't think it's in any tāla.
Hopkins: I should say that there is a regular beat structure that repeats - that is, that is repeated over and over again.
Shankar: No, no what I mean is: it is not based on any particular cycle.
Hopkins: Yes, it is.
Shankar: Is it?
Hopkins: Yes, yes - and - and this cycle is important as a background and it is -
Shankar: Yes, I can see the opening theme (sings) - but the thing is, it's not like - similar - following strict beats, you know, compared to South Indian - so - they might go a little faster and slower, or sometimes it's like 6 at the beginning, then it gets like 5-1/2 or 5, you know.
Hopkins: Do you think you could tap that out? While it's playing?
Shankar: Yes, definitely. So, that's what I was trying to get, but
  - (Shankar taps beats while first springar is played through. See example 2 for a transcription of the beginning through the first beat of the second phrase.)

Shankar: But the pattern changes.
Hopkins: Actually, they don't perceive a difference. They perceive it as the same pattern all the way through.
Shankar: Yes? Yes, kind of hard. (<u>Laughs</u>) I don't know the music, you know.

The similarity of the overall rhythmic design to the Indian <u>tāla</u> system, characterized by periodic returns to a reference point, has already been mentioned. Shankar seemed to use a cognitive structure that was already familiar to him when he focused on the larger components (the phrases) before attempting to isolate the groupings within them. He remained sceptical of the existence of a beat cycle and continued to perceive an unsteady pulse. His spoken beats were as even as the melodic figuration would allow them to be; thus he overreached the beginning of the new phrase (see example 2).[5]

Kaloyanides, in complete contrast to Shankar in his approach, attempted to build up to the larger components through tying together small clusters of twos and threes:

Kaloyanides: Oh, I get a sense of it as being - Well, I'm trying to get the number of beats, and I sense it in groups of twos and threes offhand. With all the material I sense it as being - hearing twos against threes quite often - a matter of structure. In a lot of it, gives me the sense of a triple metre; but then I hear, rather than three beats in each major division, I hear two.

Like Shankar, Kaloyanides perceived the music through known constructions - in his case, from Balkan music - as he tried out a thirteen-beat sequence whose components (3 + 3 + 3 + 2 + 2) represent an uneven beat structure. The concept if not the proportion is applicable to Norwegian music, but Kaloyanides assumed the accented second beat of the measure to be the beginning of the cycle. He did not begin clapping until the seventh measure of the piece. Thus, I have transposed his beating of an analogous phrase for comparative purposes (see example 2). After finding that the pattern could not be kept up, he commented, 'Very complicated!'

Predictably, Blitstein's perception of the rhythmic structure shows the influence of the European violin tradition, a music in which melodic and harmonic considerations have customarily determined rhythmic character (Hopkins 1967). Hence, she alone of the three musicians analysed the rhythm principally through singing (and later, playing) the melodic line.

Blitstein: Could I reproduce that much? If I think I can? (<u>sings the opening motif in the rhythm</u>). So it would be: one, two, three. Then a measure of four, a measure of three, and then a measure of four, or a measure of seven with a strong ... (<u>sings again</u>). Could I hear that much again? See if I'm right?
Hopkins: And tap while it's going on? Is that a good idea?

152 Pandora Hopkins

Example 2. Comparison of pattern perception of the first phrase of 'Jon Vestafe' (after Knut Dahle), played by Kjetil Løndal (Telemark), the structural rhythmic pattern as perceived by Shankar, Kaloyanides, and Blitstein. Musical notation does not use traditional <u>hardingfele</u> transposition; however, the pitch of all notes has been lowered, as indicated.

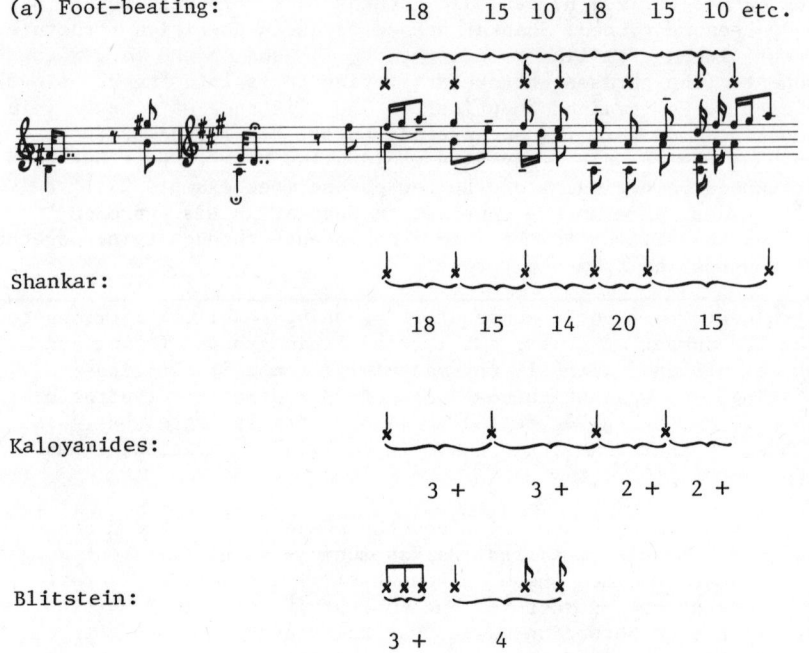

Blitstein: Okay. Let's see if it fits. (<u>First two phrases played</u>, <u>then</u>) Back to the beginning - I'm lost. What I'm doing is not <u>that</u>. (The first three phrases are replayed.) Now I get eight - four, five, six, seven, eight (<u>sings</u>).
Hopkins: Okay, try tapping it while it's going on. (<u>The first three</u> <u>phrases are played again</u>.)

The initially perceived rhythmic pattern (3 + 4) quite apparently reflects the melodic contour. Very likely it is also influenced by harmonic factors, since Blitstein carried her pattern through the first half of the fourth beat - up to the change of register (see example 2). This perception of the rhythm, like other perceptions, was constructed out of previous experience, was completed through factors of expectation, and was inaccurate in this unfamiliar context.

The different percepts were logically (indeed, skilfully) constructed according to the musical system familiar to the listener, but it was obvious to each musician that the conclusion reached did not

agree with the musical scheme. The others would have concurred with
Blitstein when she exclaimed, 'It doesn't fit at the end of each
measure or phrase. I cannot figure out the rhythmic pattern.'

3 Search for Appropriateness

'I shall proceed to define an intelligent act or an intelligent
solution as any act, or solution, which has appropriate novelty'
(Gregory 1974: 630). Shankar observed: 'Kind of hard. I don't know
the music, you know.' This kind of 'knowing' can be arrived at only
through a search for what is or is not appropriate, and this search
for appropriateness, in accordance with the above definition, is an
immensely important cognitive operation. Indeed, it was at the root
of each musician's investigation. It is apparent, however, that a
search for appropriateness (or should we call it 'meaning'?) can be
understood only in a cultural context.

Rudolph Arnheim, who applied Gestalt principles to the field of
aesthetics, demonstrated that these principles do not involve mini-
mizing 'the role of learning and experience in perception' (see
Gombrich 1960: 262):

> Gestalt psychologists, while pointing out that the capacity to
> see shapes is not brought about merely by repeated exposure to
> the stimuli, have no reason to suggest that a gestalt shows up
> with automatic spontaneity. (Arnheim 1969: 30)

> In Gestalt terms, past experience, knowledge, learning, memory
> are considered as factors of the temporal context in which a given
> phenomenon appears. Like the spatial context, on which Gestaltists
> have concentrated their attention during the early development
> of the theory, the temporal context influences the way a
> phenomenon is perceived. An object looks big or small depending
> on whether it is seen, spatially, in the company of smaller or
> larger objects. The buildings of a middle-sized town look tall
> to a farmer, small to a New Yorker, and correspondingly, their
> expression differs for the two observers ... Such examples do
> not demonstrate that there is no intrinsic connection between
> perceptual patterns and the expression they convey but simply
> that experiences must not be evaluated in isolation from their
> spatial and temporal whole-context. (Arnheim 1941: 166f.)

I have dwelt on this point because it is not easy to be aware of
the extent to which the obvious may be a perception organized by
matters of expectancy - matters that are derived from previous knowledge and experience. To again borrow an analogy from the visual
field: 'We do not always realize that the theory of perspective
developed in the fifteenth century is a scientific convention; it
is merely one way of describing space and has no absolute validity'
(Read 1956: 66f.).

It is as true for aural thinking as it is for visual thinking that
perception consists of the grasping of relevant generic features of

the object, and that a conception of structure must be present before
abstraction can take place. Thus, concept formation must be acknowledged to be present in aural forms, just as it is in visual shapes
(see Arnheim 1969: 153, 173, 27). The musicians in our experiment,
having found that their original attempts at abstraction were not
appropriate to the situation at hand, expressed perplexity. They
then began the task of restructuring in order to solve the problem
that had been set before them. At times they verbalized about the
difficulties encountered in purposefully shifting their orientation.
Blitstein, for example, explained: 'It's the end of the thing that
really throws me ... the end of that figure. I can't differentiate
between the ornamentation and the beat.' And later: 'Now the beginning
of each thing ... I'm not sure whether it's an upbeat or whether
it's the first beat or if it's an introduction ... Now I don't know
if that's the start. I'm very confused; and I think that's one of
the, one of the many things that's throwing me.'

Kaloyanides, while working on the first example, remarked: 'That's
one way I hear it. Sometimes I hear it differently -.' And, again,
in reference to the following springar: 'Well - I listen to it different ways, the different times I hear it. Sometimes I get a steady
pulse, sometimes I tend to group it different ways -. But ... sometimes I feel four strong beats, sometimes I feel three.' Later,
during the third example: 'In looking for the cycle, I have a lot
of trouble in recognizing where a phrase will end and begin, if there
is such a concept.' At the end of the entire session, Kaloyanides
summed up some of these problems: 'What sort of complicates it for
me is the lack of an introduction and a resolution of a phrase;
that's more of a musical continuum that I hear. And it sure would
take numerous listenings of the material to be able to develop a
sense of the pattern. You could discover where people see the beginning
of a phrase.'

4 Aural Concepts

The restructuring process resulted in the trying out of new and different possibilities - mental templates that might be called 'aural
concepts,' to adapt Arnheim's terminology (1969: 27). It is especially
significant that this restructuring process was carried out by each
musician according to the path already established in his or her
initial responses to the material, determined, of course, by experience. It is most interesting to see certain features come to light
in aspects that were similar enough to the familiar tradition for
enlightenment to take place.

Shankar continued to envision the aural scheme in terms of the
phrase lengths and their division. In the second example he found:

Shankar: Two different themes. Yes, two different themes. The first
 - is like four times. Then the second theme is reproduced four
 times.

In the third springar, he begins to concentrate more carefully on
the subdivisions of these periods:

155 Aural Thinking

Shankar: It starts with six beats, you know. Triplets, but let's
   beat it - . See, he improvises this on six beats - . After six
   cycles, he goes to a different register, and the same thing - .

During the playing of the fourth springar, I noticed that Shankar
was clapping a specific South-Indian tāla:

Hopkins: You were tapping rupaka?
Shankar: Yes, yes, rupaka. Rupaka tāla. And it is not extremely
   strict; but - at the same time, it goes:

Of course, it varies, also; so it's triplets also within the
three beats - Yes, sometimes.

The analogy to rupaka tāla impressed me, for, although it certainly
did not fit completely (as Shankar had implied), this tāla contains
the heavy second beat and light third beat that are characteristic
of the Telemark springar. In his analysis of the fifth and last
springar, Shankar continued to concentrate on the smaller dimensions
of the rhythmic structure and to find patterns in them somewhat
analogous to patterns in Indian music.

Kaloyanides, continuing to conceive of the music as being built
up from small groups of twos and threes, began in the fourth example
to experiment with more intricate configurations. He also extended
his analysis to the larger dimensions.

Kaloyanides: I also have the sense of - triplets. Six groups of
   triplets there.
Hopkins: Which you felt in the last one?
Kaloyanides: Yes, the same as the last one. Also, the two against
   three is there - . Sometimes, the phrases run three groups long,
   sometimes six groups long - Also I hear like a - slight delay
   before the one -
Hopkins: Could you express that slight delay in a -
Kaloyanides: Metrical frame? Yeah, I'm trying to figure how much of
   a delay it is. (Listens to example) Hearing it in six groups of
   three, it would beat like eighteen. I hear a nineteenth beat.
Hopkins: Would that correspond to any Greek rhythm? Do you know?
Kaloyanides: Something with nineteen beats? No. Anything that's in
   Greek music, anything that's really complex - and that standard
   over a long period, it's usually slow. - So you won't get something that quick.

Kaloyanides determined not only that there were six phrase subdivisions but also the degree of irregularity. However, he failed
to understand that the beats are intended to be perceived in groups
of three and that the ratio between them is an even more subtle one
(close to 4 + 4 + 3).

Blitstein, at the conclusion of her work with the third springar, recognized and articulated the problem she was up against:

Blitstein: Let me tell you, I have a great deal of trouble isolating the beat pattern from the melodic pattern.

Unlike the other musicians, who eventually found that certain mechanisms in musical systems familiar to them provided some insight into the problem at hand, Blitstein was working from knowledge of a tradition whose principles with respect to rhythm are almost antithetical to those of Norwegain fiddle music. After realizing that she was being misled by the melodic figuration, she began to concentrate on the lower voice lines - the contrapuntal motives and drone patterns - and to experiement with uneven beat patterns. The style of melodic elaboration found in hardingfele music is remarkably similar to that in Baroque violin music (Hopkins 1967), and Blitstein's adroitness in dealing with the melodic and harmonic aspects of the music was undoubtedly due to her experience with this Baroque tradition. However, the very familiarity of this aspect of the music necessarily made the rhythmic dissimilarity more difficult to accept.

Blitstein: No, I miss that ornament every time. See, the ornament comes where I don't think it's going to be.

In one instance (the third springar), melodic contour influenced all three musicians into a period of general agreement, but this lasted only through the first two sections (see example 3). The musicians perceived an even beat and triplet subdivisions, although the beats actually exhibit the typical Telemark configuration (the ratio averages out to 15/14/10), and the 'triplet' notes are not of equal length but close to ♪ ♪♪ or ♪ ♪♪ . The ear, influenced by the three-note groupings of the figuration at a lively tempo, heard in each case a familiar relationship. In the third section, which begins on the last measure of the second section (a beautiful example of phrase elision), the melodic figuration gave no help, and all three listeners were lost.

Blitstein: Now what happened? Where did it go?

The sound-wave pattern is also blurred at this point because there is a change of tempo at the beginning of the new section. Indeed, the new tempo does not become stablized for some time.

5 Judgments

In their judgments offered at the end of each interview, the musicians expressed great respect for the Norwegian tradition. Shankar pronounced it 'very intricate' and added: 'I think it will be most difficult for musicians trained in Western classical music with no experience of Indian or other non-Western musics.' Blitstein agreed and thought that even a non-musician, whose brain 'doesn't fit into all these cubbyholes,' would probably have an easier time.

157 Aural Thinking

Example 3. 'Rjukanfossen' (third springar)

Kaloyanides summarized his impressions as follows: 'Very confusing stuff. Let's see - any general things. I get a very polyrhythmic sense - a combination of things at the same time ... This is very - foreign to me ... My first impression is to grab at something familiar. Very tricky stuff!'

SUMMARY

It is of major importance that, in no case, did the initial perception include a cyclical beat pattern - even though the consultant-musicians were all informed beforehand that such a pattern existed. We should realize that the first, by far the longest, portion of each session passed without comment while the examples were played a number of times. In each instance, the musicians had to devise a method for discovering what was not readily apparent. An examination of their own words revealed the existence of the signficiant features derived from Arnheim's study of 'visual thinking.' Their search for

understanding necessitated an active exploration that involved
focusing on specific aspects over others – a simplification of the
total musical construction. The selection of certain elements was
influenced by the memory of learned knowledge, a carry-over from
the familiar tradition. Shankar's scepticism derived from his expectation concerning the nature of a recurrent beat pattern; where
he perceived an arbitrary unsteadiness, the <u>hardingfele spelemann</u>
perceives articulations within a consistently recurrent pattern.
Blitstein, inhibited by the nature of her tradition from considering
certain possibilities, made a synthesis that was logical according
to her own experience but not correct in the context of the Norwegian
tradition. All the musicians soon realized that their solutions were
not meaningful within the appropriate context. Their reappraisals
resulted in the restructuring of 'mental templates,' which resulted
in some deepening of understanding, but of course, never complete
understanding.

Aural perception, like visual perception, obviously involves the
grasping of structural features. In an attempt to apply these features across cultural boundaries, the abstraction of cognitive elements is influenced by concepts of appropriateness that are themselves determined by previous knowledge. 'No one borderline separates
a purely perceptual image – if such there is – from one completed
by memory' (Arnheim 1969: 84). In a very real sense, Arnheim's
completion by memory is a comparison, a process that must, it appears to me, go on constantly and automatically. Some years ago, I
suggested that the old name for the discipline we now call 'ethnomusicology' ('comparative musicology') was more correct than the
later term, because 'every time we transcribe a piece of ethnic
music into our notational system, we compare it with our music'
(Hopkins 1966: 312). Perhaps it would be closer to the truth to
adopt the concept that any time we hear a piece of unfamiliar music,
we perceive it automatically through comparisons with familiar music.

According to the predispositions analysed above it is now apparent
that comparisons can occur with appropriate or inappropriate mental
images. It is also true, although not so apparent, that appropriateness is a matter that has been decided by the initiates and cannot
be measured mechanically. For example, a correctly perceived triplet
rarely consists of a group of three precisely equal notes, and notes
of different vibration frequencies within a scale system may be perceived as both identical and 'in tune.' Indeed, a note that is identical in pitch with another may be perceived as 'out of tune' because
of its position in the musical scheme. Yet none of these things is a
matter of chance; every one can be accounted for and will be expected
by those 'in the know.' We remember that Seashore, not understanding
this, was shocked when he discovered that his measurements of soundwave patterns made by famous performers showed great areas of divergence from the musical notation.

Scholars interested in structural analysis are aware of the importance of non-verbal systems of human communication. They frequently
employ musical analogies to describe this concept (for example, see
Leach 1973: 40), since they have noticed that music, considered as

159 Aural Thinking

one of a number of non-verbal manifestations of thought, approximates more closely the permutations of mental patterning than does verbal communication, which is mainly limited to linearity. Lévi-Strauss used the term capacité anagrammatique for this kind of mental patterning and deliberately utilized formal musical structures to describe mythological thought patterns in his monumental work on that subject (1964-71; see also Hopkins 1977). He explained that he refused to abandon himself to 'that form of mysticism that proclaims the intuitive and ineffable character of moral and aesthetic sentiments and even at times maintains that they illuminate the consciousness independently of all intellectual apprehension of their object' (1971: 596). He was probably thinking of criticisms such as my recent complaint (1977) that they would not be tenable for an aural, improvised tradition. But the Norwegian Hardanger fiddle tradition would be neither more intellectual nor more permanent if it were associated with a written notation: the structure itself is aural, and individual elaborations on that structure have meaning only to those initiated in the tradition. Notation ceases to have meaning when the aural tradition is no longer extant, as those who do research on the performance practice of past styles well know.

The hardingfele spelemann Finn Vabø, pointing to the monumental volumes of published transcriptions for the Hardanger fiddle, remarked that new pieces could not be learned from them because 'the music is not there.' He made it quite clear that he had the utmost respect for the editors (all of whom were outstanding both as players of the instrument and as scholars) and for the edition (which has a place of honour on his bookshelf). Vabø was simply calling attention to the limitations of musical notation for prescriptive purposes with respect to the intangible aspects of his tradition - those factors that must be learned by ear. In this paper I limited my study to an examination of a single characteristic of hardingfele structure - one that cannot be adequately represented by notation but one, that, nonetheless, is freely acknowledged by the musicians themselves to be of prime importance. A strong cognitive component obviously exists in even the initial percept of this non-notatable rhythmic feature.

NOTES

1 This paper is based on research that was done from 1965 to 1979. A first draft was read at the national meeting of the Society for Ethnomusicology at Wesleyan University, October 1975. I am indebted to Thomas Burns, University of Pennsylvania, for valuable advice during the progress of research and through several drafts of this material. This version is a revision of the draft that became part of my PhD dissertation, University of Pennsylvania, 1978.
2 The hardingfele (Harding or Hardanger fiddle) has fundamentally the size and shape of a European Baroque violin, but it possesses, in addition to the usual four bowed strings, a number (usually four or five) of sympathetic strings that run under the finger-

board. It is characteristically ornamented with stylized floral decorations and intricate mother-of-pearl inlay; usually a carved dragon's head surmounts the neck of the instrument, in place of a violin scroll. Played over a much wider area today than ever before, this instrument of the southern rural areas has become a national symbol for Norway.

3 The hardingfele spelemenn Kjetil Løndal and Knut Jure (assisted by Østein Odden, Ola Øyaland, and Johannes Dahle) kindly sent me tapes recorded from the commercially recorded examples, so that I could have an authoritative version with audible foot-beating; it is upon these tapes that the measurement aspect of the project has been based. Ola Kai Ledang, Trondheim University, sent me a tape recorded by him in Telemark from the playing of Johannes Dahle in Tinn, and I have thus been able to compare his material with some of the recordings I made of Dahle's playing on field trips in 1967, 1972, and 1979.

4 Robert Apfel, Yale University, generously allowed me access to the machinery at the Mason Laboratory and gave me advice on how to use it. Burton Rosner and William Labov, University of Pennsylvania, also gave me advice on these mechanical aspects.

5 The transcriptions in this paper are not of a detailed descriptive nature but rather are designed to convey the general outline of the rhythmic structure. Broad lines over or under notes in the first measures of the examples indicate the general pattern of lengthening followed (with the flexibility necessitated by interpretive requirements) in subsequent measures.

REFERENCES

Arnheim, R. 1966 Toward a Psychology of Art (Berkeley, University of California Press)
- 1969 Visual Thinking (Berkeley, University of California Press)
Blacking, J. 1974 How Musical Is Man? (Seattle, University of Washington Press)
Diamond, S. 1974 'The Myth of Structuralism' in I. Rosse, ed. The Unconscious in Culture: The Structuralism of Claude Levi-Strauss in Perspective (New York, Dutton)
Fry, D. 1970 'Phonology' in I. Lyons, ed. New Horizons in Linguistics (Harmondsworth, England, Penguin)
Fudge, E. 1970 'Phonology and Phonetics' in T. Sebeok, ed. Current Trends in Linguistics 9 (The Hague, Mouton)
Gombrich, E. 1960 Art and Illusion (Princeton, Princeton University Press)
Gregory, R. 1974 Concepts and Mechanisms of Perception (London, Oxford University Press)
Groven, E. 1971 'Musikkstudiar - Ikkje Utgjevne for' in O. Fjalestad, ed. Eivind Groven: Heiderskrift til 70-Årsdagen (Oslo, Universitetsforlaget)
Helmholtz, H. 1857 Popular Scientific Lectures English translation by A. Ellis (New York, Dover, 1962)

Hood, M. 1960 'The Challenge of "Bi-Musicality,"' Ethnomusicology 4 (2): 55-9
Hopkins, P. 1966 'The Purposes of Transcription,' Ethnomusicology 10 (3): 310-17
- 1967 'The Hardanger Fiddle and European Tradition,' unpublished paper read at New England chapter meeting of Society for Ethnomusicology
- 1977 'The Homology of Music and Myth: Views of Lévi-Strauss on Musical Structure'.Ethnomusicology 21 (2): 247-61
Leach, E. 1973 'Structuralism in Social Anthropology' in D. Robey, ed. Structuralism: An Introduction (London, Oxford University Press)
Ledang, O. 1967 Song, Syngemate, og Stemnekarakter (Oslo, Universitetsforlaget)
Lévi-Strauss, C. 1964-71 Mythologiques, 4 vols. (Paris, Plon-Julliard)
- 1971 Mythologiques, IV. L'Homme nu (Paris, Plon-Julliard)
Meyer, L. 1956 Emotion and Meaning in Music (Chicago, University of Chicago Press)
Read, H. 1956 The Art of Sculpture (New York, Pantheon) (Quoted in Gombrich 1960)
Sapir, E. 1958 'Writings On Language' in D. Mandelbaum, ed. Selected Essays (Berkeley, University of California Press
- 1921 Language (New York, Harcourt, Brace and World)
Seashore, C. 1938 Psychology of Music (New York, Dover, 1968)
Seeger, C. 1961 'Semantic, Logical and Political Considerations Bearing upon Research in Ethnomusicology' Ethnomusicology 5 (1): 77-80
Sibley, F., (ed.) 1971 Perception: A Philosophical Symposium (London, Methuen)

CHRISTOPHER MARSHALL
Towards a Comparative Aesthetics of Music

The cross-cultural study of music is confronted by a curious anomaly. In Western culture[1] there are many explicit theories about what I shall call <u>musical experience</u> - that is, the thing that happens in a person's head when he creates, performs, or hears music. These theories are well developed and consciously discussed by artists, critics, and philosophers in Western culture and, more or less similarly, in such other elite traditions as those of India and the Islamic world. But in the non-literate cultures of the world - those of most peasants and tribespeople - it seems as though ideas about musical experience, and music in general, are almost completely lacking.

There are two ways of looking at this apparently extreme dichotomy. First, there is the question of whether traditional cultures hold any ideas and beliefs about particular aspects of musical experience. Plenty of these ideas exist in the literature of the West; aestheticians and artists have proposed many definitions and concepts to explain certain features of musical creation and appreciation. Meyer (1956), for example, held that the basis of response to music is the frustration and fulfilment of expectation, and Langer (1953) felt that musical form expresses the form of feeling. Merriam described six such beliefs that seem widely held in the West (1964: 261 ff.): that the composer or listener separates music from its context through 'psychic distance'; that form is manipulated for its own sake; that the evaluation of music is strongly connected to standards of beauty; that the sound itself of music is what communicates or produces emotion; that music is a product of purposeful 'aesthetic' intent; and that it is possible and indeed necessary to verbalize ideas and theories about music and the experience of music. All these beliefs, and many more, are used to interpret the acts of musical creation, performance, and appreciation. But the literature on traditional cultures seems to have very little to say about indigenous beliefs of these musical activities. Something is known about formal and critical aesthetic thought in non-literate societies - ideas about such things as excellence in music and art, standards of criticism, and musical form - from the studies of scholars like Sachs (1975), Fernandez (1971), and

Schneider (1956), among others. But psychological aesthetic beliefs about the interior experience of making or hearing music are far less known. The few ethnomusicologists who have tried to elicit such beliefs have reported little success. McAllester (1954), for example, noted how difficult it was to discuss musical experience with the Navaho.

The second side to this seeming dichotomy is that the difference between literate Western and traditional musical thought seems even more marked with regard to the existence of musical philosophies - mutually interdependent and consistent ideas and definitions about formal, critical, and psychological aspects of music. Western thought, of course, abounds in such philosophies. Aestheticians like Meyer and Langer have integrated many ideas into self-consistent philosophies of music, and the six ideas that Merriam described as typical of much Western thought seem, in combination, to form such a philosophy. But here more than ever the ethnomusicological literature fails to produce solid evidence of similar systems in non-literate cultures. There are descriptions of formal and critical aesthetic beliefs of some traditional peoples, and a few isolated ideas about the psychology of musical experience have also been reported. But no one, to my knowledge, has been able to show any extensive logical integration of these into a philosophy of music. As Merriam concluded in his study of Basongye and Flathead musical beliefs, 'Both societies engage in activities which lead to what we would call artistic ends; both societies clearly make evaluative judgments; but neither society has the Western aesthetic' (1964: 269).

Why should literate cultures form ideas and philosophies about musical experience in abundance, while non-literate peoples scarcely seem to form either? Perhaps it is simply because primitive people do not think about such things. Many eminent scholars seem to imply this. Hood's response to Merriam's work was: 'These 2 societies are carriers of an oral tradition of music that can be described as "tribal" or "folk" or "non-cultivated," i.e. non-fine art. It is not too surprising, therefore, when he demonstrates the absence of a concept held by a literate society and applied exclusively to fine art' (1966: 223). And the anthropologist Redfield wrote: 'I do not think that any much discussed or much considered formulation of aesthetic taste is likely to appear in an isolated primitive group where style is traditional and learned without awareness of other possibilities' (1971: 58). But this is hardly a satisfactory explanation, for it denigrates the quality of peasant and tribal thought vis-à-vis our own. It also cannot explain why cultures develop complicated ideas about the social, natural, and supernatural world (compare Lévi-Strauss 1966) but seem incapable of doing so for musical creation and perception; and it does not really supply reasons for the 'absence of artistic thought' among non-literate peoples.

Other scholars have been more willing to assume that native theories of composition, performance, and expression do exist. In the past fifty years, mainly because of the impact of linguistic theory, anthropologists and others have begun to treat music and art as cultural systems of thought and as ways of expressing meaning, and it has become possible to consider recording and studying ideas about music. Such researchers as McAllester (1954), Merriam (1964), and Nketia (1954) in music, and Bohannon (1961), Fernandez (1971), and Otten (1971) in art, have recorded much of what is known about indigenous aesthetic thought. Yet the problem has remained unsolved, an embarrassment to those with faith in cultural relativity and the psychic unity of mankind, for their discoveries do not seem to add up to anything as comprehensive and self-consistent as the musical philosophies of our culture. There is always 'the possibility that the whole conceptual approach to music is so different from our own that it remains inaccessible or at least is not understood' (Merriam: 264). But why should it remain so inaccessible? Perhaps, after all, there really is an irreducible difference in kind between the musical thought of the literate and traditional worlds.

Is this problem really of concern to ethnomusicologists? I think it should be. It may be a matter of debate whether musical thought ought to be of primary or secondary importance as an object of study for us. But the ideas that a culture uses to explain musical composition or form, or emotion in music, may also be the ones it uses to guide and shape musical creation and evaluation, and thus the ones that have great effect on the sound itself of music — surely a matter of concern to ethnomusicolgists. And if he could somehow have access to indigenous musical beliefs during musical analysis, a researcher might discover that essential points were revealed more quickly, otherwise unobserved subtleties were uncovered, and ethnocentric distortion minimized.

The apparent absence of musical thought in some cultures is therefore a challenge to the comparative nature of the discipline. As Mieczyslaw Kolinski has long stressed, it is the responsibility of ethnomusicologists studying other musical cultures to undertake 'comparative analysis ... designed to establish their distinguishing features and, ultimately, to search for universals providing a common basis for the immense variety of musical creations' (1967: 5). Here, as it is so often in ethnomusicology, the important comparison is between Western culture and other cultures. Has 'comparative analysis' of musical thought failed thus far because organized ideas about music are not universal? If so, it is incumbent on us in the West to explain why only certain cultures, such as our own, have developed them. We will also have to find some substratum of music within the mind, perhaps a less rational one, that is a true human universal. Deeper, more reflexive questions arise, such as the philosophical problem of adequacy: if music can be created and appreciated in some cultures without theory, how close can ethnomusicological theories come to explaining the music of those cultures, or any music?

But perhaps systematic philosophies of music actually are human universals. If so, we are challenged to explain why some philosophies are more inaccessible to analysis than our own. Once we could explain

Towards a Comparative Aesthetics of Music

that, we could take on the task of describing their 'distinguishing features' and the logic that binds these features into belief systems. In the end it might be possible to discover universal patterns of thought about music, patterns of which Western aesthetic philosophies are special examples, by undertaking comparative and 'broadly cross-cultural studies designed to provide new insight into that evasive phenomenon commonly called "music."' (Kolinski 1977: 77).

I hope to show why there is a good reason to suppose that organized philosophies of music are indeed human universals, and to explain why there has been so little success in discovering the musical thought of other cultures.

Any body of thought about music and musical experience must be based on ideas about experience in general; aesthetic beliefs rely on deeper, more abstract epistemological presuppositions. A work of music is a work of cognition, a product of human thought, and the perception and appreciation of the work is also an act of cognition. The acts of making and appreciating music may be regarded variously as inspiration, formal manipulation, emotional catharsis, or the voice of divinity, but they are undeniably cognitive acts. Therefore, when a theory is formed about how music is experienced, it must be based on a theory of cognition. Ideas about the creation, knowledge, feeling, and perception of music are special extensions of ideas about epistemology, that is, creation, knowledge, feeling, and perception in general.

The validity of this conclusion can be demonstrated by pointing out a few of the epistemological foundations of Western aesthetic theories. The notion of psychic distance, for example, so essential to many Western theories, depends on characteristically Western ideas of 'experience' and 'mind' (compare Ryle 1949). Psychic distance refers to the appreciation of an object in and of itself, in which the analytical mind directs its attention to certain kinds of experience, the perception and exploration of pure form. This notion of psychic distance rests on the assumption that there is such a thing as an object of thought whose features can be explored by the thinking subject; that there is an agency, the mind, which acts on objects to render them meaningful; and that experience of objects can be formal (as of musical sounds) or practical (as of everyday sounds). Clearly the concept of psychic distance requires these particular epistemological assumptions. The Western idea that composers or listeners manipulate form for its own sake requires that they be conscious of the formal elements of sound. Since this awareness in turn requires the abstraction of form from emotion and context, it is linked to the idea of psychic distance and shares the same underlying assumptions about mind and experience.

It is agreed that the evaluation of music is somehow connected with the idea of beauty. Theories vary as to whether beauty inheres in the musical object or rises out of the attitude taken towards it, but it is widely felt that the value of music is of a sort different from the value of most everyday things. This feeling, which presupposes the need to observe the object that is music in a special way and the ability to abstract form from context, also rests on epistemological assumptions of mind and experience. It seems clear, then, that these earmarks of Western aesthetic belief depend on specific notions about thinking and experience. Western aesthetic philosophies derive from Western epistemological assumptions.

But not all cultures make these same assumptions. Systematic speculation about cognition must be a cultural universal because of the retroflexive nature of thought itself (compare Marshall 1977: 53 ff.), but the actual beliefs that make up the epistemology differ widely from culture to culture. Lienhardt (1961), for example, has shown that the Dinka of the Sudan conceptualize meaning, feeling, and knowledge in ways markedly unlike our own; and Hoffman (1978) has described Javanese notions of time and circumstance that differ greatly from those of the West. This divergence in beliefs suggests a whole new way of looking at the question of musical thought. Since all cultures have their own ideas about knowledge and experience, it is logical to suppose that all have their own ideas about the knowledge and experience of music in particular. In other words, since philosophies of epistemology are universal and diverse, then philosophies of music must be both universal and diverse also.

This perspective of universal and diverse musical philosophies could be revolutionary. Musical belief systems, previously thought to be the work of only a few literate elites, now would seem to be part of every human group's cultural heritage. Ideas about musical experience must derive from a culture's epistemology, and these as yet mainly undiscovered ideas must be tremendously rich and varied, to judge from the intricate and exotic systems of epistemological thought that anthropologists are beginning to uncover (compare Castaneda 1968; Siegel 1978).

Yet we of the West have overlooked this wealth of human intellectual creation almost completely. Our error has been to assume without question that ours is the only way to conceptualize experience and knowledge; in looking at other cultures, this has attuned us to only those aesthetic beliefs that derive from our own epistemology and has blinded us to beliefs that have their roots in very different conceptions. It is no wonder that non-literate societies have always seemed deficient in aesthetic thought: we have not known what to look for. If we are to discover anything about how peasants and tribal people experience music, we shall have to discover first how they experience thought in general.

In the remainder of this article I would like to make three points: that the theoretical connection between epistemology and aesthetics has actual heuristic value; that it uncovers ideas about musical experience that would not have been discovered by other means; and that real philosophies of music exist in non-literate traditional societies, philosophies that rival Western theories in complexity and consistency. The method I propose for demonstrating these points is illustrated here in one culture but could be applied to any (for research methodology see Marshall 1977: 54 ff.).

Towards a Comparative Aesthetics of Music

The Debarčani are Macedonian peasants inhabiting an isolated valley in southwestern Yugoslavia near the town of Ohrid. Like many other Macedonians they were isolated from the larger world until relatively recently by Turkish domination and primitive communications. The older Debarčani, most of whom are illiterate, still live in a largely traditional manner, and music and song remain strong in their folk culture. In the course of nine months of field-work there in 1975,[2] I found that the Dabarčani have a philosophy of music that is well-developed, generally consistent, based on distinctive ideas about knowledge, feeling, and experience, and significantly unlike those of the literate cultures of Europe and Asia. Here I shall describe a few of these underlying epistemological notions, contrasting them with those of the West, and show how the Debarčani apply these notions in shaping a coherent theory of musical experience.

The Debarčani feel that music is the product of an internal mental agency and that items of music have the character of concepts or thoughts. This agency, known as <u>akil</u> or <u>um</u>, is only roughly analogous to our notion of 'mind.' The <u>akil</u> is like the mind in that it too is an agency of consciousness, an aspect of a person that is concerned with concepts and the awareness of concepts; beyond this <u>akil</u> and mind are quite different. In the West the mind is regarded as a powerful integrating organ of personality which is involved in storing, producing, and reflecting on feelings, memories, perceptions, and much more. A person's individuality or sense of self is largely a matter of how his mind operates and what it contains. We can never really 'lose our minds,' only our powers of reason; the mind is with all of us until death. But the <u>akil</u> is only one aspect of the Debarčani individual, and not the most important. It is possible for the <u>akil</u> to separate itself from the self: when a Debarčani cannot recall something, he may say 'I lost my mind,' meaning that the agency for apprehending memories is not with him at the moment.

Also, <u>akil</u> is neither the subject of thinking nor the shaper of reality. In the West there is a tendency to feel that there is some subjective agency that acts to comprehend reality or create meanings as the objects of its thoughts. The mind performs analytical operations upon reality, its object, or it synthesizes structures of thought within itself. But thought in this sense does not take place in Debarca: ideas and truths are not things made or shaped by a mental agency, but exist simply as immanent truths.

The concepts (<u>poimas</u>) with which the <u>akil</u> is concerned include memories, beliefs, attitudes, dreams, and items of music. These entities are not products of mental operations, for it is not felt that such operations take place; in fact, it is not felt that they originate anywhere. Beliefs, dreams, and songs originate in tradition, 'established from some time' by 'the same people' who first lived together and first made music.

The <u>akil</u> does not create or transform concepts through thought, nor does it store them within itself; it 'grasps' (<u>faka</u>, <u>zafati</u>)

them. Concepts have a permanent existence of a sort, unlocalized in time or place, but every single aspect of tradition cannot be at the forefront of one's attention. The akil is seen as the agency or power that 'grasps' certain concepts and makes them conscious. The metaphors used to describe the process are often those of physical apprehension: 'get,' 'bring over,' 'buy (for resale).' There is no implication that the process involves a selection or critical appraisal of the concept. A memory, dream, song, or other concept is grasped by the akil as a total Gestalt, not as a structured entity, and the grasping does not involve an appreciation of the structure of the concept. One thinks of, rather than about or up, things.

In Western thought, the process of expressing concepts is one of signification, the uniting of purely mental concepts with expressive systems like language, musical form, or gesture. The mind is the agency that manipulates the structure of the system to express the idea. The Debarcani see the expressive function of the akil differently: in the same way the akil 'apprehends' concepts directly without analysing or synthesizing them, it expresses concepts simply by presenting them, by revealing them and making them immanent. There is no act of joining thought with form, for thought and form are one. Concepts are indivisible packages of meaning, to be received and delivered but not opened. All the metaphors used to refer to expression indicate the direct and uncomplicated nature of the akil's action: 'drive forth,' 'deliver,' 'place.'

This unique theory of thought is most helpful in discovering and understanding Debarcani theories of musical origins, teaching of music, and talent. Pieces of music, being concepts, have no specific origin or history of formation; they exist in the same preconscious way that other concepts do, as formed truths waiting to be brought to consciousness. The subject of composition is not therefore of much interest to the Debarcani. Many of those interviewed said that all traditional music came into being when the first people were created, and the few informants that could volunteer clearer explanations of the compositional process were unable to cite any known instance of composition. This is because items of music, being concepts, exist independently of the akil; the akil grasps them but does not create them or affect them. Thus any process of composition would have to take place outside a person's akil. But for the Debarcani (unlike many other cultures), there is no recognized source for new concepts - ideas are not inspired by divinity or learned in dreams or visions - and there is no idea that concepts exist somewhere waiting to be found. Traditional culture, including music, exists in its entirety and cannot be created ex nihilo by the akil. Sources of novelty lie elsewhere - new pieces may be borrowed from outside Debarca, and errors or corruptions may occur - but composition is not a recognized source.

In Debarca music is not taught. Informants said that the best way to learn music is to expose oneself to it and listen as much as possible; that, along with a desire to learn and regular practice, is enough to make one proficient. This belief stems directly from the Debarčani theory of knowledge. A Debarčani does not achieve an understanding of a piece of music through guided analysis, for this is not how one understands something. The akil grasps the concept of the music as a whole; all that is needed is continued exposure to the music for it to 'become real' and be grasped fully. Because understanding is achieved through gnosis rather than analysis, there is no need for a teacher to break down the music for a student; a teacher is not even needed to reveal new music to a student since all traditional music already exists in accessible, audible form. It is necessary only that the concept of the music be 'driven forth' clearly and well - something any musician does during performance - to enable a listener to grasp it and make it his own.

Musical talent thus is thought to be distributed equally to all. There is no difference in degree or kind of musical understanding between the ordinary listener and the listener who wants to learn the music; the performer 'delivers' the musical concept for the audience, and the audience apprehends and experiences the immanence of the concept. The most skilful and experienced performer, it is felt, has the same grasp of the music he plays as does the average listener; it is just as real for one as the other. The difference between musician and non-musician lies not in the degree of understanding the musician has, or in any superior ability to understand, but in his desire and acquired skill to perform. This skill is not a matter of the akil: it is localized in the hands or mouth (and thus is more like a set of learned habits or muscular reflexes) and can be acquired by any normal person.

The Debarčani theory of knowledge also explains some unusual features of their theory of musical form. It does not seem surprising at first that the Debarčani have only a limited vocabulary of specifically musical terminology and that they do not seem to distinguish clearly or at all many elements of musical form - ethnomusicologists have long assumed that they know more than their informants do about the structure of music. Yet on second thought some explanation is required. Since the Debarčani produce extremely complex structures of sound, why have they not developed complicated bodies of terminology and theory to explain their musical creations? Some clues may be found in their epistemology of music, especially in the idea of music as concept.

Certain parameters of musical sound appear to be well recognized by the Debarčani, for they readily distinguish elements of form within each parameter. Some of the terms they use to refer to these elements are purely musical ones (such as 'beat' and 'pitch' in our own culture); many more terms are metaphorical and synaesthetic (such as 'tone colour,' 'high pitch'), though none the less accurate for that. But other levels of musical structure do not seem to be the objects of such elaborated thought, for an awareness of form on these levels appears to be slight or absent.

Timbre is one parameter whose terminology is well-developed. Many terms are used, all metaphorical (since the Debarčani cannot measure the overtones that make timbre the way the physicist can). 'Weak,' 'constricted,' 'stout,' 'fat,' 'strong,' 'slim,' 'clear,' and 'well-mixing' are some designations of specific timbres. Another parameter, tempo, also seems to be the object of conscious thought and elaboration. Although the terminology of tempo is limited to a few relative terms, like 'faster,' 'slow,' and 'quick' (since scientific measurements are not available), all musicians and most non-musicians have a very clear notion of the proper tempo for a given piece and can rank pieces according to tempo. Obviously the Debarcani are well aware of this aspect of form.

In other parameters of form, they do not appear to have conscious conceptual systems or vocabularies that are so well developed. I found no indications that the Debarcani are aware of scale, ambitus, or interval width as aspects of form in their music, for example. This does not mean that such parameters do not exist in the objective sound of the music, or that the Debarcani could not make distinctions within these parameters if taught to do so by an outsider; it means merely that their normal course of thought does not lead them to consider these things. There is not only no native terminology (direct or metaphorical) for talking about these parameters, but there also does not seem to be any unverbalized categorization of these things. I could not get informants to distinguish pieces in one scale from pieces in another, or narrow from wide intervals, other than to say they sounded different, perhaps.

The Debarcani seem to have a similar lack of awareness about textual structure. They have no traditional words for 'line' or 'stanza'; informants used the word zbor ('something said') to refer to words, lines, and stanzas in song. This is not to say that informants were unaware of levels of structure in their song texts. Informants were capable of dividing texts roughly into lines and stanzas after I had given them a little coaching, but the need for coaching indicates that textual structure is an issue only vaguely conceived in Debarcani thought.

That the Debarcani conceive some aspects of musical form more clearly than others can be understood by referring to the Debarcani's ideas about the general character of music. I said earlier that each piece is seen as a concept, a single entity apprehended by the akil as a total Gestalt. The concept of structure is foreign to this epistemology; the akil is not an analysing agency, and the concepts that it grasps are not seen to be structured or amenable to analysis. Given this approach to music, it is possible to be aware of certain aspects of musical structure; others, though, cannot be understood. One can form explicit and well-developed ideas about those aspects of musical form that can be seen as qualities pertaining to music sound as a whole: timbre and tempo are qualities spread equally over an entire piece of music, and so they are readily distinguished and elaborated in Debarcani thought. But other aspects of music can be discovered only by analysing a piece, separating levels of structure, and abstracting elements of form that occur some places but not others in the piece: these parameters (for example, textual structure, scales, and intervals) will not be readily elaborated by a mode of thought that eschews analytic thinking and regards the piece of music as a unitary, indivisible concept. Qualities that do not

Towards a Comparative Aesthetics of Music

involve formal analysis are objects of elaborated thought for the Debarčani; qualities that do require analysis are less so.

Much more could be said about Debarčani aesthetics and epistemology. There is not space to describe their concept of beauty, which is derived from notions of truth and tradition, or to discuss their extremely interesting theory of emotion in music which complements the idea of music as concept (Marshall 1977). But it seems clear that a great many ideas - very unlike those in the West - about musical experience do exist in this non-literate peasant society, and that these ideas about creation, learning, talent, and form in music are derivations from, or special uses of, a general theory about knowledge. It is also clear that these ideas are not isolated, vague, or ad-hoc beliefs, as might have been expected: they constitute a self-consistent logical structure which is both complex and capable of further elaboration - in other words, a philosophy of musical experience, an 'aesthetic,' which is given unity by the epistemology that informs it.

If I had gone to Debarca without realizing the connection between epistemological and aesthetic thought, I should have been forced to conclude that the natives were deficient in musical thought, with little or no knowledge of composition, learning, talent, or form. Some scholars, those looking for Western-style ideas about music among the Debarčani, would have fallen into a double error: they would have assumed that all musical belief had to resemble that of the literate West and failed to realize that the Debarčani might have a different epistemology and thus a different sort of aesthetic. Other scholars, bound less by the categories of Western aesthetics and attuned to any kind of beliefs about music, would have been somewhat more successful in discovering various isolated ideas; but they would have been unable to show how these ideas were organized into a logical aesthetic. The native beliefs they described would have seemed curiously fragmentary and disconnected - certainly nothing like a real philosophy of music. The failing of this second kind of scholar would have been the inability to penetrate to the organizing principle of the indigenous aesthetic, the epistemological assumptions upon which the aesthetic is based; the pattern in the thought would not have been observed. But when one drops the search for Western aesthetic beliefs in a traditional culture and realizes that any ideas about its music must stem from an indigenous epistemology, one discovers that such ideas and philosophies actually do exist.

This new approach seems to have unique heuristic value, and its possibilities are very exciting. All at once the range of aesthetic beliefs available for study has increased from the traditions of a few literate cultures to the living belief systems of every one of the world's cultures. We must explore and record - and compare - this wealth of human creativity. How do the musical beliefs of Plato differ from those of a Yugoslav goatherd? Do the theories of literate societies have something in common, compared to non-literate societies? Are some cultures more intellectually creative than others with respect to theories about music, and if so why? Ethnomusicology as a discipline will benefit from the description and comparison of musical thought. There will be new insights into the minds of creators, performers, and audiences of music, which will reveal more about creativity, performance, and listening universally and in specific cultures. Indigenous philosophical traditions may offer new ways of looking at old issues, such as the debate over music and its context or the question of permissible variation within a tradition. We shall realize that our professional theories rest on culturally specific epistemological assumptions, and thus become more knowledgeable theorists. And finally, once the false dichotomy between literate and traditional cultures is discarded and the full range of musical philosophies begins to be known, new searches for universals of musical thought will lead us to a fresh awareness of the beauty and power of the human mind and of music, its creation.

NOTES

1 By 'Western' I mean the elite literate cultures of Europe and the Americas in the last two centuries; I use the word for convenience and advisedly, since folk and popular ideas exist in the West as well.
2 The author wishes to acknowledge the support of the United States Office of Education and the International Research and Exchanges Board.

REFERENCES

Bohannon, Paul 1961 'Artist and Critic in an African Society' in Marian W. Smith, ed. The Artist in Tribal Society (London, Routledge and Kegan Paul)
Castaneda, Carlos 1968 The Teachings of Don Juan: A Yaqui Way of Knowledge (Berkeley, University of California Press)
Fernandez, James W. 1971 'Principles of Opposition and Vitality in Fang Art' in Carol F. Jopling, ed. Art and Aesthetics in Primitive Societies (New York, Dutton)
Hoffman, Stanley B. 1978 'Epistemology and Music: A Javanese Example' Ethnomusicology 22 (1): 68-88
Hood, Mantle 1966 'Comment on "The Anthropology of Music,"' Current Anthropology 7 (2): 222-3
Kolinski, Mieczyslaw 1967 'Recent Trends in Ethnomusicology' Ethnomusicology 11 (1): 1-24
- 1977 'Final Reply to Herndon' Ethnomusicology 21 (1): 75-84
Langer, Suzanne K. 1953 Feeling and Form (New York, Scribner)
Lévi-Strauss, Claude 1966 The Savage Mind (Chicago, University of Chicago Press)
Lienhardt, Godfrey 1961 Divinity and Experience: The Religion of the Dinka (Oxford, Clarendon Press)
Marshall, Christopher 1977 'The Aesthetics of Music in Village Macedonia,' PhD dissertation, Cornell University, Ithaca, NY

McAllester, David P. 1954 Enemy Way Music (Cambridge, Peabody Museum)
Merriam, Alan P. 1964 The Anthropology of Music (Evanston, Northwestern University Press)
Meyer, Leonard B. 1956 Emotion and Meaning in Music (Chicago, University of Chicago Press)
Nketia, J.H. Kwabena 1954 'The Role of the Drummer in Akan Society' African Music 1: 34-43
Otten, Charlotte M., ed. 1971 Anthropology and Art: Readings in Cross-cultural Aesthetics (Garden City, Natural History Press)
Redfield, Robert 1971 'Art and Icon' in Charlotte M. Otten, ed. Anthropology and Art: Readings in Cross-cultural Aesthetics (Garden City, Natural History Press) 39-65
Ryle, Gilbert 1949 The Concept of Mind (New York, Harper and Row)
Sachs, Nahoma 1975 'Meaning and Music: Musical Symbolism in a Macedonian Village' PhD dissertation, Indiana University, Bloomington, Indiana
Schneider, Harold K. 1956 'The Interpretation of Pakot Visual Art' Man 56: 103-6
Siegel, James T. 1978 The Rope of God (Berkeley, University of California Press)

ALAN P. MERRIAM
On Objections to Comparison in Ethnomusicology

> I have chosen to discuss the comparative method because I feel that anthropology ... can ill afford to give up a method, unless the method is proved to be without value. And this has never been done in the case of the comparative method. (Ackernecht 1954: 118)

In an article in 1973, Bruno Nettl discussed the general topic of comparison in ethnomusicology, citing major studies, problems, and achievements. In this paper, I wish to call attention to two specific aspects of the topic, both of which concern the objections made to comparison in ethnomusicology. The subject is important because the objections seem to me to be either half-truths or simply vague statements of the views of their proponents. Further, these anti-comparativist views have gained increasingly wide credence and influence among ethnomusicologists and by no means always with demonstrably positive results. Since the problems raised by comparison are complex and have long been the subject of pointed debate in anthropology, the literature is vast and can be only sampled here. In ethnomusicology, however, the same problems have been barely recognized in their wider context, and they badly need to be given more recognition and definition and to be the subject of clear discussion among us ethnomusicologists, for we are in danger of throwing the baby of comparativism out of the bath we are filling with the water of increasingly sophisticated methodologies. The basic argument of this paper, then, is that we should not abandon comparativism in favour of ideographic studies, no matter how great the methodological advances. Rather, we need to focus considerable attention and energy directly on comparativism in order to search for more feasible ways of making it a useful research tool in ethnomusicology.

Before pursuing the argument, I must clarify some basic positions. First, my purpose is not to annoy but to incite ethnomusicologists to a sensible discussion of how to deal with the problems raised by comparison. Second, my aim is not to scrap new methodologies for old; my aim is to call attention to the potential merits of ideas that have preceded those preoccupying us now, since I believe these older notions can assist us in our present work. And finally, in advocating

On Objections to Comparison in Ethnomusicology

new discussion on - and thus, by inference, respect for - a basically unpopular, and even disdained, approach in ethnomusicology, I realize that I risk misinterpretation of my own position. In order to avoid that complication, I wish to state that my basic position has not changed: I am still interested in the study of music as culture, and the study of music sound structure is a means to a more limited end than that which I usually wish to undertake. My purpose, then, is to remind us that structural studies clearly do have their place in ethnomusicology, that such studies lead naturally and inevitably to comparisons of structures, and that such comparisons can, under specific circumstances, lead to new and broadened knowledge of music.

ANTICOMPARATIVIST VIEWS

The two anticomparativist views I wish to use as a basis for discussion are quite different from each other, although in the broad sense their final results are the same. The first view, as phrased by Mantle Hood in several publications, is a denial of the past and present utility of any kind of comparison and, in the end, is an implication that there is no hope of future promise. The second, as propounded by John Blacking over a period of years, is a rejection of the utility of one kind of comparison - the comparison of forms - and an emphasis on the priority of another kind of comparison - that of meanings. Let us examine Hood's point of view first.

Some eighteen years ago, Hood stated his objection to comparison in the following terms: 'It seems a bit foolish in retrospection that the pioneers of our field became engrossed in the comparison of different musics before any real understanding of the musics being compared had been achieved' (1963: 233). Six years later, he expressed almost the same point of view: 'An early concern with comparative method, before the subjects under comparison could be understood, led to some imaginative theories but provided very little accurate information' (1969: 299). In both these statements the onus for the purported failure of comparison was put on past mistakes, as it was again in the following statement, which is both much stronger and much more explicit: 'I am convinced that the gross generalities that have confused and confounded comparative studies in the past ... will never expose ... [the] ... elusive universals of music' (1971: 349). And finally, this most recent word seems to be a denial of all possibility of the usefulness, or even the comprehensibility, of comparison: 'Comparative musicology? I no longer understand the term' (ibid.).

Hood, of course, is not alone in this attitude. Norma McLeod, for example, in discussin the work of Alan Lomax, wrote:

> Now, Lomax has taken another view ... He said ... that 'pieces of music relate directly to major cultural patterning.' For him, minute musical matters are symbols for major cultural patterns, such as incest, warfare, the extended family, or what have you. For example, in societies with extended families, you should

> have people singing in a certain way. He has related matters of
> internal form in music to what might be called context of cul-
> ture: the major broad patterning of culture is, he says,
> reflected within the minute details of music. Well, now, this
> is fair if he can prove it, but I don't think he can. He uses
> a comparative technique ... I find myself unable to accept broad
> generalizations of this nature: I'm not comfortable with them.
> (Herndon and Brunyate 1975: 168)

Several threads seem to run through these statements. One is that comparison has earned its obscurity through the errors made and compounded by scholars in the past. But surely we do not discard a methodology simply because it has been misused or because its users reached what we now believe - in the light of the further accumulation of knowledge - to be faulty conclusions. Indeed, error is an important part of any kind of scientific method: failure is just as crucial as success. What is important is to learn how to use the methodology correctly and to advantage.

A second thread, which is sometimes an implication and sometimes a denial, is that although comparison in the past may have been premature, it may be possible in the fugure. But simultaneously a third thread - the most serious one - is the suggestion that comparative methods will never help us (Hood) or, put differently, that broad generalizations are neither acceptable nor, by implication, desirable in ethnomusicology (McLeod). This introduces the much broader question of the methodology used by ethnomusicologists, and particularly of the implied or actual role played by comparison in that methodology.

My assumption is that ethnomusicologists attempt to operate under a combination of methods borrowed from those used in both the humanities and the social sciences. Indeed, it is this mixture of borrowings, never reconciled with each other, that has led to so much of the confusion that marks ethnomusicology. The borrowings from the social sciences are at prime issue here, since comparison is at the root of many kinds of generalization and generalization is widely assumed to be the end result of scientific methodology. Moles, for example, remarked that 'after all, an objective of science is to generalize,' and that 'through generalization we gain order and, in addition, an explanation of that order' (1977: 236). In much of anthropology and in much of ethnomusicology as well, generalization has been assumed to be based upon the inductive method, and it is in this connection that even stronger statements of the aims of science have been made. Radcliffe-Brown, for example, saw a clear homology between the physical sciences and social anthropology:

> The postulate of the inductive method is that all phenomena are
> subject to natural law, and that consequently it is possible,
> by the application of certain logical methods, to discover and
> prove certain general laws, i.e., certain general statements or
> formulae, of greater or less degree of generality, each of which
> applies to a certain range of facts or events. The essence of

On Objections to Comparison in Ethnomusicology

induction is generalisation; a particular fact is explained by being shown to be an example of a general rule. (1958: 7)

If one of the basic goals of the ethnomusicologist is generalization, which he reaches at least partly through induction, it seems to follow that the use of a comparative methodology in some form cannot be avoided since 'comparison is a basic aspect of human thought ... In all analogy, classification, definition, and divisions, comparison is involved in one form or the other' (Śarana 1975: 12). Somewhat more formally, Murdock stated the matter as follows:

Whatever other methods of investigation are employed ... the comparative method is indispensable. Without it, no combination of other methods can achieve scientifc results of universal application. At the most they can only produce culture-bound generalizations, approximately valid for a particular group of related societies during a particular segment of their history, but incapable of generalization to other societies except as highly tentative working hyoptheses, and equally incapable of predicting future developments in periods of rapid social change or even of comprehending them after they have occurred. (1965: 298)

Indeed, the process of formal comparison has been discussed repeatedly (among many others by Driver 1973; Naroll 1968; Ackernecht 1954; Schapera 1953), and it has often been suggested that its beginnings coincided roughly with the beginning of the eighteenth century (Radcliffe-Brown 1958: 144-52; Sarana 1975: 12-13; Ackernecht 1954: passim).

Besides its contribution to the inductive method, comparison has other uses. Lewis, for example (1961), suggested six specific applications, and Śarana (1975: 16 and passim) wrote that the possible end results included the establishment of inferential history, typology or classification, generalization, and formulation of generalized process. We shall return later to these matters, but it is the following string of assumptions that must occupy us here: one of the aims of ethnomusicology is to make generalizations; one of the ways of achieving generalizations is the inductive method; one of the important constituents of the inductive method is comparison. If generalization is not taken to be an aim of ethnomusicology, then comparison is not necessarily either useful or desirable. I do not believe this to be true, nor do I believe that either Hood or McLeod believes it to be true, for both have made numerous comparisons in their own work. Indeed, it is virtually impossible to conceive of a type of study that does not use comparison, if, for example, only on the simple basis of the mental opposition involved in the way 'I' make music as opposed to the way 'they' make music. Even description is based upon implicit comparison.

One final, if obvious, point remains: that induction is not the only kind of methodology employed by scientists. Indeed, deduction is equally important, although the fact does not seem to have been recognized clearly by ethnomusicologists. It is probably most accurate to say that induction and deduction go hand in hand in any investigation that operates from the initial basis of an organized problem. In writing of his approach to the study of economic anthropology Schneider expressed the basis of deduction as follows:

> In the nature of deductive reasoning the approach to the study of economic behavior is not through the ethnographic facts but by means of 'universal principles,' logico-mathematical in form, springing from the imagination. Generating the logical system necessary to deductive economics requires no cross-cultural data or facts from any system, except perhaps common-sense knowledge of the empirical realm to which the theory is to be applied. (1974: 23)

Deduction, in other words, is an artefact of the mind which is built up through the rigour of its own logic. When the ethnomusicologist creates a set of hypotheses, or a general proposition, that he wishes to test in the field, he is using deduction; in the process of testing them, he is using induction. The two are parts of the same general process, and each requires some form of the other, as Schneider observed: 'Conventional wisdom tells us that induction and deduction are concomitants of each other' (1974: 30).

But while deduction and induction are together at the basis of most field studies in ethnomusicology, neither is sufficient in itself for generalization. Deduction must be proved by induction or it leads only to the sterility of abstract and unproved theory; induction must be generated by deduction or it remains no more than pure description, no matter how inspired that description may be. I do not see the results of either Hood's or McLeod's work mired in either of these dead ends.

The second anticomparativist view, which denies the utility or the possibility of comparisons of form, has for a number of years been associated in my mind with a statement made some time ago by John Blacking:

> Statistical analyses of intervals ... are all very well, provided that we know that the same intervals have the same meanings in all the cultures whose music we are comparing. If this is not certain, we may be comparing incomparable phenomena. In other words, if we accept the view that patterns of music sound in any culture are the product of concepts and behaviour peculiar to that culture, we cannot compare them with similar patterns in another culture unless we know that the latter are derived from similar concepts and behaviour. Conversely, statistical analyses may show that the music of 2 cultures is very different, but an analysis of the cultural 'origins' of the sound patterns may reveal that they have essentially the same meaning, which has been translated into the different 'languages' of the 2 cultures. (1966: 218)

On Objections to Comparison in Ethnomusicology

Blacking repeated this point of view in subsequent publications, though tying it ever more closely to the problem of deep and surface structures (1972: 108), and other scholars have followed suit. The point of view is an old one going back at least as far as the French sociologists (see Radcliffe-Brown 1958: 161); in ethnomusicology it was voiced at least as early as 1960 by Leonard Meyer: 'Appearances are often deceptive. For instance, two cultures may appear to employ the same scale structure, but this structure might be interpreted differently by the members of each culture. Conversely, the music of two cultures may employ very different materials, but the underlying mechanism governing the organization of these materials might be the same for both' (1960: 49-50).

One of the more recent statements of this point of view came from Johnston:

> An example of false analogy would be to compare the Uganda xylophone 4th to the Tsonga musical bow 4th. The former is produced by dividing the octave into five equal intervals of 240 Cents each and beating upon alternate xylophone slats tuned to these intervals, yielding intervals of 480 Cents. The latter is produced by inverting the natural 5th of 702 Cents, yielding 498 for the musical bow's 4th. Like or nearly-alike intervals cannot be compared cross-culturally as though the social meaning of the sounds were identical, regardless of cultural attitudes and the psycho-historical background of their production and use within the society (1973: 145).

The obvious question here is how Johnston can call both intervals by the Western term 'fourth,' given the facts that they do not encompass the same number of cents, that they are not derived in the same manner, that the use of a Western term inevitably introduces a comparison into the reader's comprehension, and that Johnston's point is that they are not the same thing. Nevertheless, this particular basis of objection to comparison is clearly delineated in these quotations.

Throughout the history of the discussion of comparativism in anthropology, and more recently in ethnomusicology, debate has centred on four basic problems. The first problem, emphasized by Blacking, has been put forward in the name of functional integration; that is, that one cannot take items out of context for comparison without knowing what each means in its own context, and that if the contexts or the meanings differ, comparison becomes impossible. Nketia (1967), among many others, made the same point, but a number of commentators have taken a contrary view. Sarana, for example, wrote: 'It may be argued that [because] the parts of a culture are functionally related ... to compare an aspect of culture with that of another means that both have been torn out of their respective cultural contexts. In some extreme cases this objection may hold good. But it can be overcome by a proper definition of the units and the items of comparison and by making clear also the level of abstraction at which one proposes to work' (1975: 76). Murdock made the same basic comment, though in rather more severe terms, in commenting on Ruth Benedict's views:

> She strongly implied that the abstraction of elements for comparison with those of other cultures is illegitimate. An element has no meaning except in its context; in isolation it is meaningless. I submit that this is nonsense. Specific functions, of course, are discoverable only in context. Scientific laws or propositions, however, can be arrived at, in anthropology, as in any other science, only by abstracting and comparing features observable in many phenomena as they occur in nature (1965: 146).

The antithetical views cited here do not, of course, resolve the problem but they do suggest that a second problem must be dealt with simultaneously. This is the problem of units, that is, how units are selected, what the proper unit for comparison should be, how to make certain that the units are indeed comparable, and so on. Once again, these difficulties have been the subject of considerable discussion and debate among anthropologists. The central point was expressed briefly by Naroll, who said that 'for anthropologists ... the most urgent need is a standard set of categories and terms ... [that] follow the most general and most nearly validated system at hand' (1968: 269). Leach discussed in lengthier terms the basic problems that he felt mitigate against this possibility:

> An essential part of this scientific procedure is the development of precisely defined concepts (such as species, elements, molecules, atoms, elementary particles, mass, energy, pressure, spatial dimension, temperature), which together provide an internationally agreed upon frame of reference in terms of which the particular phenomena observed by different investigators may be described. Scientific progress is possible only because all the specialists in a given discipline use units of description that are commonly understood and have precisely defined meaning ... These characteristics of natural science have been consciously imitated by leading theorists of the social sciences, but they have been reluctant to admit that the two fields are analogous rather than homologous ... The units of ordinary anthropological description - expressions like 'patrilineal descent,' 'uxorilocal residence,' ... are not in any way comparable to the precisely defined diagnostic elements which form the units of discourse in natural science. This is the heart of the whole matter (1968: 339, 340-1).

Such a general statement would be denied by many anthropologists whose interests lie in cross-cultural comparison (for example, Murdock 1949), and many scholars have worked intensively on solving the problems presented (for example, Moles 1977; Naroll 1968), but

181 On Objections to Comparison in Ethnomusicology

since these discussions are anthropological rather than ethnomusicological, they will not be presented further here. Attention may be called, however, to one of the most frequently cited methodologies, that of 'controlled comparison,' suggested by Eggan (1950) and further discussed in its application in ethnomusicology (Merriam 1964: passim).

Other scholars have suggested that certain kinds of phenomena are much more difficult to handle than others. This was emphasized by Osgood, for example, when he noted that 'comparisons across cultures are particularly difficult when what anthropologists term "non-material traits" are involved. I shall use the term "subjective culture." It is one thing to compare skull shapes, blood types or artifacts; it is quite another to compare peoples' values, stereotypes, attitudes, feelings or, most generally, meanings'(1967: 6). Presumably Osgood would include music in his 'non-material traits,' but would this classification, in fact, be accurate? It seems plausible to consider music as both material and non-material, depending upon which part is being studied; that is, the sound structure may well be regarded as made up of 'material' traits, and the meaning of music falls under 'subjective culture.' Whether or not this is true, some ethnomusicologists deny that any sort of comparisons can be made simply because 'you can't get comparable data.' This is the recent view of McLeod, who presumably intends to solve the problem by beginning again with the inductive method: since comparable data cannot be obtained, 'what we do instead is to say, "this society does this: does anybody know another one that does anything like it?" In other words, we take baby steps' (Herndon and Brunyate 1975: 178).

This in turn leads us to a third objection to comparison. In this argument it is held that one well-chosen example or one well-done experiment is all that is necessary to document a general principle. This approach seems to be animating much of ethnomusicological research today, not perhaps so much in the sense that a single example is taken to stand for all examples (which is the inevitable result of McLeod's statement that it is impossible to generalize), as in the sense of limited goals. Herndon, for example, expressed the view that 'the discovery of native categories should be a primary goal, a logical place to begin our investigations' (1976: 221), but it seems to me that this is rather precisely where many of us have already begun and, in any event, that it is by no means the only place to begin. Herndon was here apparently expressing her basic interest in goals that were 'limited, particularistic and pragmatic' (1976: 229), and although I see no possible objection to these goals, neither do I see them as the only possible goals. The idea of limited goals in anthropology today has been well expressed by Šarana: 'The contemporary anthropologists in general firmly believe that ... intensive field studies, aiming at tackling limited problems, are more useful for understanding the nature of human society and culture than aspiring for all-embracing generalizations covering the whole of mankind' (1975: 94). I believe this to be a reasonable statement of the situation as it exists now in both anthropology and ethnomusicology, but I would deplore the statement had not Śarana continued: 'We do not say that the latter are not at all worth pursuing. We all know, however, that at this stage of the development of our discipline we cannot attempt generalizations on a broader scale, with the same depth and authority, as we can do at the level of our microscopic and intensive fieldwork studies' (1975: 94-5). I am not quite sure I understand the self-contradiction in this statement but I am willing to take it at surface value as long as it is understood to mean that attempts at generalization are equally important as microscopic studies.

This recent emphasis on the particular leads us into the difference between two basic kinds of studies in both anthropology and ethnomusicology, as described by Naroll:

> Systematic comparative studies have long been carried out in cultural anthropology for two distinct ends. First, <u>idiographic</u>, historical studies have been carried out in an effort to reconstruct the specific culture history of certain regions or certain traits. Second, <u>nomothetic</u>, sociological studies have been carried out in an effort to discover or verify basic laws of society or culture, basic principles which presumably would hold good at least as tendencies in any society, anywhere, any time.
>
> Idiographic generalizations hold good only about the specific cultures compared. But nomothetic generalizations explicitly or implicitly hold good for the entire universe studied, at least as tendencies. Consequently, if valid, they permit predictions about cultures not yet studied, indeed about cultures not yet in existence ...
>
> This distinction has long been made between the purpose of idiographic and nomothetic studies. By an idiographic study is thus meant one whose purpose is to describe a particular sequence of events ... By a nomothetic study is meant one whose purpose is to discern a repetitive pattern which reflects a general characteristic of society or culture (1968: 236-7).

Selection of limited goals does not necessarily negate comparison per se (Harris 1968: 576, 579), but neither does it solve the question of comparable units. Rather it represents a choice of research strategy, a choice that may be made on the simple basis of preference or because one strategy seems to its user to be more powerful than another. It is this argument that animated the recent published debate between Herndon and Kolinski (Herndon 1974, 1976; Kolinski 1976, 1977), in which Herndon maintained that Kolinski's units were, in effect, imposed from the outside, and thus unverifiable on a cross-cultural basis. Her key observation was: 'Put quite simply, if we are going to compare musics, we must have testable, consistent units with which to compare; Kolinski's units, while consistent, are intuitive, rather than formal. Their utility as a classificatory device is not in question ... [but] ... their utility as a comparative instrument cannot be checked, and this is where one of the major problems with the system lies' (1976: 218). Herndon would presumably make exactly the same objection to Nketia's remarks concerning units of melodic organization and their utility in comparison:

> There are features of melodic organization which the concept of scale patterns enables us to handle, namely features of melodic movement - especially the choice of melodic patterns formed out of the steps of a given scale, patterns which constitute the basic vocabulary of the musician, or the building blocks that he uses in creating and re-creating music. Thus the patterns used in pentatonic melodies (whatever their pitch realizations) or those used in other scale patterns can be abstracted and compared where comparative stylistic analysis is required (1972a: 17).

The question at this point is whether the units that traditionally have been used in ethnomusicology, that is, Western units of analysis, are applicable to music of other cultures and, if so, whether they are suitable for use in comparative problems. At this point, the question of the meanings of such units is suspended; we are concerned for the moment only with the question of form. That form and meaning can be separated conceptually is also taken for granted (for example, Linton 1936: 403 and passim). Whether they should be separated is another kind of question to which I shall return later.

Surely there can be no argument about whether it is possible to abstract form from all other attributes of music and deal with it separately, for countless studies in musicology and ethnomusicology have done precisely that and have resulted in an accumulation of valuable information. In the simplest kind of example, suppose one were to select at random six songs of the Washo Indians of the Great Basin area and six songs of the Lakota Indians of the northern Plains, to present the figures on the tonal ranges alone to someone who had not heard music from either group, and ask that person to select which songs came from one group and which from the other. While this information alone would not enable the neophyte to identify which group was Washo and which Lakota, the chances are very high indeed that six tonal ranges would fall into one group and six into the other, and the chances are equally good that the division would be Washo : Lakota accurate. No reference is made to meaning, use, function, context, or any other variable: the sole criterion is form. Furthermore, it has been demonstrated through mathematical proofs that such formal distributions of elements of music are both constant and identifying (Freeman and Merriam 1956). The point is not that this is the best way of doing things, the only way of doing things, the best way of doing some thing, or that it is applicable in all cases, but rather that it <u>can</u> be done, and that doing it produces certain kinds of verifiable results which do have worthwhile applications.

That this is so can hardly be of surprise to us. Similar procedures, with all the same advantages and disadvantages, have been applied, for example, in folklore with the concepts of motif and tale type, in dance with the elements isolated in Labanotation, and perhaps most notably in linguistics which, in certain of its operations, has relied exclusively and highly successfully on the level of form.

While we are well-advised to keep firmly in mind Feld's strictures (1974) concerning the applicability of linguistic models in ethnomusicology, it is clear that the linguist is in a better position to make much more powerful statements of form than is the ethnomusicologist. Again on a simple level, Fromkin and Rodman made the assertion, almost casually, that 'we find, for example, that the same, relatively small set of phonetic properties characterize all human speech sounds, that the same classes of these sounds are utilized in languages spoken from the Arctic Circle to the Cape of Good Hope, and that the same kinds of regular patterns of speech sounds occur all over the world' (1974: 69).

To the best of my knowledge, ethnomusicologists cannot make a statement like this, or even one analogous to it, for we simply do not have the requisite information. This is not to argue that a parallel statement about music would be a positive statement; rather, it is to say that we have not asked this kind of question seriously, that the present investigative mood in ethnomusicology seems to be precluding us from asking such a question, and that the same general mood makes us look askance at those who might like to ask it. It is perfectly evident that Kolinski has taught us some things, both positive and negative, about music, and so has Herndon; despite the polemics, neither is entirely correct or in a position to answer all our questions. Although the debate was useful, since it clarified basic problems, neither participant was the winner; rather, we all are winners if the result has been the widening of valid approaches to the study of music.

A final objection made to comparison is subsumed under the rubric of extreme relativism. The matter has been put clearly by Śarana:

> An anthropologist's exclusive concern with a single people at a certain period of their existence may give rise to a viewpoint opposing all comparisons. In such a case it is contended that every culture is unique and possesses a set of values which is not easy to define. But an anthropologist, with his long and close association with the people, may experience and understand it. The uniqueness of each culture is inviolable. So there can be no comparison of cultures or parts of cultures (1975: 75).

I have not seen this precise viewpoint in the published literature of ethnomusicology but I have discussed it in private and in correspondence with several of my colleagues. The philosophy, it seems to me, is essentially one of both particularism and despair, and I am inclined to agree strongly with Śarana when he writes: 'Extreme or arch-relativism, if accepted and practiced generally, becomes an impediment in the development of any scientific discipline. In its reasonably restricted form cultural relativism is one of anthropology's notable contributions' (1975: 76).

RESULTS OF COMPARISON

Assuming that comparison in ethnomusicology is possible, what kinds of results can we hope to obtain, and have any such studies been

made? Among the suggested objectives is what Śarana (1975) calls
'inferential history,' and the ethnomusicological literature
includes a number of such studies. Nketia, for example, begins
his work concerning the sources of data on music in Africa by
noting that 'our task is to discover what is old, to isolate it
from the new by comparative methods, so that we can proceed from
the present to the past' (1972b: 43). McLeod, in her study of
musical instruments in Madagascar, tells us that 'this paper is
presented in the hope that the materials from Madagascar will aid
in a better understanding of one of the most puzzling problems of
historical relationship: that between Africa and Indonesia' (1977:
189), and the method used is compartive. Wachsmann uses the same
method for historical purposes in his study of music history in
East Africa (1971: 97). Lomax both infers and postulates history
directly upon a comparative method (1968), and many other examples
could be cited. The utility of comparison for the establishment of
inferential history in ethnomusicology can hardly be disputed.

Nor can we attack comparison as a technique for the study of
distribution and typology. One of the uses of comparative data for
this purpose has been the postulation of music areas, all of which
have been organized on the basis of individual traits of music
style, and all of which combine the two factors into distributional-
typological schemes. What is interesting about this particular usage
is that aside from inevitable slight modification, each successive
area mapping shows not only continuity but also very little basic
difference from one effort to the next. Thus Nettl's mapping of
North-American Indian music-style areas (1954) is not strikingly
different from that of Roberts, which preceded Nettl's by eighteen
years (1936); nor, for Africa, are Merriam's (1959) from Lomax's
(1970). Distributional and typological studies give us certain
types of information and do not give us others. The point, however,
is that they do give us reliable information of the type they are
capable of giving, and this is attested to by the continuity and
similarity of the successive results obtained.

A third objective of comparison is to suggest generalizations,
and again ethnomusicologists have not failed. The work of Lomax
(1968) comes readily to mind, and also the quite different sort of
generalization by McAllester, who finds it possible to speak of
what he calls 'near-universals' in music. While the units are
stated far less precisely than in other instances, McAllester had
to have engaged in comparisons of elements of style in order to be
able to write:

> Almost everywhere there is some sense of the tonic, some kind of
> a tonal centre in music. Almost everywhere music establishes a
> tendency. It seems to be going somewhere, whatever its terms are,
> and the joy that the performers of that music feel has to do with
> the way in which that tendency is realized ... Music in almost
> every tradition seems to have a beginning and an end. Everywhere
> there is a development of some kind and form of some kind. There
> is pattern, there are formulae, there are special signs that all the
> practitioners of a particular music recognize ... (1971: 379-80).

Not every ethnomusicologist would agree with these generalizations, but none the less they are generalizations and they have been reached on the basis of comparison.

Other generalizations are made in flat assertive terms, such as Harwood's suggestion that octave stretching and four other identifiable aspects of musical sensation and perception are human musical universals (1976: 525-8). It is impossible to reach such conclusions without the use of comparison. Finally, potential generalizations are sometimes expressed as hypotheses, as in the suggestion that in Flathead Indian music slow tempo has a number of correlates, and that this may conceivably be true of other kinds of music, and even of all music (Merriam 1967: 323-4).

Closely related to the purpose of generalization through comparison is what Šarana calls 'generalized process' (1975: 48-51), that is, generalization about processes that show transition through time. This type of generalization has been applied in the use of Gluckman's theory of structural duration (1968) to explain change in music viewed as a social institution (Merriam 1977: 839-41). Other similar studies are to be found in the literature.

If we can easily cite comparative studies in ethnomusicology, and if we can accept the fact that they are solidly grounded and provide us with sound new information, then why are such strong objections to comparison voiced by Blacking and others? Two answers seem possible. The first is simply that the objectors feel other kinds of problems and procedures are more important and powerful in ethnomusicology than those suggested by a formal comparative approach. I will return to this point in a moment.

The second answer, also a matter of opinion concerning the relative merits of different kinds of approaches, specifically involves the question of levels of analysis. Blacking's urgent suggestion is that comparison is invalid unless it includes the component of meaning, that is, he would not study form alone but only form and meaning together. But intellectual endeavours are full of level-dichotomies, and the kinds of questions asked and the procedures used differ among schools, by preference, through conviction, and via other variables which are a matter of choice. Radcliffe-Brown, for example, referred frequently to the distinction between 'psychology and social anthropology,' which he saw as the extremely important difference between studying 'individual behaviour in its relation to the individual' and 'the behaviour of groups or collective bodies of individuals in its relation to the group' (1958: 17, passim), but I do not recall his suggesting that psychology be abandoned. Similarly, Hanson insists on a clear distinction between what he calls 'individual' and 'institutional' questions (1975); he does not suggest that we stop asking one kind or the other but rather that we understand the distinctions and their implications. Similarly we may study a group versus groups, the diachronic or the synchronic, or any one of a number of other possibilities. The point is that we can ask any set of questions of our data (though of course questions contemplated in advance will affect the ways in which the data are gathered). Are the questions valid? Of course they are, assuming that we know the basis on which the data were collected, that we hold that basis constant, and that the basis is not a palpably foolish one. Thus it must be concluded that we are entitled to ask questions about form as we are to ask them about meaning or about form and meaning combined. My objection arises when we claim that one kind of question is invalid merely because we believe that the kind of question we ourselves wish to ask is more important, feasible, or productive. While the latter may in fact be true, in itself it does not invalidate the utility of the former. We <u>must</u> ask different kinds of questions; catholicity of approach is the life-blood of intellectual investigation viewed large, and dismissal of valid methodology simply because it does not interest us is at best parochial.

It should be perfectly clear by this time that I am arguing here for the validity of a variety of techniques and applications in the field of ethnomusicology. If we are to learn as much as possible, in the most economical way, about music taken as a socio-cultural phenomenon, then we cannot cut ourselves off from any reasonable approach. Lest there be misunderstanding, I wish to reiterate that ethnomusicology for me is the study of music as culture, and that does not preclude the study of form; indeed we cannot proceed without it.

The most fruitful studies of music, I believe, will be of the kind that seeks broader goals than those that can be achieved by comparison alone; or, in the words of Blacking:

> More important to me than the possibility of comparing different styles of music is the prospect of knowing what music really <u>is</u> as an expression of human behaviour, and to what extent its generating processes are musical and specific to the human species ... we shall not be able to investigate these problems until analyses of music include the deep, as well as the surface structures, and we pay as much attention to man the music-maker as we do to the music man makes (1972: 108).

The proposition seems hardly arguable to me, and it has been accepted and stated by others, among them Meyer (1960: 50), Leach (1968: 341), and Harwood (1976: 531). But part of the process of reaching this kind of understanding has depended in the past, and will depend in the future, on careful, limited, controlled comparison. It does us no good to maintain that the comparison of form is to be abandoned because other problems are more cogent, or far-reaching, or interesting. We need the process of comparison as we need other techniques of analysis, and I suggest that instead of thinking of reasons for discarding it, we need to devote concentrated attention to making comparison a more workable weapon in the ethnomusicological arsenal.

REFERENCES

Ackernecht, Erwin H. 1954 'On the Comparative Method in Anthropology' in Robert F. Spencer, ed. Method and Perspective in Anthropology (Minneapolis, University of Minnesota Press) 117-25
Blacking, John 1966 'Review: The Anthropology of Music' Current Anthropology 7: 218-19
- 1972 'Deep and Surface Structures in Venda Music' 1971 Yearbook of the International Folk Music Council 3: 91-108
Driver, Harold E. 1973 'Cross-cultural Studies' in John J. Honigmann, ed. Handbook of Social and Cultural Anthropology (Chicago, Rand McNally) 327-67
Eggan, Fred 1950 Social Organization of the Western Pueblos (Chicago, University of Chicago Press)
Feld, Steven 1974 'Linguistic Models in Ethnomusicology' Ethnomusicology 18 (2): 197-217
Freeman, Linton C., and Merriam, Alan P. 1956 'Statistical Classification in Anthropology: An Application to Ethnomusicology' American Anthropologist 58: 464-72
Fromkin, Victoria, and Rodman, Robert 1974 An Introduction to Language (New York, Holt, Rinehart and Winston)
Gluckman, Max 1968 'The Utility of the Equilibrium Model in the Study of Social Change' American Anthropologist 70: 219-37
Hanson, F. Allan 1975 Meaning in Culture (London, Routledge & Kegan Paul)
Harris, Marvin 1968 The Rise of Anthropological Theory (New York, Thomas Y. Crowell)
Harwood, Dane L. 1976 'Universals in Music: A Perspective from Cognitive Psychology' Ethnomusicology 20 (3): 521-33
Herndon, Marcia 1974 'Analysis: Herding of Sacred Cows?' Ethnomusicology 18: 219-62
- 1976 'Reply to Kolinski: Tarus Omicida' Ethnomusicology 20 (2): 217-31
Herndon, Marcia, and Brunyate, Roger 1975 Form in Performance (Austin, Office of the College of Fine Arts, University of Texas)
Hood, Mantle 1963 'Music, the Unknown,' in Frank L. Harrison, Mantle Hood, and Claude V. Palisca Musicology (Englewood Cliffs, NJ, Prentice-Hall) 215-326
- 1969 'Ethnomusicology' in Willi Apel, ed. Harvard Dictionary of Music (Cambridge, Harvard University Press) 2d ed., 298-300
- 1971 The Ethnomusicologist (New York, McGraw-Hill)
Johnston, Thomas F. 1973 'The Cultural Role of Tsonga Beer-Drink Music' Yearbook of the International Folk Music Council 5: 132-55
Kolinski, Mieczyslaw 1976 'Herndon's Verdict on Analysis: tabula rasa,' Ethnomusicology 20 (1): 1-22
- 1977 'Final Reply to Herndon' Ethnomusicology 21 (1): 75-83
Leach, Edmund R. 1968 'The Comparative Method in Anthropology' in David L. Sills, ed. International Encyclopedia of the Social Sciences 1: 339-45
Lewis, Oscar 1961 'Comparisons in Cultural Anthropology' in Frank W. Moore, ed. Readings in Cross-cultural Methodology (New Haven, HRAF Press) 55-88

Linton, Ralph 1936 The Study of Man: An Introduction (New York, D. Appleton-Century)
Lomax, Alan 1968 Folk Song and Culture (Washington, DC, American Association for the Advancement of Science)
- 1970 'The Homogeneity of African-Afro-American Musical Style' in Norman E. Whitten, Jr. and John F. Szwed, eds. Afro-American Anthropology: Comparative Perspectives (New York, Free Press) 181-201
McAllester, David P. 1971 'Some Thoughts on "Universals" in World Music' Ethnomusicology 15 (3) 379-80
McLeod, Norma 1977 'Musical Instruments and History in Madagascar' in Essays for a Humanist: An Offering to Klaus Wachsmann (New York, Town House Press) 189-215
Merriam, Alan P. 1959 'African Music' in William R. Bascom and Melville J. Herskovits, eds. Continuity and Change in African Cultures (Chicago, University of Chicago Press) 49-86
- 1964 The Anthropology of Music (Evanston, Northwestern University Press)
- 1967 Ethnomusicology of the Flathead Indians (Chicago, Aldine)
- 1977 'Music Change in a Basongye Village (Zaïre)' Anthropos 72: 806-46
Meyer, Leonard B. 1960 'Universalims and Relativism in the Study of Ethnic Music' Ethnomusicology 4 (1): 49-54
Moles, Jerry A. 1977 'Standardization and Measurement in Cultural Anthropology: A Neglected Area' Current Anthropology 18: 235-58
Murdock, George Peter 1949 Social Structure (New York, Macmillan)
- 1965 Culture and Society (Pittsburgh, University of Pittsburgh Press
Naroll, Raoul 1968 'Some Thoughts on Comparative Method in Cultural Anthropology' in Hubert M. Blalock, Jr. and Ann B. Blalock, eds. Methodology in Social Research (New York, McGraw-Hill) 236-77
Nettl, Bruno 1954 North American Indian Musical Styles (Philadelphia, American Folklore Society Memoir 45)
- 1973 'Comparison and Comparative Method in Ethnomusicology' Yearbook of the Institute of Latin American Studies 9: 148-61
Nketia, J.H. Kwabena 1967 'Musicology and African Music: A Review of Problems and Areas of Research' in David Brokensha and Michael Crowder, eds. Africa in the Wider World (Oxford, Pergamon Press) 12-35
- 1972a 'The Musical Languages of Subsaharan Africa' in African Music. Meeting in Yaoundé (Cameroon) (Paris, La Revue musicale) 7-42
- 1972b 'Sources of Historical Data on the Musical Cultures in African Music. Meeting in Yaoundé (Cameroon) (Paris, La Revue musicale) 43-9
Osgood, Charles E. 1967 'On the Strategy of Cross-national Research into Subjective Culture' Social Science Information 6: 5-37
Radcliffe-Brown, A.R. 1958 Method in Social Anthropology edited by M.N. Srinivas (Chicago, University of Chicago Press)
Roberts, Helen H. 1936 Musical Areas in Aboriginal North America (New Haven, Yale University Publications in Anthroplogy No. 12)

Contributors

John Beckwith
University of Toronto, Toronto, Ontario

Charles Lafayette Boilès
Université de Montréal, Montreal, Quebec

W. Jay Dowling
University of Texas at Dallas, Texas

Pandora Hopkins
Rutgers University, Newark, New Jersey

Christopher Marshall
Unity College, Unity, Maine

Timothy J. McGee
University of Toronto, Toronto, Ontario

Alan P. Merriam (deceased)
Indiana University, Bloomington, Indiana

Jean-Jacques Nattiez
Université de Montréal, Montreal, Quebec

Bruno Nettl
University of Illinois, Urbana, Illinois

Jay Rahn
York University, Toronto, Ontario

George D. Sawa
University of Toronto, Toronto, Ontario

Song Bang-song
National Classical Music Institute, Seoul, Korea

David Waterhouse
University of Toronto, Toronto, Ontario

DATE DUE

OCT 2 3 1986			
NOV 2 0 1986			
JAN 1 1987			

DEMCO 38-297